The Judas Syndrome

James Farrell

FULTON-HALL

FULTON-HALL PUBLISHING CO.
595 Buckingham Way
San Francisco, CA 94132

ISBN 0-918756-03

To the children
of our nation whose
rightful inheritance is being
wasted before their time.

TABLE OF CONTENTS

TABLE OF CONTENTS

"NINE-TENTHS OF WISDOM CONSISTS IN BEING
WISE IN TIME."

Theodore Roosevelt

Certainly one of our most courageous Presidents, Teddy had a lot more to say than just his famous remark *"Walk softly and carry a big stick."* While knowledge or *"wisdom"* has always been important, never has the relationship between *"wisdom"* and *"time"* been so critical to our national survival as it is today.

FOREWORD

It is generally accepted in the scientific world that human
e on this planet dates back at least three million years.
'hatever figure one chooses to believe, we know that it
ok until the year 1830 for the world to reach the one
llion population mark. The second billion inhabitants,
owever, came along in only 100 more years (1930). The
ird billion was with us thirty years later (1960), and we
ssed the four billion mark during 1975, a mere fifteen
ears later.

It is an inescapable fact that if the human species is to sur-
ve on this earth it will be the result of intelligent beings
aking rational decision based on the factors as they actual-
exist. There is no place for sentiment, superstition, or,
uch less, for wishful thinking in the decision making pro-
ss of a "life-or-death" situation.

The planet earth has given notice it will no longer harbor
competent planners and managers as tenants. The next
cade may well determine for all times who, if any, will sur-
ve, and at least from the level of governmental leadership,
ne can say that they failed to receive proper notice.

As American citizens we have learned the hard way (and
rhaps to our amazement) that what America wants — or
en wishes for the World-at-large — has had little or no
neficial impact on its present state of being. Our nation's
lf-appointed role (following WW II) as the paternal guar-
an of mankind, while initially successful in individual
ses, has long since exceeded the rational boundaries of
th expectations and tenure.

The primary purpose of this book is to illustrate that while playing the role of World-guardian, we have neglected to pay attention to what is happening in our own house. Problems that were emerging decades ago have been left to fester, while politicians "buffooned" our heads with the idea that it is America's responsibility to take care of the world. Of particular concern is the manner in which our nation's political process has been altered to accommodate ideologies foreign to the concept of what made this nation something special in the first place.

The system of complementary "checks and balances," as envisioned by our nation's founders, has degenerated into a condition of "checkmate." What is not invalidated through the judicial process, lingers on only to be mitigated by bureaucratic policies which often reach 180 degrees at variance with each other. Consequently, government has become **unworkable** — while the cost of accomplishing **nothing** continued to skyrocket.

Think of it! If it took 2,999,830 years for the world to achieve a population of **one**-billion inhabitants — but only 15 years to acquire the **fourth** — then indeed, "rough" waters" lie ahead and the "oars" of this nation had better begin stroking in unison. If America is to survive as a nation in the coming — most turbulent period in the history of mankind, national policy can no longer be predicated on the basis of "how many votes it is worth?"

CHAPTER 1
REMEMBER ME AT THE POLLS

"The people who had once bestowed commands, consul-ships, legions, and all else now longs eagerly for just two things, bread and circus games."

So wrote the Roman poet Juvenal as he watched the decaying Roman Empire. The contemporary historian George Santayana sums up history in this manner: "Those who cannot remember the past are condemned to relive it."

Separated by almost two milleniums, these wise sages were commenting (and perhaps unknowingly) about incompetent, inefficient, deceitful, and self-centered political charlatans who could care less about the fall of the Empire or the State of the Union. Get elected or re-elected and to hell with posterity. This messge couldn't be clearer or the evidence more damning.

The once mighty U.S. dollar continues to plunge in value alongside the world's stable currencies and may soon be replaced as the bench mark of international trading by the yen or the mark. Inflation is leading the nation into domestic chaos while our soaring balance-of-payments deficit shows no sign or even hope of reversing itself. It should be obvious that if America can't balance its foreign trade bills with money (and we can't), then our nation faces an insidious form of "foreclosure" which has already begun and is described in later chapters.

Traditional American mobility is being doomed to inevitable gas rationing and ultimately, designated living areas by a population that is outgrowing its resources. Our concept of "one nation, indivisible" is no longer applicable. Political opportunists seeking to establish powerful voting-blocs are systematically and deliberately dividing the United States into little more than a multi-racial, multi-lingual, and multi-ethnic campground. "Separatism" that will eventually lead to a separation of the Union.

In this 20th Century A.D., the "money changers" still occupy the favored positions in the temple, extracting their usury from the population with both the blessing and cooperation of government. America's backbone, the middle class, has become an endangered species gravitating towards the poorhouse while only a few escape the pull of inflation to become rich — and many of the already rich become the super-rich. Crime, poverty, drug addiction and ghettos are replacing self-respect, self-reliance, morality and productiveness as our nation's most notable hallmarks.

Americans raced halfway around the world to fight a "no win" war in defense of something or someone in Asia, only to have our incompetent politicians allow a two-bit dictator to extort the Panama Canal from us on the premise that the world will love us for being an idiot. Without having contributed a single drop of blood, sweat, tears or "grey matter" to the most meaningful engineering achievement in history, Panama will soon become landlord of this vital waterway along with several billion dollars of other American assets in the Canal Zone. Not even the "Godfather" could have foisted more humiliating treaties on the United States than those recently ratified by our Senate. And to make our "humble pie" even more unpalatable, for the next 20 years while we are packing pajamas and toothbrushes, America will be paying Panama upwards of $50,000,000 in yearly tribute. Tribute or reparations apparently intended to compensate Panama for our losses. For the purpose of clarity we should repeat that statement: Panama will not be paying us for our assets; we will be paying them for our losses. No longer can we harbor even a reasonable doubt that the welfare-mentality of our politicians is without bounds. It also becomes more evident each day that the legacy of Benedict Arnold has outlived those of Washington, Lincoln and Teddy Roosevelt. What some day is sure to be regarded as the most incredible blunder in history, is examined in detail in Chapter 2.

But as the inimitable Al Jolson might have said, "Folks you ain't heard anything yet."

While America's political incompetents continue to roam the earth in search of needy people and worthy causes, the United States is spending over $100,000,000,000 annually for national defense. Defense against what? Defense against whom? America is being **invaded,** and has been for the past several years by millions of illegal aliens. The fact that this insurgent army may or may not carry weapons in no way lessens its destructive impact. The invaders are millions of additional liabilities who contribute enormously to every major problem facing our nation.

No one (not even in government) denies that the cost of

ur present fuel imports is leading us into bankruptcy. And
•hat is our Administration's answer to this dilemma? It is
•erely to contemplate a variety of penalties and restrictions
•gainst our own citizens, together with creation of yet
•nother huge federal bureaucratic agency. Meanwhile,
•assive waves of illegal aliens pour across our borders, and
•ongress seeks refuge in yet another "study" of the im-
•igration problem . . . Studies of which have been going on
•ow for some **fifteen years.**

We know it is the imbalance between supply and demand
•hich contributes most heavily to the inflationary process.
•on't we?) This fact is particularly evident in the soaring
•ost and growing scarcity of housing, as more and more
•eople come into the market seeking homes, both renters
•nd buyers.

The tremendous combined burden of welfare programs,
•nemployment compensation, low-cost housing projects for
•e poor, multilingual requirements and the **administration**
f **preferential minority employment and educational op-
ortunities** has become so overwhelming and un-
•anageable that it is literally "driving us up the wall". And
•gain, the administration in Washington is aware of these
•cts, and so are our legislators.

As if the massive influx of Spanish-surname minorities
•ere not enough, in 1978 Mr. Carter sent his Vice-
•resident to Southeast Asia to bring back Oriental refugees.
•r. Mondale's initial catch was some 25,000 people, to be
•llowed by similar amounts each year; a figure which has
•ubsequently been raised to 188,000 annually. Humani-
•arianism? Hardly. After all, Mr. Carter is well aware of the
•ct that even if the U.S. were to permit immigration of
•5,000,000 needy Asians every year, the bottom of the
•sian refugee barrel would **never** be reached. Population in
•e Third World nations is multiplying so rapidly that im-
•igration serves only as a stimulus to the cycle rather than a
•lution to the real problem. In the long run, America is do-
•g nothing to help these nations by accepting their excess
•opulations. At best, we are only momentarily delaying
•eir "moment of truth", while in turn becoming a part of the
•roblem ourselves.

3

The arrival of millions of new minorities serves only to aggravate our own existing problems well beyond what might be indicated by the mere statistical numbers. The Civil Rights Act of 1964 relegated our **non-minority** Americans to a lesser degree of "citizenship rights". It did that specifically in an attempt to upgrade the status of our present minorities. Quite obviously, this has become an exercise in futility, since the effort expended toward that goal constantly keeps being diluted by the arrival of wave after wave of new minorities.

Examining America's past approach to improving minority conditions by two measures of achievement, it becomes evident that we have failed. First, progress has not kept pace with retrogression. Second, the small degree of improvement in certain areas is largely at the expense of increasingly disastrous impediments to the whole. A totally unimaginative concept of "levelling" has resulted in stunting the nation's potential to a far greater extent than it has succeeded in achieving the realistic expectations of individual segments of our society. Could it be that our politicians recognize this, and have decided that the easiest solution to the problem lies in converting the "minorities" into the "majority"? Admittedly a silly suggestion, but what else are we to conclude?

Contrary to the claims of many politicians, since World War II America has done more to create a "minority problem" than to alleviate the basic economic and cultural poverty which spawns the problem. Merely pointing to the thousands of minorities now occupying lofty jobs as evidence that we are making progress is an outright fraud. We are not making progress. We need only to view the millions of minorities turning many of our largest cities into almost total ghettos to arrive at the truth. Temporary social programs can act as a "penicillin" treatment in helping to cure an economic illness. But trying to mix permanent socialism with a democratic form of government is as deadly as prescribing penicillin as a daily dietary supplement. That's precisely what has taken place over the past few decades, while government itself has grown like a cancer, eating away at the core of our productive society.

4

Although the logistical problems of massive immigration are obvious, the political, social and ideological ramifications are downright frightening. During the June, 1978, primary election in San Francisco, a twelve-member team from the U.S. Attorney's office was assigned to monitor compliance with our nation's new multi-lingual voting requirements. The head of this bureaucratic task force complained that San Francisco's Registrar of Voters had not assigned enough bi-lingual interpreters to the polls, stating that America was "no longer an English-speaking nation." Isn't that nice to hear?

During his campaign for the Presidency, Mr. Carter acknowledged that America has a serious illegal alien problem. To date, however, all that he has done to combat it is to suggest amnesty, along with changing the official terminology for illegal aliens to "undocumented workers". Such actions can only be defined as typical strokes of administrative genius in problem solving. Unfortunately, neither of these courageous moves succeeded in halting the invasion. In July of 1978, Gregorio Villalopez, leader of a Chicano group known as the Brown Berets, conducted a mass rally in Larado, Texas demanding *"independence from the United States"* and *"all land between Texas and California inclusive . . . We are only seeking a free nation with a proper flag, more legal than this one, the United States,"* said Villalopez. Was this merely an isolated incident? Not at all. It is a phenomenon which grows in intensity proportionate with the mass migration. Adding just a "pinch of gall" to the situation is the fact that American taxpayers support Chicano study programs in many of our universities which, in essence, both stimulate and subsidize this type of ethnic divisiveness.

The point of the above observation is that for too many years our government has operated like a stupified drunk who can't remember from one moment to the next the problems at hand. Consequently, we find our politicians going on year after year creating new or expanded government agencies for the purpose of taking on new areas of responsibility. Which raises the question, "How long can a nation survive with bureaucrats who find **administering** to problems more advantageous than **solving** them?"

Our federal budget for the present year (1980) will approximate 532 billion dollars. If laid end-to-end, this amount in $1 bills would reach to the moon and back 218 times. Astronomical indeed, but after spending this $532,000,000,000 will our nation be any better off than we were at the beginning of the year? Will we have eradicated even one of our many serious problems or will we again find much of this budget being used to create **new problems** and **more bureaucracy?** If past performance is a valid indicator, then the answer is all too obvious. While no citizen truly objects to the burden of supporting legitimate government functions, there is a rising tide of indignation from taxpayers evolving around the question of "legitimacy". What are the valid and legitimate functions of government, versus those which government has either assumed or usurped?

The Declaration of Independence specifically enunciated the reasons our forefathers found it necessary to overthrow the English monarchy's control of the American colonies and establish our independence. In reference to the oppression by England, it decribes *"usurpations, all having in direct object the establishment of an absolute tyranny over these States".* If the ability to exercise blackmail by the threat of withholding funds which our present federal government usurped under the guise of "revenue sharing" is not *"the establishment of an absolute tyranny over these States,"* it is certainly not far from it. The federal government has often used this "club" in forcing its irrational demands upon state and city governments, as well as on local school boards.

The same Declaration says of the King, *"He has erected a multitude of new offices, and sent hither swarms of Officers to harass our People, and eat out their substance."* The many analogies to be found here are obvious.

The Ninth Amendment to the Constitution states: *"The enumeration in the Constitution, of certain rights, shall not be construed to deny or disparage others retained by the people."* The Tenth Amendment reiterates that principle in these words: *"The powers not delegated to the United States by the Constitution nor prohibited by it to the States, are reserved to the States respectively, or to the people."* But with some 200,000 new laws being passed each year at the various levels of government, it would be almost presumptuous to believe that the American citizen still retains the right to breathe.

We have indeed strayed a long way from our nation's founding concept of government being the servant of the people. Although it is the individual American citizen who supports government, through clever perversion of our complex political system, the "kept" are in essence becoming our "keepers".

Again, what is the legitimate role of government? We know that government, per se, does not squeeze oranges, mend shoes, repair televison sets, drive taxis or draw beer. It doesn't build houses, can chili, tailor suits, give permanents, sell furniture, straighten fenders, fill cavities or operate theaters. These are all the normal functions and interplay of commerce between our citizens. Yet, at the federal, state and local levels, government now consumes over 40% of the gross national product. In other words, two days out of every five-day work week go to support government spending. Obviously, that is not the way our system was intended to operate.

Stupidity, incompetence and irresponsibility are as disastrous to the operation of a nation as they are to the management of any business enterprise. General Motors, IBM or AT&T would collapse within a month if they were to condone the malfeasance in management which the American people have tolerated for so long in their government. Unfortunately, many people seem to think that governments are immune to the consequences of mismanagement. They do not believe that a country such as ours could actually "go belly-up". A wishful illusion, however, as history is full of once-great nations that have literally perished from the face of this earth. To assume that America holds a God-granted exemption from such a fate is simply to court catastrophe.

The paralyzing stock market crash of 1929 was precipitated mainly by "kiting" inflated stock prices far above their actual values. Our spendthrift economy of today is based on much the same false foundation. We have managed to "kite" our economic well-being on an ever increasing national debt and a soaring balance-of-payments deficit, which sooner or later will have to be paid. There is, however, one important difference between these two situations. In 1929, America had an incredible abundance of natural resources and living space which greatly aided and assured ultimate recovery from the Depression. Today we have no such abundance to fall back upon for cushions.

It is indeed difficult to understand how America, once the richest and most powerful nation on earth, could have degenerated so quickly into what is now a very precarious position. Difficult, but not impossible. The first step in such an analysis is to recognize the process. For the past several decades our nation's inner strength has been vandalized by a breed of political hypocrites that essentially are little more than common cheats. Cheaters that have used the "corporate bank account" (U.S. Treasury) as an almost unlimited source with which to purchase votes, and in turn, political muscle. Unfortunately, these charlatans have succeeded in hypnotizing large segments of our population into believing that government is an inexhaustible fountain of blessings. A magic fountain which is capable of replacing ambition, resourcefulness, hard work and personal sacrifice as the ultimate source of individual sustenance. A preposterous illusion that must inevitably vanish just as all mirages do.

The most dangerous part of this charade, however, is that in the process, government has become an empire within a nation. A separate entity more powerful than the people who support it, and consequently, one that expends more energy in perpetuation of itself than it does for the Union. Over a hundred years ago Abraham Lincoln said, "You cannot help the poor by destroying the rich. You cannot keep out of trouble by spending more than you earn. You cannot build character and courage by taking away a man's initiative. You cannot help men permanently by doing for them what they could and should do for themselves." These are inescapable truths that apply not only to our domestic situation, but to our international relationships as well.

What should be of most urgent concern to the American

people is the question of who is actually pulling the strings of government in Washington. Such a consistent pattern of departures from what were once considered as American ideals and standards would seem to belie the possibility of mere chance, fate or accident. Who, for example, decided that Americans, by law, should be divided into different categories of citizens according to their racial, ethnic, or linguistic heritage? Such is surely not "the will of the people." And who decided that the exercising of freedom of choice by one citizen in dealing with another shall be a federal crime? The point, of course, is that a government that can, and does, punish even one of its citizens for exercising the most basic element of liberty, the **freedom to choose,** is not only capable, but will eventually deny that freedom to all.

Such radical departures from the fundamental principles on which this nation was founded have been fed to us gradually, much like a deliberate case of arsenic poisoning. In each instance, politicians have told us "these changes are for the good of the nation". But couching such ideological meanderings in flowery language does not make them innocuous. Indeed no. They are still serious abrogations of our basic rights and liberties, which ultimately, will adversely affect every citizen.

Government "by the people", and "for the people", is largely becoming more of a motto than it is an actual fact. Through illusion and subterfuge, our nation's legal establishment (a de facto dictatorship) have usurped much of the real power formerly vested in the people and their elected representatives. What good are laws reflecting the "will of the people", when our courts (often liberal to the point of being subversive) interpret them as **they** damn-well please. And when this happens, which it so often does, it is not the **intentions** of our legislators — but the **interpretation** by the courts — which become **the law of the land.**

Under the guise of protecting the constitutional "rights" of the criminal element, our judicial system, has in fact, deprived lawful society of most of its tangible protection. Most notably, the inability of peaceful citizens to feel safe and secure even in their homes — while our streets become "nightmare alleys" for the elderly.

But such insidious legal practices are not reserved for individuals, alone; America is virtually the only nation on earth that actually subsidizes (with taxpayer money) revolutionary organizations which openly advocate the destruction of our country. In essence, it now appears that through the legal process our nation is literally being programmed to — "self-destruct".

Unfortunately, most Americans seem to view the incredible transformation taking place in our government — in our lifestyle — even in our culture and personal values — as occurring through a "natural process of evolution". That is, "changing" — as opposed to — "being changed" by a small proportion of the population whose vested interests are completely alien to every concept of the American Dream.

Like a tiger snared in a net, America's once-powerful democratic process has becme entrapped in a maze of extraneous overhead-factors which now threaten to render it unworkable. It would be nice to believe that our leaders do not actually know what is happening to our country. But such an assumption is ridiculous. It would appear more logical to conclude that America's current crises have come about by design rather than by chance. A fairly obvious case of the "Judas syndrome" emerges as we begin piecing together the jigsaw puzzle of political chicanery. "Big brother" governments are not created overnight, nor are they the result of any single act or cause. Historically, they are the end-product of many subtle entrapments which finally bring on social, moral and economic collapse.

The real destroyer of the liberties of any people is he who spreads among them bounties, donations and largesse.

PLUTARCH (circa 46-120A D)

While we have not yet reached the point of no return, the trend is unmistakable. Like the "yellow brick road" trends always lead somewhere, and it is time the American people recognize the ultimate destination of our dangerous political, social, economic and ideological policies.

Meanwhile, at the international level, our world has become one of rapidly accelerating problems of enormous consequences. Problems and situations for which there are

10

no precedents to guide us. In 1973 Peking announced that the population of mainland China had surpassed 800 million. On May 1, 1978 the Chinese reported reaching the 900 million mark. That is 100,000,000 additional inhabitants that have been added to the world's survival problems by one nation alone in a mere five years. Think of it! This **increase** is equal to almost half the total population of the United States. Unfortunately, birth rates in many parts of the world (including a number of nations in the Western Hemisphere) are even higher. Are these figures statistical trivia or are they important and valid indicators of things to come?

If it rains for an unusually long period of time in the mountains, we have past experience to tell us that it will flood in the valley and we can plan accordingly. There are no precdents, however, to guide us in this matter. We can only rely on common sense, logic and, above all, foresight. Yet those whom we pay so handsomely to perform such services, have time and again demonstrated their inability to even utilize hindsight.

In formulating policies based on foresight, it might do well to consider the following hypotheses. **Even if the inhabitants of this earth were all of one race, one religion, and one political philosophy, the world would still be headed toward conflict. Conflict of one nature or another because of sheer numbers.** There is no way to avoid this inevitability as long as the world's population continues to mushroom; and any politician who tells us otherwise is either a fool, a liar, or both. We are well past the point in history where we can pass the problem on to the next generation to worry about. Serious conflict resulting from too many people for not enough resources will occur within the coming decade. We know they why; the only uncertainty is the where, when and how.

America's greatest danger, however, is from our own politicians, many of whom are deliberately misleading our citizens into a false sense of security. In February of 1978, another 85 U.S. military installations (some dating back to 1776) were under consideration for possible closing. While there may be a measure of economic prudence behind some of these proposed shutdowns, if this is being done to create the illusion that enlightenment has antiquated preparedness, beware. Or if these economies are necessary for the purpose of expanding social programs, it would again be a dangerous trade-off. The welfare state is not a first line of defense against anything, internal or external. The very idea that by giving away American possessions, massive foreign aid, or showering the earth with brotherly love, the world will soon become a Utopian paradise is utter nonsense.

America has learned the hard way that we cannot police the world. It is even more illogical to assume that we can provide sustenance or refuge for political, social or ideological mentalities who refuse to acknoweledge the mathematical limitations of their nation's habitability factors. **The right to procreate carries with it the equal responsibility to provide for that which has been propagated.** Unfortunately, it is the failure to acknowledge and accept this resposibility which incubates tragedy at every level of existence where it occurs.

The purpose of this book is **not** intended to create animoslty towards illegal aliens. After all, no one can be blamed for trying to better themselves and, in doing so, for challenging our "toothless" immigration posture. As American citizens, however, we do have every right to express through the ballot our just indignation toward the irresponsible politicians who continue to court ethnic voting-bloc power for their own benefit at the expense of national interests. We referred earlier in this text to the non-legitimate functions of government. At this point, it would be an enormous improvement if the federal government would simply carry out its assigned **responsibilities.** Section 4 of Article IV of our Constitution states: *"The United States shall guarantee to every State in this Union . . . and shall protect each of them against invasion."* Well?

It is doubtful that anyone can accurately sum up what will happen to the world by the year 1990. But of the wide range of possibilities, one that would appear to have no chance at all of making the list of even the top one hundred would be "stability and peaceful coexistence." In other words, the odds for what is desirable just are not now high enough to bet our lives on. Wishing for the best is fine, but we must do our planning somewhat more in conformance with the world realities. Failure to plan, in essence, is simply **planning to fail.**

This does not mean that America has to start conducting tself like a "bad guy". It does, however, mean that we must top acting as though there isn't going to be a tomorrow — or there won't be. It shouldn't be necessary to make excuses or to apologize for exercising a prudent management of our nation. Unfortunately, there are a great many hypocrites (and not all are in government) who would like to saddle those who stand up for the American interest with a guilt omplex. It's almost as though there were something immoral or indecent about looking out for ourselves. Ridiculous. It is simply a matter of "getting our act together" in the interest of national survival.

Our nation desperately needs to regain its sense of priorities. We must recongize and define what is important, what's less important, and what we shouldn't be doing at all. If we can identify that last point first, the other objectives should fall in line relatively easy. One prerequisite to an intelligent re-alignment of priorities is that we must immediately stop **exacerbating** the many serious problems we already have. That would seem to make sense, or does it? Apparently it does not in Washington.

Next, we must face the unpleasant facts. We're not about to get honest answers, much less sensible management, from a crop of politicians who have consistently demonstrated their inadequacy. True, we do have a number of responsible and truly dedicated legislators and officials, but it seems they constitute only a minority influence. If anything of constructive and lasting value is to be achieved, it will come only through the demands of an informed and involved electorate. The average American citizen can no longer afford the luxury of assuming that everything is being taken care of "topside". It isn't, and it hasn't been for quite some time.

This book contains some material originally published in 1975 (revised in 1976) under the title **GIVE US YOUR POOR (The Immigration Bomb).** Material that has purposely been included to illustrate that the problems of 1975-76 are not only still with us, but in most instances have been severely compounded.

The problem of massive immigration is no longer just a single concern. It is inextricably tied to every major political, social, economic and ideological issue at hand. As such, it is imperative that we understand this phenomenon in complete perspective with the realities of today's world.

Now, in a somewhat calmer vein, let us examine in detail the consequences of a government establishment becoming so involved in **everthing** — that it actually takes care of **nothing.**

CHAPTER 2
THE PANAMA CANAL

The new Panama Canal treaties which were recently rammed through the Senate and down the throats of an objecting American public may well be the final chapter in the history of America's greatness as a world power.

Nobody likes a coward, and no one respects an idiot. Yet our government insisted on playing both of these roles to the hilt. The willful deceit practiced by both Panama and the United States, in failing accurately and honestly to present the facts of this issue to their citizens would, in almost any court on earth, warrant charges of criminal fraud. Misrepresentation was not an isolated or occasional incident. It was the foundation upon which the proceedings took place. While it is fruitless to "cry over spilt milk," it is essential that we review the history of this affair in order to prevent the loss of other states and territories through the same process.

The United States was not "hatched - as is" in 1776. Starting with the original 13 colonies, we have become the present United States of America through a long series of acquisitions. In 1803 America bought the huge area known as the Louisiana Purchase from France at a cost of $15,000,000. We acquired Florida from Spain in 1819 at a cost of $5,000,000. In 1863 we purchased Alaska from Russia for $7,200,000, and though there have been other acquisitions since, these fairly represent the "going price of the day" for undeveloped territory. Did the United States steal the Canal Zone through an act of "gunboat diplomacy" as some allege, or did we justly compensate all concerned in this affair?

Initially, America paid the sum of $40,000,000 to the French company which still held the "right of way" and which had made an enormous investment in attempting to build a canal across Panama. We paid $10,000,000 to the new nation of Panama, and we purchased at handsome prices all privately owned lands within the Canal Zone, including those occupied by "squatters." (We should not judge these sums in terms of today's inflated currency. The ten million dollars we paid Panama was equal to perhaps several times that nation's annual gross national product.) Later, in 1921, to compensate Colombia for the loss of its former territory and at the same time ease tensions between all parties concerned, the United States awarded Colombia $25,000,000 in exchange for official recognition of Panama as an independent, sovereign nation.

America not only purchased the rights to the Canal Zone, but in essence, we actually bought and paid for the entire nation of Panama. Let us, however, limit this inquiry of "fair and square" versus "swindle" to the Canal Zone alone. Without considering any of the subsequent payments to Panama, or our enormous investment in developing this area, America's total outlay of cash for our rights to the Canal Zone amounted to some $500 per acre. We might contrast this with the 13 cents an acre we paid for Florida, the three cents an acre for the Louisiana Purchase, and the two cents an acre we paid for Alaska.

Five hundred dollars an acre for what was then a virtually uninhabitable "cesspool" is indeed a "swindle." But who was the victim? Certainly not Panama.

America's legal right to possession of the Canal Zone is unquestionable. Since there has been so much said about this "proud" little nation of Panama whose sovereignty has been trampled upon by a big, bad "colonial power," it's time we examined the issue from a moral standpoint.

Until the 19th Century, the area which now comprises the nation of Panama was simply a pirate hangout, sacked at will by each next marauding invader. Not until 1821 did the area become a part of the old Grenada Confederacy, which later became the nation of Columbia. It was America's enforcement of the Monroe Doctrine that time and again provided the Isthmus with a long period of relative tranquility. Tranquility, but not progress.

The entire area remained mostly uninhabited and uninhabitable. The only significant towns, Colon on the Caribbean and Panama on the Pacific, were often paralyzed by outbreaks of deadly yellow fever, dysentery and malaria. Without an adequate water supply (much less sewage or sanitation), fire was a constant plague. The French com-

16

any that had earlier built the Suez Canal, tried the same at across Panama in 1878. It spent $180,000,000 on the oject, lost 40,000 lives in the attempt, and failed. When merica took on this project, we assumed what amounted the greatest gamble in all of recorded history.

There have been so many serious and sinister allegations how, to the detriment of poor little Panama, the United ates happened to build a canal there, that it's time to let e record reveal the truth.

For a number of years America had surveyed alternate utes across the Isthmus. Two separate commissions had rveyed the problem and recommended the crossing be ade through Nicaragua. Many of our senators and other mericans also preferred this route, which would have been)0 miles closer to the United States. When our negotia-)ns with Colombia broke down, and America had all but ecided on the Nicaraguan route, Panamanians, fearing this ould leave them still no more than an isolated pesthole, eclared their independence for the express purpose of egotiating directly with the United States. Even the ugaboo about the initial treaties being signed on behalf of anama by a Frenchman rather than a Panamanian citizen as been purposely distorted out of context with reality.

The Panamanian revolt was a well-timed movement. The enchman who headed up their canal effort was perhaps e only person capable of selling the Panama crossing to merica. Bunau-Varilla, who was in the United States egotiating on Panama's behalf at the time of the uprising, bled the following message to the new government:

"GOVERNMENT OF THE REPUBLIC OF PANAMA:

I have fought during 17 years for the triumph of the Panama Canal against every conceivable obstacle, natural difficulties as well as human ignorance, even harder to overcome. I thank the Government for having confided to me the exalted mission, in permitting me to exert my energies in the defense of the new Republic, whose birth assures the realization of the most stupendous conception of the human mind.

As first official notice, I have the honour to inform you of the of- ficial recognition of the Republic of Panama by the Government of the United States, which has likewise notified Bogota of its decision in terms equivalent to a formal interdiction to undertake any

BUNAU-VARILLA, New York, Nov. 7, 1903"
(Panama's Star & Herald — Nov. 11, 1903)

Between 1899 and 1903, Colombia proper had suffered a disastrous civil war which left that nation physically and financially prostrate. It was then, at the end of this conflict that Panama seceded from Colombia in a totally bloodless coup. When considering the moral rights involved, one should remember that it was American lives that were lost in building the canal and making the area habitable, and no Panama in its liberation movement.

It took almost two and a half years to conquer yellow fever and bring sanitation to the entire area before we could even begin work on the canal. After this, all that remained was no less than the achievement of an engineering miracle. It is impossible to convey to present generations the enormity of this gamble. The experienced French company had tried and failed; why should we be any more fortunate? It was a gamble we might well have lost had we not been able to eradicate the deadly yellow fever. Panama did not contribute financially, technologically, nor did she even provide manpower for the effort. The building of the canal was totally an American project, but it is Panama that has reaped the lion's share of benefits from this incredible achievement.

The conduct of business between nations is essentially the same as it is between individuals. It is based on the fair and equitable exchange of values. In the Panama affair, in exchange for approximately 500 square miles (1.8 percent of the total area of Panama, which constitutes the Canal Zone), we have provided to the inhabitants and nation of Panama over 28,000 square miles of pestilence-free habitable living area. Had there been no monetary consideration whatsoever, this alone would have been a "fair and equitable" transaction for Panama. But America's contributions to that nation did not stop there. We have installed and maintained sewage and sanitation systems in their cities, paved their roads, built giant breakwaters to provide them safe harbors on both coasts, and it is the canal which Americans built that supplies Panama, directly and indirectly, with a substantial portion of its everyday economy. No ven an idiot could honestly describe that sort of conduct on ur part as "Yankee imperialism" or "exploitation." Parcularly so, when America has operated the canal not for ur own selfish interests, but as an economic blessing nefiting the entire world.

At the time, a great many Americans resented our choice f the Panama route and didn't hesitate to voice their suspicions of a little Panamanian "hanky-panky" in the transacon. To illustrate the seriousness of our consideration of the icaraguan route, even as late as 1916 (after the Panama anal was completed), the United States paid Nicaragua 3,000,000 for an option on that route. The idea was later andoned in favor of greater development of the Panama anal. Far from just sitting back after the canal was opened r use in 1914, and harvesting the tolls (as many of our tizens were led to believe), America's history on the thmus has been one of continual investment and improvent, for the benefit of Panama as well as for our canal peration.

In 1936 we built a huge dam across the Chagres River in anama proper, which not only helps to stabilize the flow of ater into the canal system but also provides light, power nd water to other parts of that nation. To assure uninterpted use of the canal in the event of damage to one set of cks, a duplicate set was added in the 1940's at a cost of most 200 million dollars.

Contrary to another popular notion, even the argument y "pro-treaty" forces that the canal "divides Panama in alf" twists the facts to misrepresent the true situation. The anal separates Panamanians little more than the Mississippi iver or the Rocky Mountains separate Americans. In practal application, the canal's location is actually to their enefit. Had the canal been built at either extremity of anama, half of the indirect benefits they now derive would e going to Costa Rica or Colombia.

President Carter's televised presentation of the canal issue the American people on February 1, 1978 was totally eceptive. In appearing to answer objections to the new eaties, his biased views distorted the facts almost beyond cognition. An example: Most Americans wondered first,

19

why we were giving the canal away / and second, if w
must, why we were compounding this stupidity by agreein
to pay Panama upwards of 50 million dollars annually fc
the next 22 years. Mr. Carter's answer: *"Are we payin
Panama to take the canal? We are not. Under the new trec
ty, any payments to Panama will come from tolls paid b
ships which use the canal."* Well, that's hardly a truthfu
answer. Where would those tolls go if they didn't go t
Panama? Obviously, to the nation that paid for the right c
way, paid for the construction, and is paying the costs c
operating the canal. So regardless of which pocket we ar
taking it out of, we are still paying Panama to rob us.

Next, the President's message conveyed the idea that th
new treaties included a "bonus" option for America: that
at some future time it should be necessary to build a sea
level canal across Panama, America would be given the firs
priority to do so. Again, a slight distortion of the facts: Arti
cle XII of the new treaty which the President referred t
spells out that America is **prohibited** from negotiating witl
any other country for the construction of an inter-oceani
canal in the Western Hemisphere without the **consent** of th
Panamanian Government. Factually stated then this articl
gives Panama the right to **veto** our building a canal acros
Nicaragua or anywhere else in the Western Hemisphere
even across the United States.

In attempting to answer the objection, "Why should w
give away something that Americans bought and paid for?
Mr. Carter stated: *"I must repeat a very important point: W
do not own the Panama Canal Zone. We have never hac
sovereignty over it. We have had only the right to use it . .
From the beginning, we have made annual payment t
Panama to use their land. You do not pay rent on your ow
land."*

Again, while not necessarily an outright lie, it was in
deed quite a bit short of the "God's honest truth," regar
ding the circumstances of our annual payments t
Panama. There was no mention of **rent** or **lease** i
our 1903 Treaty or its amendments. The purpose of ou
annual payment to Panama was to compensate that na
tion for the loss of revenues from a pre-existing agree

ment regarding a railroad across the Isthmus which Americans had also built, back in 1863. When the French took on their canal project in 1878, they also took over the railroad and the payments. When we bought out the French, once again we assumed control of the railroad, and the sole purpose of those annual payments was to compensate the Panamanians for that loss of revenue. Whether our original treaties with Panama spelled out "buy" or not, such terminology could not be more overriding than other provisions of this accord, which was to apply *"in perpetuity" (forever),* and *"to the entire exclusion of the exercise by the Republic of Panama of any such sovereign rights, power or authority."* What could be clearer as to intent?

With the opening of the canal, and the accompanying loss of revenue from the railroad, America began paying Panama $50,000 per year. This was later raised to $430,000 when America abandoned the gold standard, and were gradually increased to $2.3 million annually.

Perhaps the most important point in Mr. Carter's fireside chat urging Americans to accept the new treaties was his statement that ratification would "demonstrate that as a large and powerful country, we are able to deal fairly and honorably with a proud but smaller nation."

Must a bank turn over its money to a bandit to prove that it is a "fair and honorable" institution? Isn't there just a touch of silliness in President Carter's selection of words? Virtually every pro-treaty advocate has constantly referred to *Panamanian pride.* Unfortunately, none bothered to explain what it is that Panamanians are so "proud of."

Panamanians did not conceive the ingenious set of locks by which giant ocean liners are raised 86 feet above sea level, the engineering brilliance that made possible the building of the canal. They didn't suffer the dangerous hardships of penetrating the swamp and jungle breeding grounds of lethal yellow fever, seeking out and destroying the deadly killer that had made most of their nation uninhabitable. They didn't contribute in any way to the actual building of the canal. Almost everything of tangible value in their nation was either built for them by Americans, built with American financial aid, or is the legacy of our presence in the Canal Zone.

It is evident that a great many of our politicians considered America's **just** pride secondary to Panama's **assumed** pride. But pride alone in any case should never be the determining factor in important decision making. The real issue at stake in the Canal Zone issue was the universally accepted **"right to possess"** that which one has lawfully obtained through **purchase** or **creation.** This right is basic to civilization and cannot be abrogated without serious impairment to the concept of civilized society. Americans who sacrificed their lives to build the canal, together with the generations since who have contributed blood, sweat and tears in the form of taxes to provide some **7,000 million dollars** worth of American assets in the Canal Zone, have been defrauded of this right.

The most shameful part of the entire affair, is that loss of this territory was achieved not so much by act of Panama as it was through the scare tactics employed by our own politicians and bureaucrats. Scare tactics that succeeded in convincing a number of people that trying to hold the canal would lead to "another Vietnam." Again, not only a complete distortion of the facts, but also of the moral values involved. For whom were we fighting some 9,000 miles away in Vietnam? Certainly not for American homes and property, and not against direct aggression aimed at the United States. There were no legitimate analogies to be drawn between the two situations. Sol Linowitz, our own chief negotiator on the new treaties, not only "parroted" the extortion threats of General Torrijos, he amplified them to enormously unreal proportions. Panama's armed forces consist only of approximately 2,000 national guard troops, who already have their hands full keeping Panama in subjection to the dictatorial rule of General Torrijos.

Had these treaties been rejected by our Senate for the outright piracy they represented, initially there might have been attempts to sabotage the canal. None, however, could have succeeded were we determined to prevent such action. Chamberlain's appeasement of Hitler did not prevent World War II; it merely encouraged the process of lawless aggression. Contrary to the emotional eyewash that flowed so freely from our pro-treaty forces, the realities of the canal issue were not based on humanitarian concerns for the Panamanian people. The Panamanians were merely the dupes in the transaction, the pawns, the phony excuse used by yet another ambitious dictator.

In addition to the obvious value of the canal, our Canal Zone encompassed billions of dollars worth of gigantic cranes, warehouses, machine shops, highways, docking facilities, hospitals, international airports and their support activities, housing and recreation areas, all bought and paid for by the American taxpayer. These assets will now be "milked" by the small handful of greedy "Generalissimos" and "El Supremos" who will emerge from time to time to fight over the spoils of this monumental economic windfall. In the long run, the average Panamanian citizen will gain little from this act of piracy. Historical evidence of the area points more to the likelihood of an endless series of uprisings and civil wars for control of this unearned bonanza, and a general disaster for the people of Panama.

This power struggle alone promises to bring chaos and turmoil to the world's most important shipping artery. Regardless of all other considerations which should have dictated a "no" for the new treaties, American withdrawal from the Canal Zone can be counted upon to incubate disaster. Crisis after crisis will arise in which we are certain to become involved, and in which we may surely expect to suffer far greater losses than if we had shown the courage to defend our just rights and territory.

It will indeed be difficult for future historians to understand anything about this totally illogical transaction. The often touted premise that it will gain us the friendship of Latin America is perhaps the most idiotic assumption of all. Every day that the American worker steps behind a sales counter, operates a lathe, drives a truck, saws a board, ploughs a field, or descends into the black hole of a coal mine; a part of that day has been spent working for the benefit of the people living in Central and South America. Since 1945, the United States has unselfishly provided billions of dollars in foreign aid to help nations of the Western Hemisphere improve their economic conditions, and this includes Panama. The enormously significant point, however, is that this aid was not obtained by them through extortion or threats. If our track record to date has not earned their friendship, giving away a canal can add nothing towards that goal. Quite the contrary.

Latin Americans are predominantly a "macho" people. They admire courage and despise weakness. It is their hereditary nature, and not even Mr. Carter, can change that fact. But what are the economic realities that pertain to Latin America and the Panama Canal? Considering our 59-year record of benevolent operation of the canal, what do the nations of South and Central America stand to gain by this transfer of ownership? The answer is: absolutely nothing. The unbiased right of all nations of the world to use our canal at fair and reasonable rates has played a major role in the economic development of Latin America. The new treaty, which goes into effect when Panama assumes complete control of the canal, says nothing about the toll-rates Panama may charge. As an inefficient, unstable and poorly run government, Panama may be expected to "milk" the canal for all it's worth. We cannot even be sure that Torrijos, as an acknowledged friend and admirer of Fidel Castro, or Torrijos' successors, will not selectively "juice" or favor certain Latin American nations with the objective of bringing them into the communist camp.

With nothing to gain and everything to lose by a change in Canal management, one has to wonder at the kind of pressures used by the Carter administration to gain the tacit approval of Latin American governments; much less to prevent their vehement opposition to the new treaties. We must also consider the process and the "shenanigans" of our President in swinging the votes of senators who had previously opposed the treaties. Anyone who listened intently and objectively to the Senate proceedings on this matter would have had to conclude, from the evidence presented, that the Senate would vote 100 to 0 against ratification. Unfortunately, those senators who so valiantly presented the overwhelming case for the American people — and against the treaties — were not debating **anyone**. They were simply talking to the walls. There is no way that solid evidence and logic can be argued against meaningless ethereal rhetoric. The fact that these treaties which represent a plain case of piracy even reached the Senate for so-called "debate" was itself a national disgrace.

Senator Paul Laxalt of Nevada, who, with "down to earth" facts and reasoning defended America's interest as ably as Abe Lincoln might have done, has provided us with perhaps the only plausible clues to this mystery. In his opening day address to the Senate debating the new treaties, Senator Laxalt stated:

> "It looks like big business is concerned enought about insuring its investments in Panama to back the treaty. It is no secret that the Torrijos regime is teetering close to the edge of financial collapse. What is less well known is that many U.S. companies have created offshore investment centers in Panama, taking advantage of Panama's lax banking and tax laws, and pouring literally hundreds of millions of dollars there.

> "If the walls caved in on the Torrijos government, American dollars heavily invested in the country would be lost. With this treaty and its extravagant payoff plans, the Panamanian economy would be pumped up and many American businessmen saved from a financial drubbing. Additionally, I think the business community has bought the 'violence argument' and is willing to have taxpayer dollars bail them out of imagined Latin difficulties.

> "The third leg of the establishment triad offering support for the Panama Canal Treaty is the leadership of big labor. There is so much politics tied in with this endorsement that I am not sure the merits of the treaty were a consideration. The polls show that the rank and file members do not support the treaty. Perhaps not all the leadership does either, but I cannot tell, due to the heavyhandedness of George Meany. Louis Fattorosi is strongly against the treaty. Last month he was scheduled to speak out against the treaties as a member

of the Panama Truth Squad However, he was warned by
the AFL-CIO head office that if he did so the AFL-CIO
would revoke the charters of the Canal Zone unions."

Envy is the easiest of all potions to sell to a troubled
populace. And typical of the political opportunist he is,
General Torrijos climbed to power on "hate Yankee" propaganda. But envy clothed in spurious compassion or any
other false garb is insufficient justification for appropriating
the fruit of what has been achieved through the blood, sweat
and sacrifices of another. If we should accept such a
premise, then the world would surely descend again into the
abyss of the Dark Ages.

There is no question that treaties of long duration should
be open to modification where reasonable justification exists. The American taxpayer supports the largest and best-
paid State Department of any nation on earth. But is
diplomacy no more than attending cocktail parties? Or does
it also entail the ability to recognize potentially bad situations, and to attend to them promptly before they reach
crisis proportions? There can be no excuse for taking 13
years to negotiate a treaty of surrender, rather than a
mutually acceptable compromise.

Admittedly, Panamanian citizens did have a number of
legitimate grievances that needed redress. Often they were
held to only menial employment on the canal, being denied
the satisfaction of participating in the higher paying skilled
positions. But this, and other such irritability factors should
have been negotiable.

With hundreds of alternatives and options available to the
United States, why did we choose complete capitulation? In
addition to our annual gratuities, between 1945 and 1975
America has provided Panama some 446 million dollars in
foreign aid and development loans and grants. They didn't
have the "Chinese boot" on our foot; pressures can work in
both directions. We could have made concessions, including increased revenues from the canal operation. We
might have helped them with more realistic aid in the
economic sector. Or, as a last resort, we might even have
gone to the other extreme and taken over the whole of

Panama — which we did buy and pay for!

All of the Senate's haggling over amendments to the treaties regarding our rights to defend the canal or to move American warships to the head of the line in the event of hostilities was little more than a face-saving exercise. After all, what good is moving to the head of the line if we have to depend on someone else to open the gates?

An incredible irony emerged in answer to the question who are we giving the canal to? Pro-treaty forces never stopped throwing insinuations of imperialism, colonialism, and exploitation at the American people. But we are not giving our canal to the native Indians who are indigenous to the isthmus. Instead, in an ironic twist to charges of imperialism, we are turning it over to the same small clique of ruling families that have exploited Panama from the day their conquistador ancestors first stepped ashore.

We have relinquished possession of the greatest single peaceful achievement of our two-hundred-year history, the most meaningful contribution ever made by one nation for the benefit of all nations. We sadly deceive ourselves if we believe this to be the end of our problems in that area. More accurately, it signals the beginning of our troubles.

CHAPTER 3
CHINA AND TAIWAN

For the past thirty years, the Chinese government on Taiwan and the United States have been as close as any two allies on earth. Trust and loyalty are an essential part of such a relationship. The Taiwanese have proven themselves extraordinarily endowed with these qualities, and our alliance with them has served America well.

During the Korean War, and later in the Vietnam War, our military bases on that stragetically located island, and the Chinese cooperation in other support matters during those conflicts, provided America with greatly needed aid in time of dire need. Conversely, we know that in both of those conflicts, American soldiers were dying at the hands of the Red Chinese war machine. Succinctly stated, the Taiwan Chinese have been our proven friends, and the mainland Chinese our enemies. But "friend or foe" is by no means the major distinguishing feature between these two completely separate bodies of Chinese-speaking peoples.

The communist regime of Red China is a tyrannical government which is estimated to have slaughtered upwards of sixty million of its own citizens while indoctrinating them with the "blessings" of communism. Opposition is not tolerated on the mainland other than at the pleasure of the government, and then only for the purpose of purging one mistaken line of thought or policy and inaugurating a new one. It may even be said that "planned dissension" has been a key element in the survival of communism on the mainland, just as it is in most other communist nations. When things go wrong under communism, which they so often do, planned dissension provides scapegoats for the occasion who are then simply liquidated as "enemies of the people."

Incredible a it may seem, it is merely a matter of semantics which assures the survival of communism as a totally oppressive and dehumanizing form of government. Under other forms of tyranny, dissenters are labeled "enemies of the government," a term which often backfires by rallying popular support. But "enemies of the people" — what a magnificent choice of words — actually adds an aura of legitimacy to the liquidation of any and all who dare to oppose the regime. Consequently, Red China's population has become virtual living puppets whose entire lives are dictated for them by the all-powerful Communist Party.

On the other side of the China question, we find the Chinese of Taiwan, a people whose love of freedom and liberty caused them to establish a form of government very much like our own. As a free and democratic society, the nation and people of Taiwan have prospered immensely since their founding to escape the oppression of communism back in 1949.

When comparing the esthetic values of these two nations, one must wonder at what could have prompted the President of the United States on December 15, 1978 to reverse and repudiate the principles for which Americans have fought and died in every war we have waged in the 20th Century. The millions of Americans who lost lives or limbs in these conflicts believed their sacrifices were helping to make the world safe for democracy. Now, unfortunately, Mr. Carter would have us believe that the world-wide supremacy of the Coca-Cola Company is far more important than such ideals.

Anyone doubting our description of mainland China might ask themselves: How did a population of almost one billion people who only yesterday were screaming for the blood of the "Yankee imperialist pig" suddenly "put on a happy face"? The answer is obvious: when the regime says "growl," the people growl; "smile," and the people smile. Nothing is by choice or by chance. With the Sword of Damocles constantly hanging over their heads, the conduct of the citizens of Red China is understandable. What is not understandable is how such a regime can tell the president of a nation seven thousand miles away to "dance," and indeed, he dances.

The question of whether or not we should conduct business with mainland China is not the issue. The door was opened for the eventual resumption of such trade by the Nixon administration, and sooner or later would have occurred. The issue, absolutely critical, was at what price and on whose terms? Unfortunately, as the Carter administration has repeatedly demonstrated, they cannot recognize a "buyer's" from a "seller's" market when dealing with foreign powers.

Red China, whose population is expected to surpass 1.4 billion people by the year 2000, has reached the absolute boundaries of its isolationist policies. No longer can the Red Chinese survive without the modern technologies of the West, and particularly, trade with the United States. America not only has the technology they so desperately need, but also has the market for their raw materials and products which would enable them to purchase that technology. In the "poker game" of world politics — just as in Panama — Mr. Jimmy Carter has again "folded" America's winning hand. Unfortunately, in this case the ultimate consequences may be even more disastrous. In the Panama affair, our president merely sold out his own country. When, however, without even bothering to consult Congress (and with only seven hours notice to the Taiwan government) he reversed 30 years of policies and priciples by selling out a close friend and ally, he ended all semblance of credibility for the argument that the United States is a nation to be trusted.

It is simply inconceivable that what we see on the surface is the true picture. America held all the trump cards and could have lived indefinitey without resuming trade and diplomatic relations with the communist mainland. Conversely, we know that Red China now desperately needs this association. With such knowledge readily available to the administration, why then did Mr. Carter so willingly submit to conditions tantamount to unconditional surrender? Our president not only categorically accepted Peking's demands for abrogation of our mutual defense pact with Taiwan, removal of all American troops from that island, and the severing of diplomatic relations with a good friend, but he went a step further, adding insult to the already seriously injured Chinese of Taiwan.

Contained in his announcement that America would "divorce" the free Chinese and "marry" those of the communist mainland, was his incredible and totally unnecessary statement: "There is but one China and Taiwan is part of it." While such an idea might sound reasonable to the casual observer, the citizens of Taiwan know that this pronouncement sounded their death warrant. There is simply no way that a nation of twenty million people, who for almost half a century have experienced the blessings of freedom, can be integrated peacefully into a nation of slaves. Nor is there any way for the masters of a slave state to allow the survival of twenty million heretics who, as long as they lived, would constitute a veritable cancer to its ideologies.

The seemingly lenient terms offered by communist Vice Premier Deng Xiaoping (Teng Hsiao-ping) for reunification of the two Chinas, which were made public shortly after Mr. Carter's "bombshell" announcement, were simply so much balm for the Western world: an "act" of cooperation by Beijing (Peking) well calculated to temper the impact and blur the realities of this inconceivably dishonorable deed by our administration. The Taiwan government hasn't even bothered to respond to this offer, knowing full well that reunification is impossible — it is surrender that is demanded of them.

With literally nothing to gain under the superficial terms of their offer, why is Beijing so adamant about "immediate reunification"? Obviously they know, as do the Chinese of Taiwan, that given even the slightest "toe-hold" on that island, they would soon manage to destroy it from within. There is not one chance in a million for a peaceful and safe reunification of these two nations whose ideologies at this time are as far apart as the North and South Poles. How long will it take for each to move sufficiently toward an acceptable middle ground? If ever, perhaps two or more decades would be an optimistic projection. In the meantime, if Red China were to follow its avowed intentions, Mr. Carter would have condemned to death twenty million friends.

The decision to recognize Red China was a closely guarded secret, not only from the American people, but from the Congress as well. However, according to the Washington, D.C. weekly newspaper *The Spotlight* (Jan. 15, 1979), it was probably no secret to such multi-national corporate

31

giants as the Coca Cola Company, or David Rockefeller's Chase Manhattan Bank. *(The Spotlight* is a publication of Liberty Lobby, Inc., a patriotic non-profit organization whose "hatchet" falls with equal severity on both major political parties.)

If we can believe the genealogy of the Carter administration as outlined in *The Spotlight,* it is indeed as intriguing as a James Bond 007 movie plot. Moreover, we can begin to make sense out of what (at least superficially) appears to have been an act of sheer stupidity.

According to *The Spotlight,* President Carter, along with Secretary of State Cyrus Vance and National Security Council chief Zbigniew Brzezinski, are all former members of David Rockefeller's "Trilateral Commission." The Trilateral Commission is a consortium of North American, European and Japanese businessmen formed by Mr. Rockefeller in the early 1970's, the membership of which includes Coca Cola board chairman and close Carter confidante J. Paul Austin. Also noted in this genealogy is Attorney General Griffin Bell, former member of the Atlanta-based law firm of King and Spaulding, attorneys for the Coca Cola Company — which also happens to be headquartered in Atlanta. Another name of the list is that of HEW Secretary Joseph Califano, whose former Washington, D.C. law firm had represented Coca Cola in the nation's capital. Fascinating reading, to say the least.

A little farther down in the same article, we find that Charles W. Duncan, a former president of the Coca Cola Company, had been allowed by Mr. Carter to keep his millions of dollars worth of "Coke" stock while assuming a post that is responsible for the day to day running of our multi-billion dollar defense complex, that of Undersecretary of Defense.

Within one day of the President's announcement of full recognition of Red China, the Coca Cola Company was able to present to the press their new Chinese language "Coke" bottle; design studies which normally take months to accomplish. But then, the CARTER/"COKE" connection seems to spawn such coincidences: With the advent of his Egypt-Israeli peace treaty (and its generous U.S. subsidies),

"Coke" again entered the Egyptian market after 12 years of banishment from that nation.

While Bell and Califano "bit the dust" in Mr. Carter's "crisis of confidence" purge, Charles Duncan (with absolutely no experience in that field), has been promoted to secretary of our nation's new multi-billion dollar Department of Energy.

Although it has been suggested for many years that it is the giant multi-national corporations and banking houses who "pull the strings" and in essence wield the real power of government, relatively few Americans have given such ideas serious consideration. "Full stomachs" rarely ask questions no matter how suspect the circumstances. However, we find in the best-seller book *None Dare Call It Conspiracy*, by Gary Allen (Concord Press, 1971), and a follow-up offering by the same author, *The Rockefeller File* ('76 Press, 1976), a fairly convincing argument for such an hypothesis. Mr. Allen's books pull no punches, citing names, dates, places, and secret societies in establishing the conspiracy angle.

In spite of the fact that some of the highest public officials and most prominent family names in America were openly used, neither book has resulted in libel or slander suits. Perhaps even more amazing is that each book carried an introduction by a United States congressman.

Conspiracy or coincidence, less than 24 hours before Mr. Carter announced his decision to abandon our allies on Taiwan, the communist Hsinhua News Agency reported that Chase Manhattan Bank president Willard D. Butcher was in Beijing (Peking) exploring business opportunities with top mainland China officials. According to this dispatch, Mr. Butcher "expressed willingness to strengthen cooperation with the Bank of China and to make useful contributions to China's four modernizations: of agriculture, industry, *national defense,* and science and technology, before the end of this century."

Obviously, any contributions that help to modernize a nation that at present is over 80 percent peasant farmers would indirectly increase its military potential. But going beyond that, as suggested by Mr. Butcher, and directly helping to modernize the war-machine of a single nation whose inhabitants number nearly one-fourth of the population of the entire world, seems slightly insane, if not downright suicidal.

The very idea that this momentous decision was taken without the consent of Congress — and was held secret from the American people until "after the fact" — is itself highly suspect. What other surprises could Mr. Carter have in store for us? There is no great body of water separating East and West Germany — merely a barbed wire fence. What a tantalizing target this must be for a man with an apparently compulsive give-away complex.

Since the intrigue of Mr. Carter's "China caper" is beyond the comprehension of all but the real "insiders," the best we can do at this point is to wait and to watch as the details of our new relationship with the China mainland unfold. There are two points in particular that Americans should look for and scrutinize in detail:

1. Will our commerce with Red China be conducted on the basis of "cash and carry" or under *long-term credits*? If it is the latter, it means that our government will underwrite the investments of big business, which will profit enormously, while the average American citizen is again relegated to the role of "chump" to pay for it. Our nation's economy and balance-of-payments deficit cannot afford to support any more leeches.

2. Communist China's nuclear and national defense capabilities are not fit recipients of American technological assistance. America has already meddled far too much in maintaining "balance of power" structures throughout the world. While it has proven good business for the arms merchants, it has seriously drained our economy and undermined respect for America as a nation. The very idea of helping to create a third military super-power on this tiny little world of ours is downright terrifying. Perhaps the biggest single factor in our detente with Russia is that we both have *something to lose*. On the other hand, Red China, already in the process of exterminating herself by over-population, would not be faced with that same consideration. To entertain for one moment the thought that nuclear war between

China and Russia might solve our problems is totally preposterous. Nuclear fallout from such a massive conflagration would surely destroy most of the world.

There is one final point to consider in our decision to help modernize a nation of almost one billion inhabitants. Eighty percent of China's population at present is peasant farmers who are living an "ecologically sound" life style. Will our aid in industrializing this huge nation include sufficient emphasis on the need for environmental protection? And even if it is offered, can a government faced with the necessity of such massive immediate achievements afford the costs of such long-term considerations? Air pollution, as we know, travels on the winds, and polluting of the oceans can affect the entire world.

Modernization of mainland China will mean that in the very near future that country will be generating millions of tons annually of toxic chemical wastes along with a substantial amount of nuclear waste material. Dumped either directly into, or in a manner so that it eventually reaches the ocean, it is wholly conceivable that such pollution, if it didn't void the waters of all marine life altogether, might nevertheless render many of the world's staple seafood commodities unfit for human consumption.

CHAPTER 4
SOUTH AFRICA

The Carter administration's policy of casting America's friends to the wolves would seem to befit a place in the Guiness Book of World Records. A dubious honor, perhaps, but no less a record. As in the case of Taiwan, the nation of South Africa has done nothing to alienate their long friendship with the United States. Yet, almost from the day he assumed office, Mr. Carter has set about deliberately trying to topple that government.

The purpose of this chapter is not to defend the internal policies of South Africa. It is, however, concerned with politicians who choose to play domestic politics with our foreign policy, at the expense of the vital interests of America and all of its people.

Traditionally one of America's staunchest allies, during World War I there were 231,591 South African troops, mostly of European descent, fighting alongside our "Doughboys." In World War II, this very small but sturdy nation provided 332,323 troops to aid our effort to halt the Axis onslaught. When the fate of West Berlin was seriously in doubt, SAAF air crews distinguished themselves by carrying out 1,240 flights of urgently needed supplies on the Berlin airlift. And how quickly we seem to have forgotten that during the Korean conflict, SAAF squadrons flew a total of 12,405 combat sorties as a **part of America's 18th Fighter-Bomber Wing (USAF).**

In helping to destroy one of America's **few proven friends,** we couldn't possibly do more to aid Fidel Castro in his bid to establish an "anti-America" African empire. From a tactical standpoint alone, the alienation of this small but dependable and powerful ally is sheer insanity. South Africa is the free world's only major source of nickel, platinum, chrome, cobalt, and titanium — strategic metals required in the building of airplanes, turbine wheels, satellites, tanks, and almost every other conceivable piece of industrial machinery. The United States must now import nearly 80 percent of its strategic metal requirements. Where do we go if we lose this source? Russia is the world's only other major producer of these critical materials.

The Cape of Good Hope shipping lanes, which pass within sight of Capetown, are an integral part of the world's most important water routes. Over 20 percent of America's oil supply travels that route as does 90 percent of the oil requirements of our European NATO allies. More than 60 percent of all commerce between Europe and the Far East passes around the Cape.

Some 12,000 ships a year put into modern, well-equipped South African ports, while another 14,000 are able to pass safely by, afforded navigational aids and search and rescue assistance by the South African government. At the Simonstown naval base, support facilities are available to the fleets of the United States and other free nations of the world to safeguard this vital route around the Cape and the busy shipping lanes of the Indian Ocean. A few miles from the Simonstown naval base is the Silver Mine communications center. This huge underground complex is one of the world's most sophisticated electronic installations. It has the capability of pinpointing the exact geographical location of every ship sailing the southern hemisphere, and even identifies type, nationality and armament. It has the ability to communicate instantly with ships, aircraft and submarines in the area from South America to the Indian Ocean, and as far south as Antarctica.

Until 1968 there were no Russian naval vessels operating in the Indian Ocean. Since then, Russia has been able to establish support bases in Angola, Mozambique and Guinea Bissau. Russia's influence in Africa grows daily with the aid of Fidel Castro. South Africa is the only nation on the entire continent with the capability, modern facilities, and willingness to support American naval and air units in time of need. In contrast to Russian and Cuban expansion in Africa, September 30, 1978 marked the end of our last outpost on that continent with the closing of our military base at Kenitra, Morocco.

Any objective discussion of South Africa should begin with an historical foundation. Contrary to popular opinion, and unlike most other areas of European colonization (including America), the southern tip of the African continent which now comprises the nation of South Africa, was almost totally uninhabited by permanent tribes until the arrival of European settlers in the 1600's. It was the European development of this region which later lured the mass migrations from the north.

As a nation we must maintain foreign relations with other countries. But what are the legitimate boundaries of such relations? Where does being a good, well-meaning neighbor leave off, and being an ignorant, peace-disturbing meddler begin?

In April of 1978 President Carter made a whirlwind trip to Africa, visiting the countries of Nigeria and Liberia. What prompted this sudden safari remains somewhat of a mystery. Considerably more of a puzzle, however, is how he chose "racism in South Africa" and "human rights" as the main topic of his public utterances. To understand this dismal exhibition of ignorance on the part of a high ranking American official, we must first understand the nations in which he made his incredibly naive statements. Statements made not to the Norwegian parliament or to the Vatican, but in Liberia and Nigeria.

Liberia is the nation founded by white Americans prior to our Civil War period to serve as a refuge for emancipated slaves. It is a nation that restricts citizenship to **blacks only,** and since its founding has been cited more often than any other country on earth for the actual practice of **slavery.** Next we have Nigeria, and what more illogical place, either in geography or history, could be found in which to condemn "racism" and lack of "human rights" in other parts of Africa? Between 1967 and 1969 more than 1,000,000 Biafrans were slaughtered in Nigeria's war of genocide against the Ibo tribe. Historians would indeed have a difficult task finding another war in which so many senseless atrocities occurred.

The point of the above observation: What was Mr. Carter's real reason for choosing Nigeria and Liberia as his pulpits from which to denounce racism and human rights in South Africa? One would hardly pick the annual "Godfathers" convention as the place in which to fault a newspaper-boy who occasionally misses a subscriber. No,

Mr. Carter's reason was simply to "make points" at home. This highly unusual setting provided the President with millions of dollars worth of headlines and front page news stories designed to endear him to his own various voting blocs.

But America has no monopoly on political hypocrites. In order to better understand (to borrow a phrase from the vernacular of today's youth) how "our heads are being played with," we must examine the entire African situation in somewhat more detail.

Why, for example, was there no great outcry by the World Council of Churches, or the United Nations, for economic sanctions against the Central African Republic when President Bokassa's palace was burglarized and he ordered all common criminals then in custody to have their skulls crushed with rifle butts? And what did we hear regarding the "dignity of man" when President Macias Nguema of Equitorial Guinea celebrated Christmas Eve of 1975 with an "entertainment spectacular," using a stadium to execute one group of political prisoners by hanging and another by shooting; all this to the accompaniment of pop music? Since coming to power ten years ago, this fine little fellow has used his powerful Fang tribe to exterminate some 50,000 of his nation's minority tribesmen. Nearly two-thirds of that country's original National Assembly and senior officials have been massacred in this well-defined program of genocide. And while Idi Amin of Uganda has received some publicity for liquidating up to 300,000 of his own people, it's not because those executions were often carried out with savage cruelty. Not at all. It's simply because colorful Idi, before his recent downfall, made "good copy" worthy of the press coverage.

The absolute hypocrisy of many Third World nations and their liberal Western apologist-agitators in using South Africa as a "whipping boy" defies all reason and logic. Actual genocide is not just a pastime, it is the national sport throughout much of the Third World. If we were to consider the half million black Sudanese slaughtered by the Arabs in the Sudan, the 100,000 Karens and Shans sent to the "happy hunting ground" by the majority in Burma, or the more than 100,000 Ahams and Nagas of Assam who died fighting for their religious and political freedom in India (the land of the peace-loving Gurus), then perhaps we may begin to understand the enormous fraud of the South African situation.

Only a few short years ago, Beirut was known as "the Paris of the Middle East." But now how often can we pick up the newspaper and **not** read about Christians slaughtering Moslems or Moslems killing Christians in Lebanon? Racism is prevelant and practiced in almost every nation on earth. It is not, as the world's political hypocrites would have us believe, a phenomenon peculiar to the nation of South Africa.

If there is any measure of truth in the foregoing, why then is South Africa constantly being subjected to censure? Quite obviously, much of it is of their own making. Theirs is the only country in the world that openly and honestly admits to having racial problems. (Other nations simply bury their problems. **Literally.**) This fact has made South Africa an irresistible target for every political opportunist wanting to take a "cheap shot" at an admitted racist. What we seldom hear about, however, is that the most severe critics and active agitators for reform measures within that nation are to be found in the white, rather than the non-white, population. While it is the non-white leaders financed from outside sources who make the headlines agitating for revolutionary changes, it is still the white elements who are making meaningful changes through orderly and peaceful evolution.

Nothing is quite as shattering to the peace and tranquility, and in turn, progress, of a nation earnestly trying to make meaningful reforms (and South Africa is) as the meddling of outside busybodies who totally ignore and refuse to acknowledge the complexities of the South African situation. Particularly, the meddling of a self-appointed "Messiah" who has far less regard for the human suffering his remarks might bring than for the publicity they would garner for him at home.

Just what did Mr. Carter hope to accomplish with his inflammatory statements demanding black rule, majority rule, in all of Africa? Of the 45 nations that now comprise the continent of Africa, less than half-dozen have any form of democracy whatsoever. Most of these nations have cruel repressive dictatorships, and many (with millions of inhabitants) have simply **one-man rule.** Now that's some kind of "majority rule." But assuming that Mr. Carter's remarks were to be taken seriously throughout Africa, what might we expect?

South Africa is a nation of some four and half million whites who over a 300-year period have created a modern oasis out of a wilderness; and another 18 million non-whites who, for the most part, have migrated to the area to seek whatever improvement they might be able to find in this new habitat. What, then, would sudden "majority rule" mean in such a country? Would it result in the whites of that nation becoming "shish-kebab" on some tribal menu? Or would it simply mean four and a half million refugees looking for another homeland? The answer is neither. The people who created that nation are not about to sit back and meekly ac-

A world that learns nothing from past experience, past examples, and past historical fact, is indeed in a sorry and stupid state. The end of World War II saw the founding of the United Nations and an almost hysterical effort to foster self-rule for the European colonial possessions in Africa. Little thought was given to important considerations such as: Are they ready for self-rule? Who lives there? What are the logical boundaries? And what are the potential ramifications and consequences of "instant autonomy"? No, "humanitarianism" must be satisfied regardless of the carnage it may bring. As a result of this incredibly naive mandate, Black Africa has suffered a succession of wars, civil wars, and tribal uprisings that in terms of savage horror leave the death camps of Dachau and Buchenwald pale by comparison.

There is far more evidence to support a conclusion that this world of ours may be destroyed through the **thoughtless** efforts of humanitarians, than by the **deliberate** acts of barbarians. The South African situation is certainly a fine example of that hypothesis. Evolutionary change from within (and it is constantly taking place) will eventually solve most of that nation's racial problems, pro-

41

viding South Africa is freed of outside meddling and allowed to find meaningful, lasting, and workable solutions. If not, what is the alternative? A holocaust in which millions of human beings of every racial origin go up in smoke.

While such a catastrophe might please the "holier than thou" sector, how would it affect the continent of Africa as a whole? Contrary to the general opinion, South Africa is not a nation of pith-helmeted "Lord Jim's" working copra plantations. Far from it. It is a modern, highly industrialized country that provides the backbone of almost everything the rest of that continent needs. In time of plague and other disasters, which is the first nation others on the continent turn to for help? It is South Africa. And what do we hear about this little nation having the finest scientific research facilities on the continent, and that these facilities are available to all? We hear very little about that side of South Africa because such knowledge would be counterproductive to the **humanitarians'** goal. While this examination of the South African issue was never intended to portray that nation as a country without racial and human rights problems (it has lots of them), for the sake of all concerned, it's time we looked at them in perspective with reality.

Since 1945 less than **one thousand** people have died as the result of racial strife in the nation of South Africa. During this same period, however, **several million** human beings have been slaughtered throughout the rest of the world in deliberate, premeditated programs of genocide. (The United States alone has suffered more human casualties from racial frictions and not less than a **hundred times** the amount of property damage in racial riots than have occurred in South Africa.)

The non-whites in the nation of South Africa enjoy more political freedom and opportunity than is **actually available** to non-whites anywhere else on that continent. (In how many nations of Africa, with the exception of South Africa, is there **any** political freedom whatsoever?)

Because, and only because, of the industry and technological know-how of the white population, South Africa is the only nation on that continent in which there is **no starvation**. (South Africa is one of only eight remaining **net ex-**

porters of food left in the world.)

South African non-whites enjoy far better educational opportunities and immensely better health care than is available to non-whites anywhere else on the continent.

Last but not least, South Africa's policy of segregation and separate development (which we attack so vehemently) works **both ways.** Under the Group Area Act, whites are **prohibited** from operating businesses in those areas. As a result of this policy, non-whites who otherwise would have been unable to compete financially with the whites, now own and operate fine hotels, restaurants, service stations, and practically every other conceivable type of business. (We might contrast this point with the fact that in our own country, in the ghettos that now plague every one of our major cities, over 90 percent of all ghetto businesses are operated by non-ghetto residents.)

If our President were truly concerned about "human rights," he would not have to travel halfway around the world to find an object lesson. He might have started right here at home with the tens of thousands of our own elderly citizens who each year are beated to death, or savagely crippled for the remainder of their lives. Or he might even have directed his efforts towards freeing from economic slavery the almost five millions of our own citizens who, because of incompetent government (and those who don't work at all), find it necessary to work at two jobs in order to support their families.

The most serious of all the "sins of ignorance" committed by our politicians is that of trying to force the model of a "Crabtree Corners" America onto some nation of Afghanistucci (wherever that may be). Outside of an occasional "McDonald's" or "Kentucy Fried Chicken" shack, anyone who has ever traveled abroad soon realizes that America is different from any other place on this earth. Not necessarily better, not worse, simply different. The point, of course, is that we should stop trying to measure what is right or wrong with the world by our own particular standards, and then saying, "you must do it our way."

In February of 1978 our Justice Department ordered the closing of Rhodesia's information office in the United States, feeling that Americans shouldn't hear whatever they might have to say on their own behalf. On September 23, 1978, President Carter vigorously defended the U.S. information office of the Palestine Liberation Organization with the statement that they are entitled to freedom of speech in the United States. But again in September of 1978, the U.S. government requested a number of American clergymen to register as "foreign agents" because they had agreed to allow ministers from the nation of South Africa to address their congregations. It is thus apparent that, at the discretion of the President and his administration, we now have direct censorship as in the case of Rhodesia, and "censorship by intimidation" as in the case of South Africa.

Then, too, the American public is also faced with the problem of "censorship by perspective," which often is carried out by a not always fair and objective news media. For example, the "attention getter" on the **front page** of the May 14, 1979 edition of the San Francisco Examiner was a huge photo of a black woman in South Africa being consoled by friends. The woman had just learned that her **23-year old niece** had been sentenced to two years in prison as the **leader** of the 1976 student riots. However, in the same issue of that newspaper, we must turn to page 17 to find a small article on a report by Amnesty International that detailed how approximately 100 children ranging in age from **8 to 16** years were suffocated, stoned, bayoneted, and beaten to death with spiked clubs in the Central African Empire. Apparently we are to conclude that the mothers and fathers of children butchered by a black ruler do not suffer the same anguish as an aunt who learns that her niece has been sentenced to jail by a white government. The massacre of those children for protesting the wearing of uniforms in school (just one of many such incidents), was the final straw which later in the same year brought about the downfall of Emperor Bokassa I — by his own people, and not through the efforts of the western press.

If America is going to tie its foreign-policy to "human rights" issues, let us at least be, fair, impartial, and above all — realistic in our expectations.

CHAPTER 5
THE UNITED NATIONS
and other annoyances

For the year 1979, America had been scheduled to pro-vide Israel with three-quarters of a billion dollars in foreign aid, and approximately the same amount to a number of her Arab adversaries. With the negotiation of the Arab-Israeli peace treaty the ante was upped: As the "price" we pay to "buy" peace in the Middle East, we have agreed to furnish yet **another $5-billion**, split between Egypt and Israel, over the next three years, part of it as long term loans.

There is probably some logic in maintaining a "balance of power" as a deterrent to conflict, but the example cited is fairly typical of our past record of financing all sides of every confrontation. The net result can ultimately be nothing short of the bankruptcy of our own country. Nothing could more dramatically illustrate the peculiar nature of our policy in foreign affairs than the fact that in the past twenty years America has **financed both sides in 14 wars.**

United States involvement in the United Nations organization is perhaps the prime example of the departure from reality in our foreign policy. Like its predecessor, the League of Nations which was formed after World War I, the United Nations was born in 1945 amid dreams and hopes that this institution would forever banish war. A good theory, but unfortunately, the human intellect, unlike mechanical contrivances, does not always follow good theory with good practice. "Good theory" for one nation too often becomes "cake" for another, and this has been the historical record throughout the three decades and more of the United Nations' existence. Millions of speeches and thousands of resolutions have echoed through UN chambers, but it is doubtful that the course of humanity has veered even one degree to the right or left of its determined path as a result of all this splendid oratory.

The immediately recognizable flaw in the concept of the United Nations is that it operates too much like our own bureaucratic establishments. Somebody else pays the bills!

Consequently, this organization has grown like a cancer, become involved in everything, accomplished little, and often created as many problems as it solved. It is by far the "plushest" and most opulent institution this side of OPEC, and as such has become little more than a "Job Corps" for the world's elite. Of particular concern, however, is that more often than not, it is dominated by ideologies completely foreign to America's best interests. Which means, again, that this is yet one more case in which we are subsidizing our problems.

The United States is only one of more than 130 nations that comprise the UN membership. Yet America picks up 25 percent of UN operating costs (100 million dollars in 1978), plus the same percentage of the bills of such subsidiaries as the UN Food and Agriculture Organization, the UN Educational, Scientific and Cultural Organization, and the World Health Organization. America's total cost in 1978: $385 million for the UN's 46 sub-units.

While there was undoubtedly merit in America's generosity thirty-five years ago, when we were the richest nation on earth, how can we justify such outlays today? Going back no further than 1960 we see a pattern of America's general decline while other nations increased their financial leverage, and many have since soared to prosperity. In 1960 America's Total Reserve Assets (gold, convertible foreign currencies, special drawing rights, and reserve position in the International Monetary Fund) amounted to 33 percent of the free world's total reserve assets. By 1965, however, we had dropped to 19 percent, on down to 16 percent in 1970, and a further decline to less than 8 percent in 1978. That's the good news. Now for the bad.

With the value of the American dollar plunging almost daily in terms of the world's stable currencies, and having suffered several consecutive years of balance-of-payments deficits in our world trade, it is indeed doubtful that America now holds any Reserve position whatsoever. If we must remain in the United Nations, which is often simply an expensive duplication of other world organizations, then let us begin to pay our fair share and not another penny more.

In the narrative portion of **The Budget of the United States Government - Fiscal Year 1979** under the section titled "Foreign economic and financial assistance," we read: "The administration is firmly committed to increasing economic aid levels substantially over the next 5 years and to improving aid effectiveness. Proposed budget authority for this mission will grow by 23 percent in 1979."

Since 1945 the United States has provided foreign aid to every free nation (and many not so free) that by now totals almost $200,000,000,000. Isn't it time that we asked ourselves: What has this incredible sacrifice by the American people accomplished? True, we have helped nations that were willing to help themselves to get back on their feet again. But how about the vast majority of nations, the world at large? Is the world any more peaceful today than it was in 1946? Are the realistic prospects for survival of the world as good now as they were in 1946? If we examine the evidence, the answer to those questions must be an emphatic **No**.

An outstanding example of misguided humanitarianism that has literally financed catastrophe, and brought about even greater human suffering, is our American aid programs in Middle South Asia. In 1950 the combined populations of India, Pakistan and Bangladesh totalled about 400 million people. Since World War II the United States has provided India 9.2 billion, Pakistan 5.0 billion, and Bangladesh over one billion dollars (through 1978) in foreign aid. Are these nations actually better off today because of our help. Again, the answer is no. Our massive aid to India has allowed that nation to devote much of its own resources to the development of a nuclear bomb. But does the world really need another giant firecracker? The total population of those three nations now stands at approximately 830 million, and at their current growth rates it is estimated they will reach 1,351,000,000 by the year 2000. These nations couldn't feed themselves in 1950. They are far less able to do so today, and it shouldn't be necessary to go on with the scenario of their anticipated predicament for the year 2000 by which time their 1950 population will have tripled.

While the above are obvious examples of a good idea gone "sour," they are by no means the only such examples. We are doing precisely the same thing to the underdeveloped nations in Africa, Asia, and Central and South

America. It is American dollars that are financing a world situation in which wars of aggression are not only inevitable but will even become desirable. Now that, indeed, is some kind of humanitarianism!

As Americans we should take note of the fact that 200 years ago the topography of America differed little from that of the rest of the world. We had our swamps, impenetrable wildernesses, parched plains, and uninhabitable deserts. The transformation of this land was not accomplished with foreign aid, nor by a divine blessing. It required incredible sacrifice and unrelenting hard work by our people. During the building period, America's birth rate was as high as that anywhere on earth, but, as in most European nations, it has levelled off dramatically as we have reached the saturation point in habitable living space. The point of this observation is that we cannot possibly help those nations of the world that refuse to acknowledge — and attempt to treat — their own root problems; regardless of the amount of aid we might be able to bestow upon them. Thirty-five years of experience have surely provided enough evidence to support such a conclusion.

Our proposed foreign aid budget for 1981 contains the following items:

- Foreign economic and financial assistance . $7,456,000,000
- Military assistance   594,000,000
- Conduct of foreign affairs 1,554,000,000
- Foreign information & exchange activities . .   565,000,000
- International financial programs 6,859,000,000

Under the Food for Peace plan (Public Law 480), the United States will provide an estimated $1,129,000,000 in assistance during FY 81, which is about **two-thirds** of the total worldwide food aid target set by the United Nations **for all donors combined**. Of special significance, however, is this notation contained in the 1979 budget: "U.S. capability to provide food aid where it is needed most will be substantially increased with the establishment of the proposed international emergency wheat reserve which can be drawn on in periods of shortage." Translated into indisputable fact, this statement means that our simple-minded politicians had learned nothing, absolutely nothing, in the preceding 33 years. Not content with creating a welfare state at home, they are determined to create a world dependency as well.

Unfortunately, politicians always manage to find an area of "tokenism" to point to in refuting such statements. In this particular case, it is the millions of dollars that America has squandered on useless "family planning" programs through such organizations as the Agency for International Development (AID). The amount of money spent is indeed not "tokenism"; rather, it is the results which have been virtually nothing. If we examine a policy statement from AID's annual report for 1975, we can understand why nothing has been achieved despite these enormous expenditures. It reads: ". . . the Agency does not advocate any specific population policy for another country nor any particular method of family planning. Its aim is to provide needed assistance upon request so that the people of assisted countries may have freedom to control their reproduction as they desire." Now there's a revolutionary approach to population stabilization. Haven't people always had the "freedom to control their reproduction as they desire," and isn't it the fact that people in the nations most unable to feed themselves generally desire unusually large families?

Even the noble concept of "caring and sharing" can be carried to the extreme of a disaster, and indeed, America's foreign aid programs have reached that extent. American citizens should not allow our government to give even another penny to any nation suffering from a population problem, that does not itself make a dramatic effort to solve its dilemma. And all future aid, if any, should be contingent upon positive results of such efforts.

It is perhaps as futile as attacking "baseball and apple-pie" — to expect our leaders to re-examine America's support of the United Nations Organization. The U.N.'s ill-fated attempt at negotiating and freeing the 53 American citizens held hostage in Iran, should, however, have dramatically illustrated the impotency of this organization. But then, why castigate a fraternal organization for their failure in a situation that was not of their own making. The Iranian Crisis occurred because our own government made it happen.

Iranian officials had warned the Carter administration ahead of time that allowing the Shah to re-enter the United States would result in severe repercussions: And since our embassy in Teheran had been captured only a year earlier by the same forces, was there any reason to doubt the sincerity of this threat? This is not to infer that the United States should have bowed to the demands of any foreign nation regarding who we allow to enter our country. But it certainly dictated the need of applying a little common sense in handling the matter. The very least we could have done in preparing for such a contingency, would have been the removal of American personnel from our embassy, along with the destruction of any and all potentially compromising documents. We apparently did neither, and as a conse- quence; the most humiliating degradation of one nation at the hands of another since WW I. But the incredible farce of the situation, is that as of this writing (March 1980) the ad- ministration still feigns surprise that it happened.

To digress for a moment, we should put the history of America's involvement with the Shah and his government into perspective. Since the hostage situation broke out, there has been an enormous amount of emphasis placed on our cooperation with the Shah's secret police. Our normal foreign-aid packages to any nation, particularly, if it includes significant military hardware, runs the complete gamut from A to Z. In the lesser developed nations, which Iran was when we began our aid, such cooperation includes, how to: diaper a baby, plant corn, build an "A" frame, and heal the sick. On a slightly larger scale, it also includes projects in- volving irrigation, sewage and sanitation, education, rehabilitation of slum areas, ad infinitum. But those little achievements are not recalled by the Iranians, nor by their militant students in this country. American cooperation with the Shah's secret police is the only item they can call to mind. But let's take a realistic look at that point, too:

As an oil rich nation, Iran was not without potential enemies in that region, nor are they today. In response to this danger America was furnishing Iran with billions of dollars worth of the most sophisticated military hardware in the world, much of it still "top secret." And to do so without attempting to keep our finger "on the pulse" of that nation's stability, would indeed have been a gross dereliction of duty to our own citizens.

As for the Shah, he was certainly no worse — and perhaps considerably better than a great many leaders of the emerging nations around the world. It is undeniable that he, and he alone, took Iran out of the Dark Ages and made it a formidable 20th Century power. He brought prosperity and hope to his poverty-ridden country, but in doing so, he, or his advisors made one fatal mistake: Early in his regime he confiscated much of the vast land holdings of the Muhlahs (holy men), and at the same time stopped their state subsidies. And this was the mistake that inevitably led to his downfall: In a nation of zealots, no one can fight the "holy men" and come out on top. While we are hearing much today about the Shah's cruel and repressive dictatorship — we hear very little about the numerous acts of sabotage and terrorism which brought about such actions.

Since the hostage crisis began (150 days ago as of this writing). American sentiment has ranged from agreeing with the president's "do nothing policy" — all the way to "dropping the big-one on them." The latter certainly wouldn't have gotten the hostages back alive, but, Mr. Carter's policy hasn't either. And while the primary objective indeed should be the safety of the hostages — the administration's approach to the dilemma provided neither assurance of their safety, nor, a recognizable platform (by world standards) upon which to proceed. When Iran seized our embassy in Teheran, they literally severed diplomatic relations with the United States. When they failed to safely expel all members of our embassy staff, but instead chose to hold them hostage, they not only committed an act of war — but breached the cardinal rule of international law (or negotiations) — and that is diplomatic immunity for embassy personnel.

With the above in mind, why our government continued to conduct "business as usual" with their **official** representatives in Washington is impossible to understand. In replying to Iranian demands (but only through a third-party), the administration should have stated both emphatically and bluntly — "There is nothing to talk about while our embassy is closed and our citizens held hostage." While such a posture may or may not have resulted in release of the hostages, it would have at least appeared, even to such cannibals, that we do have a credible government in Washington. Instead, the administration chose to dignify this act of piracy by carrying on diplomatic relations with both those who sanctioned, and those who perpetrated the deed.

Once we got into this mess, a "do nothing policy' of up to three weeks duration was undoubtedly prudent. This waiting period, however, should not have been spent sitting on our hands: At the end of this period we should have started deporting **Iranian nationals** just as fast as we could possibly lay our hands on them. **Not maliciously**, but simply in accordance with standard international procedures that apply when one nation breaks off diplomatic relations with another.

Unfortunately, the moment our immigration officials even started checking on the **validity** of the tens-of-thousands of Iranian students in this country, the ACLU (American Civil Liberties Union) immediately sprang to their aid, opposing the action. On December 14, 1979, the U.S. Court of Appeals in Washington, D.C. ruled that the Immigration and Naturalization Service may continue checking on the status of Iranian students, but may **not** deport them even if found to be illegal. This decision came in response to an appeal by the Justice Department from a December 11th ruling by U.S. District Judge Joyce Green, who not only blocked any deportation proceedings; but relieved the Iranians of even responding to the inquiries of immigration officials. When our judicial system here at home exhibits no respect for immigration laws designed to protect the **rights** of **American citizens** — can there be any wonder at why our citizens are held in contempt — and hostage abroad?

Although the administration's handling of the Iranian Crisis began badly, it has since progressed to unreal — to downright "weird." Instead of deporting Iranian **nationals**, we are continuing to **import** them at an even faster rate than before. Since our embassy and its personnel were seized on November 4, 1979 (thru March 1980) more than 11,000 Iranians have been allowed to enter this country. And according to a UPI (United Press International) investigation made public on March 26, 1980, there has been so much pressure put on the Immigration Service, by the administration, **not to anger** Iranian nationals; that in at least one case it resulted in the entry of an Iranian student who had in his possession a manual on **how to build bombs.**

The very idea that America can "buy" friendships abroad, particularly, among the lesser-developed nations, has proved to be a disaster. There could be no better evidence to support such a conclusion than that which occurred in Pakistan in November of 1979: Unlike the Iranian incident in which there were alleged "grievances" between our two nations, such was not the case in Pakistan. Yet, because of a **rumor** that America has something to do with the take-over of the holy Moslem mosk in Mecca, our embassy in that nation was viciously attacked by the Pakistani people. Again, an act of war resulting in the deaths of two American servicemen attached to the embassy staff. It took seven hours of pleading while being assaulted with fire bombs and other weapons, before the government of Pakistan finally came to their aid; even though adequate forces were only minutes away. We see here an all too typical example of both a government and its people "biting the hand that fed them." In spite of the fact that the American people have provided more than **five-thousand-million dollars** ($5,000,000,000) in foreign -aid to the nation of Pakistan — that country, its government and its people; still subjected American citizens to seven of the most terrifying hours that any human being could possibly undergo.

The above discussion merely scratches the surface of the many ways in which our hard-earned tax dollars are being wasted abroad on misbegotten theories. Our massive give-away programs border on lunacy: They neither "buy" anything, nor do they accomplish anything of lasting purpose. After 35 years of accumulated evidence, it should be evident to even the most skeptical, that America can no longer afford playing the role of "Daddy Warbucks" to the world. Our nation is already on the brink of bankruptcy.

CHAPTER 6
ILLUSIONS

Politics has always been somewhat a game of illusions ever since the first group of people recognized that they needed some form of government. From ancient civilizations, right up to the 20th Century, a certain amount of illusion was perhaps even desirable in government, since in most cases, all power rested in government. It wasn't, however, until the mid-1930's that the use of illusion truly reached the state of an art in the United States. At that time, America was suffering a severe economic depression, and our population was ready to buy almost any idea, no questions asked. Indeed, the propitious moment had arrived for politicians to stop being "chintzy" with their illusions.

Unfortunately, as we have later learned to our regret, illusions are not appropriate to a Republic — if it is to be a government "of the people, by the people, and for the people." Kidding ourselves is a disastrous form of deceit.

In the early days of our nation, taxes were few, simple, direct, and understandable. This condition remained relatively intact until the 1930's, when America embarked on the first of its "grand illusions," the Social Security Act of 1937. There is certainly nothing wrong with the idea that prudent people should salt away something for the winter months of their lives, even if by government decree. The concept was excellent. What was wrong was that we spoiled a very noble idea by injecting an "illusion" into the basic format. This plan called for the wage-earner to contribute 1 percent of his earnings to the Social Security pot, while the employer also kicked in 1 percent. The idea that "someone else would pay it" (or half of it) was only a small illusion at the time, but one that has been the harbinger of our present state of economic chaos. (Each contributes 6.13% today.)

When our not too honorable (or bright) politicians realized they had "hit pay dirt" with their first illusion, a political dynasty of fraud and deceit took root. The format was so simple and foolproof that it was almost diabolical. "Promise the people anything — and let them believe that somebody else will pay for it." Armed with this new manifesto, government set about inventing and establishing a tax on virtually every product and transaction in the nation. Particular care, however, has always been taken to minimize as much as possible the reference to direct income taxes, which are so obvious and so repugnant.

It is also essential to the theme of this fraud that politicians speak paternally of the poor, the "little fellow," and the middle class who constitute the majority of voters. When mentioning something so intrusive as new or larger taxes, it is best to speak only of business taxes, particularly levies against "big business." After all, what voter could be alienated by a politician who wants to "sock it to the rich" — even the assumed rich. There is only one slight problem, however, when this theory is put into practice: *business doesn't pay taxes*. Business is simply a Tax Collector for government.

This isn't to say that the incredible burden of taxes and tax collection doesn't drive a lot of small operators out of business; it does. Nor is it to say that unreasonably heavy taxes don't hurt big businesses; they do. But only to the extent that such taxes adversely affect the overall business environment. Businesses merely pass their taxes on to the consumer (the poor, the middle class, everyone), because if they didn't, such enterprises would soon go broke, leaving jobs for no one. Today there is no such thing as an untaxed product or service. Thus came into our lives and our vocabulary the term "hidden taxes."

According to a California-based organization, The American Tax Reduction Movement, the average $8,000 automobile price includes some $4,000 in taxes. They also state there are 116 different taxes levied on a simple loaf of bread, in spite of the fact that most states do not charge sales tax on retail food purchases. The American Legislative Exchange Council of Washington, D.C., estimates that the average American family pays at least 41 percent of its hard-earned income in taxes, and that the average worker spent the first 131 days of 1979 working to support the federal, state, and local bureaucracies.

But America is not really suffering from taxes nearly as much as from the illusion that it is somebody else that is paying them. Going back to the original Social Security concept, this fact becomes evident. We know that the price consumers pay for every product and service has been marked up to compensate for the employer's contribution to the Social Security fund. They have to be, and there is nothing wrong with that. In essence, it is merely part of what employers have to pay for labor. But had these funds gone directly to the employees, who would then make the full contribution to the pot, assuredly they would have had a much better understanding of just how much of the "fruit of their labor" was going towards their own retirement. In such a case, it is doubtful that they would have stood by apathetically while their "nest egg" for the future was dissipated by incompetent government management.

The answer to "why?" government and taxes by illusion is really quite simple. A people that doesn't understand just how much it is actually paying in taxes, is far less likely to worry about how those funds are being used, abused, or squandered. Many years ago the *Reader's Digest* magazine conducted a survey of "second generation" welfare families. At a time when television sets were still somewhat of a rarity, this survey found many welfare recipients purchasing expensive TV sets, motor boats, fancy automobiles and other luxury items that a great many working families couldn't afford. Confronted with the evidence of this seemingly illogical situation, the almost standard answer received from welfare officials was: "So what? It's their money to spend as they see fit."

The conclusion of this fine bit of investigative reporting was that "nobody cared." Unfortunately, that conclusion was mistaken: government officials cared very much. After all, it is the number of welfare caseloads that determines the number of social workers required, which in turn establishes the number of supervisors needed to create one of the branches it takes to make the several divisions which constitute a department. With so much at stake, how could anyone conclude that "government doesn't care"? As a result of this attitude, we now find the bureaucracy administering to the needs of a great many third-generation welfare families.

But outright welfare is merely a small fraction of the

welfare mentality of our government. There has to be something immoral or indecent about a government (or those in government) who insist on "fondling" their people. The obvious objection to this form of "love" is the fact that there is virtually nothing that people cannot do for themselves far more efficiently and effectively than government can do for them. Even in such vital areas of the public need as health care, we find that Americans were receiving much better service from the medical profession (discounting technological advancements) prior to the invention of Medicare and Medicaide than they are receiving today.

While HEW (the Department of Health, Education, and Welfare) boastfully points to statistics on the number of Americans attending colleges today versus enrollments of 40 to 50 years ago, such statistics are grossly misleading. How many of today's college students can actually read, write, or perform simple math as accurately as the 8th grade student of several decades ago? The point here is that the billions of dollars that have been lavished on education by the federal government, particularly over the past two decades, really haven't purchased an awful lot of "smarts" for anyone.

There is little doubt that some justification exists for almost everything that government dabbles in. But this should not be used to excuse the cancerous growth of government and its never ending quest for more power and control over our lives.

In April of 1978 HEW celebrated its 25th anniversary as a full-fledged cabinet level department. While some of the functions consolidated under HEW go well back in our nation's history, it wasn't until this organization reached cabinet status that it began to acquire the characteristics of crabgrass. A strange analogy perhaps, but nothing could be more descriptive of HEW's operation. Everywhere this organization establishes a new function, like crabgrass, down go permanent, indestructible roots, which in turn sprout new runners which also take root.

Today HEW comprises a staff of almost 150,000 people, administering more than 350 different programs, which in FY 1979 cost 184 billion dollars, and is budgeted at over

205 billions for FY 1980. If that last figure is hard to visualize, look at it this way: that's enough to make 205,000 instant millionaires. A substantial portion of that budget will go for necessary and worthwhile purposes; much of it will not. And it's the "much that will not" that concerns us. To the average citizen, a problem represents a "challenge," something to be conquered. But to the bureaucrat, a problem means "opportunity" — usually for a *lifetime of escalating job importance*.

The function of educating our children is primarily a state and local obligation, with particular emphasis at the community level. The federal government first got into this business back in 1867 with a budget of $25,000 and a staff of four people. Since then our nation's population has increased approximately five-fold; staffing for the new federal Department of Education has multiplied by over 4,500 times; and the budget for that office by over 660,000 times. And the primary responsibility for our public schools *still* rests at the state and community level.

With such enormous help from the federal government, it should hardly be presumptuous to assume that Americans are now all geniuses. Unfortunately, it hasn't turned out that way. Virtually every nationwide survey of the educational situation shows that it is little better than a "disaster area." In other words, the massive federal presence — dictatorial and often counterproductive in its demands and requirements — has become the "Typhoid Mary" rather than the "guardian angel" of our public school system.

In the document *THE BUDGET OF THE UNITED STATES GOVERNMENT FISCAL YEAR 1980,* under the heading "Education, Training, Employment and Social Services," we find these major programs:

★ Elementary, secondary, and vocational educational programs: $7.7 billion.

★ Higher education: $5.2 billion.

★ Research and general education aids: $1.4 billion.

★ Training and employment: $10.6 billion.

★ Other labor services: $0.5 billion.

★ Social services: $5.4 billion.

To understand how a large part of such monies are spent, we need only to look at one of the sub-programs under the major category of "Research and general education aids." From the narrative portion of the 1979 budget document we read:

"In 1979, the National Institute of Education will focus its research toward solving the educational problems that particularly affect disadvantaged groups. Budget authority requested for the National Institute of Education rises from $90 million in 1978 to $100 million in 1979. Basic research will be substantially increased but with emphasis also on the dissemination of research results."

In the comparable narrative section of the 1980 budget document, we read (although the figures don't altogether jibe):

"Budget authority of $98 million is requested for the National Institute of Education for 1980, compared to $92 million in 1979. The Institute will focus on increasing educational equity and improving education practice. In addition, the Institute will conduct research on testing proficiencies in the basic skills."

As we note from the above, this is not a "one-time" study. It goes on year after year (though at least in 1979 they apparently had planned to let us know what they found out). If the findings of such research don't read: "Get to class on time, bring a pencil and note-pad, and pay attention to your teachers," then the taxpayers will have been swindled again out of another 98 to 100 million dollars.

As with the above example, for the past 30 or more years our government has spent billions of dollars on programs emanating from studies of "why people are poor." Again, these vast research projects come up with a variety of reasons which inevitably are translated to mean discrimination, but which rarely if ever mention the *obvious*. Admittedly, discrimination has posed an obstacle to numerous ethnic groups at various times and places throughout our history. But obstacles are not barriers, and there are too many examples of those who have surmounted such obstacles by their own efforts to consider them as barriers.

Similarly, and perhaps even better evidence, when we find so many others who have never suffered from ethnic discrimination to be among the *habitually poor,* then it's time we looked to other common denominators for answers.

There are only three *major* reasons why any person not physically or mentally handicapped is *perennially poor:*

1. Lack of ambition and the unwillingness to make personal sacrifices in order to succeed.

2. Becoming entrapped by family responsibilities (often of ever-increasing magnitude) before having achieved the ability even to support themselves.

3. Interference by the United States government, which has made being poor a tolerable, and often preferred lifestyle.

If the foregoing sounds callous, it is certainly no less compassionate than official policies which result in virtually destroying the self-reliance of millions of our citizens. But what is "self-reliance" and who really needs it? From the very beginnings of our nation, self-reliance is perhaps the one single trait that truly distinguished Americans from the other peoples of the world. Unlike the riddle of "the chicken or the egg," we know that liberty and freedom were gained by self-reliant people, and not vice versa. But as this concept wanes, so atrophies their progeny.

The phenomenal growth of the "Moonies," the "Jonestowners," and other such cults is ample evidence of the increasing number of Americans who have lost the ability and the will to depend upon themselves. Consequently, such people offer themselves up as little more than unthinking "zombies" to what they consider a higher mentality. The point here is, that under the illusion of humanitarianism, the United States government is deliberately fostering the curse of dependency upon its citizens.

Since 1945, the economic sector of the United States has produced more than enough material wealth to have stamped out poverty in America a hundred times over. If it hasn't — and we know it hasn't — then we have only the ideological "hanky-panky" of political charlatans to blame for he profligate dissipation of this wealth. It is apparent from government programs that our politicians have misread the real meaning in the parable "Give a man a fish and he will eat for a day; teach him to fish and he will eat for a lifetime.

Teaching our population to "fish" should not begin at the Job Corps stage of life, but rather at the kindergarten level, with the inculcation of self-reliance and personal responsibility. Such qualities of character not only lead to skills, but will also sustain the individual long after they have lost the ability to perform them. When, and only when, we see our children leaving school thoroughly imbued with the knowledge that the only permanent antidote for poverty is themselves, then indeed we will have wiped out poverty in this country.

In examining the self-reliance factor of our population, we might usefully ponder for a moment the evidence as to just the direct food assistance programs, alone:

School Lunch Program: Under the 1946 National School Lunch Act some 11 million children received free or reduced-price lunches in 1978. *School Breakfast Program:* Begun as a pilot project in 1966 and given permanent status by Congress in 1975, this program served breakfast each school day to more than two million children in 1977. *Summer Feeding Program:* Initiated in 1968, this program provides free meals to children participating in summer recreational programs. *Child Care Food Program:* In 1966 Congress authorized free meals for children enrolled in Project Headstart, day care centers, and after shcool care facilities. *Special Milk Program:* This program furnishes extra free milk to poor children in schools, summer camps, and child care centers. *WIC (Women, Infants and Children):* Developed in 1972, this program provides extra protein-rich food to pregnant women, nursing mothers, infants and young children. *Title VII of the Older Americans Act:* Under this program, some 400,000 elderly persons are served one meal daily (5 days a week), usually in churches or recreation centers.

In *addition* to the above, however, in 1978 there were over 17 million Americans enrolled in the *Food Stamp program.* This observation is not intended to question the need,

61

the cost, or even the propriety of any or all of the above programs. We do, however, challenge the integrity of a government that year after year accepts the *need* of such programs without seriously questioning their *cause*. When, after almost four decades of incredible national prosperity, we find some 26 million Americans living below the official poverty level ($6,200 for an urban family of four), and the problem continues to mushroom, what are we to conclude? The only logical conclusion is that the intended remedies were not solutions at all, but merely more illusions.

We might also ask: With such a dangerous trend taking place during prosperity, what would be our reserve or "emergency" position in the event of a *serious* economic crisis? Unfortunately, there is a strange paradox in the professed ideologies of both our government and its handmaidens, the publicly funded schools, which at present make impossible a reversal of the trend. While each denounces the immorality of direct slavery, both are this nation's chief advocates of collective, or "anonymous" slavery through social programs. If there is a moral point to be found in such a stance, it is almost indefinable.

It is high time the American people woke up to the ever-increasing number and magnitude of such social programs. Who are the real beneficiaries, the *big* beneficiaries, of this massive government spending? First, we know it isn't the "unfortunately poor." If it were, could we possibly have so many "permanently poor" still with us after decades of such massive so-called "assistance"? Who then?

Quite obviously, the primary beneficiaries are the numerous morally-bankrupt politicians who have built such sizeable voting constituencies out of such dependencies. But this is only the political half of the answer. On the economic side, we have the middle levels and upper strata of the bureaucracy (many in the $40,000 to $60,000 per year bracket) who indeed have found a "home" in the business of ministering to the needs of the poor. But there are others, too, outside the bureaucracy, who also profit handsomely from social programs of every size, shape and description — along with some that almost defy description.

In no way is this intended to imply that we should stop helping the unfortunately poor and the truly disadvantaged to meet their essential needs. It does mean, however, that we should begin recognizing the real motives behind many of these programs. As a typical example we might point out the new federal agency, the Legal Services Corporation. On page 281 of *THE BUDGET OF THE UNITED STATES GOVERNMENT - FISCAL YEAR 1980*, we read:

"The Legal Services Corporation funds local programs that provide free civil legal assistance to the poor. Corporation outlays have grown from $71 million in 1975 to an estimated $261 million in 1979. In 1980, outlays of $281 million are proposed. Title XX (social services) general revenue sharing, and other Federal programs outside of the administration of justice function will provide about $60 million more for legal services. Because the primary obligation for legal services rests with the private bar, the administration requests additional funds to encourage and coordinate fulfillment of these obligations. The budget also includes a $13 million increase above 1979 for Legal Services Corporation guarantees." (1981 budget — $329 million)

As the reader might already have noticed, prior to its establishment in *1975*, somehow for *199 years* the citizens of this country had managed to get along without a *Legal Services Corporation*. A certain amount of free legal advice is always available from such public entities as the city attorney's office, and from other government functions that employ a legal staff. There is also no shortage of private attorneys who will generally accept a *good* case on a contingency basis. And of course, there is the Public Defenders Office always available in criminal matters. It would thus appear that the true primary function of the Legal Services Corporation is to serve as a "Job Corps" for guaranteed full employment for members of the legal profession.

But perhaps we shouldn't confine our scanning of the budget document to serious matters only. There is also great humor to be found in this document. For example, on page 3, the opening lines under the heading "Budget Message of the President":

To the Congress of the United States:

"This budget for fiscal year 1980 is lean and austere."

Now there, indeed, is a "one-liner" that Bob Hope will never top.

CHAPTER 7
MONETARY MISCHIEF

One of the most widely used American colloquialisms used to be the old expression "sound as the American dollar." It was a euphemism indicating unquestionable value, because our nation's paper money, unlike the currencies of many foreign countries, was backed by real money: gold and silver It is doubtful that many of our post-World War II generation have ever heard this expression, and there is reason for its passing.

Prior to the "New Deal" administration of President Franklin D. Roosevelt, American currency carried a notation at the top of the bill which read: "THIS CERTIFIES THAT THERE HAVE BEEN DEPOSITED IN THE TREASURY OF THE UNITED STATES OF AMERICA" — and at the bottom, below the denomination of the bill, the words: "IN GOLD COIN PAYABLE TO THE BEARER ON DEMAND." Now this wasn't real money (paper is never real money), but they were *honest* certificates indicating that the bearer could redeem them at any time for real money (gold). There were other phrases used on different series of currency, such as: "REDEEMABLE IN GOLD ON DEMAND AT THE UNITED STATES TREASURY OR IN GOLD OR LAWFUL MONEY AT ANY FEDERAL RESERVE BANK." The "LAWFUL MONEY" referred to above were Silver Certificates, which carried the same guaranteed redemption clause, only in silver, which is also real money.

The Gold Reserve Act of 1934 removed the guaranteed redemption clause from our currency, while at the same time it made the possession of gold bullion by American citizens, or the harboring of gold coins (other than in limited quantities for purely numismatic purposes) a crime. Because of the obvious bulk of any significant amount of silver, the government allowed the continued use of Silver Certificates until 1963. At that time the price of silver began to catch up with inflation, and the "feds" withdrew all Silver Certificates from circulation.

It is important that we understand the difference between real money (gold and silver) and its more convenient substitute currency, popularly called "paper money." Real money (gold and silver) is acceptable anywhere on earth, and the issuing country is of no concern. The value is determined by the actual gold or silver content of such coinage. In fact, it isn't even necessary that the gold or silver be in the form of coins for it to constitute "real money."

To see how the United States government has actually stolen billions of dollars from its citizens when it confiscated their gold and issued them bogus "script" in lieu of "payable on demand" dollars, we need only to consider the following example: Everyone who exchanged a $20 gold-piece for a "non-redeemable" $20 bill in 1934 has today, in 1980, just that: a $20 bill — a piece of paper. At our currently inflated prices, such a bill would just about cover the cost of one dinner, a glass of wine, and the tip, at a moderately priced restaurant. On the other hand, that same $20 gold-piece, at the price of gold at this moment, would be worth approximately $650 — and that's not considering its numismatic value.

But the incredible irony of what was undoubtedly the largest single robbery in history has by no means satisfied the habit of our "spending junkies" in Washington. In the interim they have managed to run up a national debt of over 800 billion dollars, and this is still only the "tip of the iceberg" of their fiscal irresponsibility. In addition to the existing debt, the grossly under-funded future liabilities of the Social Security system, along with numerous totally *unfunded* government retirement programs, now reaches well into the *trillions* of dollars of debt.

But as might be expected, incompetent minds logically turn to irrational solutions for hope, which in this case happens to be *government-sponsored inflation.* "Why, that's ridiculous," many will say. "Mr. Carter is so concerned about this problem that he has even hired (at taxpayer expense) a special 'inflation fighter' named Alfred Kahn." But let's ignore the lip service given this problem by all politicians and simply consider the facts: First, we know that it is the enormous burden of a gargantuan bureaucracy and its wasteful spending which fuels the inflationary process. And isn't the bureaucratic establishment under Mr. Carter's direction mushrooming now faster than ever?

Next, we know that every time the federal government prints and puts into circulation more paper money (script) than is reflected in the actual assets of our economy (and they are constantly doing this), it simply dilutes the purchasing power of every dollar already held by the American citizenry. And again, isn't that factor inflationary? In private enterprise, the practice described above is called "watering the stock," and it is illegal. If a corporation were to issue additional stock without the express consent of the existing stockholders, the officers of such a company would be guilty of a serious violation of the Security and Exchange Commission statutes and would be sent to prison. But of course, considering the magnitude of the conspiracy and number of conspirators in this case, incarceration would be altogether impractical unless, perhaps, we put a barbed wire fence around the entire city of Washington, D.C.

Government's excuse for expanding the money supply faster than the actual assets of our economy warrant, is that it is necessary in order to meet the demands of our growing Gross National Product. But of course, it is government itself that compiles the statistics which comprise our Gross National Product, and since government computations include every transaction, including such non-tangibles as waste in government, the GNP is by no means an accurate measure of either our nation's productivity, or the state of our economy. We must remember that the only reason for money in the first place is to serve as a convenience factor, replacing the unwieldy aspects of the barter system. But in this capacity, if a monetary system is to be sound, money and the assets of the economy must be interchangeable at relatively par value, back and forth almost endlessly, plus or minus depreciation for "wear and tear;" with only temporary fluctuations caused by the pressures of supply and demand in the marketplace. This is how a monetary system works in a stable economy.

Unfortunately, inflation is simply another scheme by which government manages to steal billions of dollars from its citizens who have invested their money in cash-value life insurance policies, retirement income plans, savings accounts, and every other conceivable form of cash savings. And while inflation is robbing these citizens of their purchasing power, higher prices across the board are providing government with enormously higher tax revenues. But again, if our slippery politicians think for one moment that inflation is the answer to meeting future obligations, they are sadly mistaken. The inflation factor will also carry over to the other end, negating whatever illusory accumulations are made in the present.

When we examine the growing future liabilities of the Social Security system, along with the rest of the national debt structure, it becomes apparent that there is just no way that future taxpayers are going to be able (much less willing) to pay out 70, 80, even 90 percent of their incomes in order to meet such obligations. Particularly when they recognize the fact that many of these liabilities were in the building long before they were even born; were the consequences of irresponsible promises made by politicians on a "vote buying binge"; and above all, were *incurred without their consent*. After all, would anyone in his right mind *willingly* pay off the debts of a neighbor who had borrowed money, much of which was simply squandered or given away? Hardly.

The point of this observation is that citizens now looking forward to Social Security for their retirement needs a little "further down the road of life" would be well advised to add alternative measures to their retirement plans. Particularly if they still have several income-producing years ahead of them.

It's almot as though "infectious insanity" has plagued our capital for the past several decades. The federal government has gone on, year after year, spending more than it collects in taxes, and has thereby literally *mortgaged* the productivity and earning capacity of children not yet born. What kind of contemptible b-----ds could do such a thing?

Unfortunatley, those responsible for this incredible predicament (administrations that nurtured the cancerous growth of the bureaucracy, along with members of Congress who consistently legislated spending programs resulting in deficit budgets) are not generally thought of in such terms. No, quite the contrary. For the most part, they are considered to be compassionate humanitarians. And, as such, they will continue their successful modus operandi of promising the people "something that someone else will pay for" — and in all likelihood, be returned to office until this bubble finally bursts.

In 1981, the **first** $67.2 billion (67,200 X's ONE-MILLION DOLLARS) that Americans pay in federal taxes will not buy a typewriter ribbon, a lead pencil or even a paper-clip to help run the federal government. No, that money will go merely to pay the **interest** on money borrowed and already spent (much of it squandered) in year after year of deficit spending programs. To put it another way; that much money would have given us a **free** federal government (no taxes) in the year 1955. And still a better example of the cost of irresponsible government is this example: Our interest bill for the year 1981 amounts to more than **twice** the cost of running the federal government for the entire **decade** of the 1920's.

In looking at other areas of governmental incompetence, we can only assume that such politicians are living in hope that some other catastrophe will "strike the United States dead" before the collapse of our financial system exposes their true character.

CHAPTER 8
PLAYING WITH THE ECONOMY

That the administration believes raising interest rates, with the intentional goal of slowing down the economy — even moderately increasing unemployment, could be the answer to inflation seems absurd. We know that shortages of sugar, coffee, and gasoline did not lead to lower prices. The same principle applies to all commodities. Essentially, it is "supply and demand" that dictates "price" in the market place, and any decrease in productive output (supply) invariably is followed by higher prices. This is particularly true in our country, where the unemployed, through a variety of social welfare programs (including unemployment compensation), still maintain a relatively high purchasing power (demand) without contributing to the other side of the economic equation. The only logical solution to our inflation problem lies precisely in the opposite direction: a greater, not lesser, **productivity factor.**

"Productivity" is the term used to measure the amount of goods and services that are produced per hour worked, and from the following measurements we may begin to understand the real cause of inflation. During the 20-year period from 1947 to 1967, America's productivity factor increased at an average of 3.3 percent annually. Throughout this period, improvements in technology managed to compensate for, and even exceed, other factors that tend to lower productivity. During the next ten-year period (through 1977), however, our rate of increase in productivity slowed to 1.8 percent per year, and by 1980 plunged through the "zero-increase" mark to a minus factor.

Since we know that "productivity" provides us with the creature comforts of life, what then are the factors that generally tend to lower our standard of living? Basically, it is anything and everything which costs money but does not return a usable product or service. While their numbers are legion, they invariably fall within one or more of the major categories listed below:

1. The ridiculously high "overhead" factor of inefficiency and outright waste generated at **all three levels of**

government. Since this particular point is emphasized again and again throughout this text, it needs no further amplification here.

2. High interest rates. We might begin this observation by noting the incredible number of new Savings and Loan and other financial institutions that seem to be "springing up" on virtually every vacant lot. Institutions which offer phenomenal interest rates to savers, and whose advertising often warns potential investors about the dangers of "speculation." The scare tactics of some of their commercials even go so far as to make direct reference to the stock market crash of 1929. While there is certainly nothing wrong with savings accounts — and indeed, they should be a mandatory part of every person's economic portfolio — they should not be thought of as a primary vehicle in the earning and accumulation of wealth for the future. In most cases, the interest paid on such accounts in recent years hasn't even come close to compensating for the erosion of purchasing power through inflation. In other words, the unhappy "saver" comes up with a net loss in terms of true value.

The majority of these institutions now pay as high as 15 percent interest (depending on which "plan" the saver chooses), and we don't have to wonder at what rates these funds are in turned loaned out for in order for the institution to make a profit. But straight interest rates alone may be somewhat deceiving. There are other special "gimmicks" in the money-manipulating business, such as Finder's Fees, Brokerage or Mortgage Points, and Finance Charges, which again — further and unnecessarily — escalate the end cost of everything for the consumers. No wonder we have spiraling inflation — when so much of the capital required for operating expenses and for the development and expansion of our productivity process is first ballooned by as much as 12, 18, or even 24 percent at the very beginning!

The "money racket" is indeed a racket, and government per se is a very active partner in the overall scheme. When the federal government borrows money (much of it to be squandered if not actually given away) through "T-bills" and other instrumentalities at high interest rates (15.7% in March of 1980), it thereby becomes itself a part of the siphoning process that reduces the amount of money available for direct investment and ownership of productivity. And isn't it our government that sets the interest rates which banks and other such institutions can offer as well as charge?

The point of the above is that the incredibly high interest rates offered today drastically undermines the incentive for individuals to participate **directly** in ownership of the wealth-producing forces of our national productivity. The whole scheme is an ironic farce: On the one hand we have their advertising commercials which tend to indicate the saver's money is absolutely safe — being held in a vault (such is not the case, though admittedly it is safe enough, usually being judiciously managed). On the other hand is the fact that the majority of these funds are being funneled by those institutions into the mainstream of America's productivity, which their own advertising so pointedly cautions the individual saver to "beware of."

This entire concept of our nation's economic interrelationships has three very clear disadvantages:

First, the idea of a "middle man" (and often several, in a chain) whose participation "balloons" the end cost of everything: **that is inflation.** Second, the process tends to make the already-rich (those who understand the delicate intricacies of "latching onto" institutional money) even richer. It is the third point, however, that is by far the most important of the three: That the individual is being "tossed a bone" (high interest) in exchange for **not** participating in **ownership.** Thus, through this process, the **power of ownership** is increasingly being concentrated into the hands of fewer and fewer entities, and that, indeed, is not a healthy situation.

In spite of the generally higher wages in 1979, due to a 13 percent inflation factor, the real income (purchasing power) of American citizens declined by 5 percent. We might contrast this common individual predicament with the way the "money lenders" fared. For the year 1978, J.P. Morgan & Company, parent of the nation's fifth largest bank, Morgan

Guaranty Trust, reported a net profit of $266.9 million — up 22 percent from 1977. On the other side of the continent, Bank of America ("numero uno" in the nation) profits surged an amazing 25.6 percent for the year, to $497.9 million. Other such financial institutions reported even higher growth rates in earnings, and that's just their "take home" pay. Bank of America's **net revenues from interest** for the year amounted to a staggering $2.287 **billion.**

If there is a salient point to be extracted from the above, it is that government-sponsored "high interest rates" are, in effect — and perhaps intentionally, weaning away the average citizen from participation in and ownership of the productivity (wealth-producing) process. As further evidence of this phenomenon, we note that there are now five million fewer individuals participating in the stock market than there were a decade ago. Consequently, the Dow Jones Average (adjusted for inflation) of the New York Stock Exchange now stands at only about fifty percent of its value of ten years ago. Again, we should contrast this vital indicator of our nation's economic well-being with the almost obscene growth of financial institutions (the middle man).

At present it might be said that the greater portion of the "power of ownership" possessed by the greatest number of our citizens lies in home-ownership, and this, predominantly, is by those over the age of thirty. But what about the young people who are becoming adults today and those who will follow? As a result of two adverse forces, inflation, and the competition-factor of an increasing population competing for a diminishing supply of land and other natural resources, home ownership — the cherished dream of most Americans — is rapidly going the way of the dinosaur.

Instead, as we are already seeing today, large corporations with ready access to institution money are building rental properties which if successful, and large enough, will eventually be taken over by the multi-national giants — who have even greater access to the resources of the lending institutions.

On March 31, 1980, President Carter signed into law a

bill that on a graduated scale between now and 1986, will remove all limits on interest rates both offered and charged. This bill immediately raises the maximum limit on credit union loans from 12 to 15%. It also abolishes state usury laws limiting interest rates on home mortgages and other types of large loans, unless individual states choose to reverse this rule within one year. With a simple stroke of his pen, Mr. Carter abolished the concept of home-ownership for all but the extremely rich.

The Bible calls usury a crime, as does every other covenant of economic transactions between civilized human beings. But, as he has solved all such problems, our "Bible-pounding" President has solved the crime of usury by legalizing it. In signing this bill into law, Mr. Carter stated that it "will help control inflation, strengthen our financial institutions and help small savers." And taking those marvelous attributes in order, indeed he is at least partly right:

When the average person can no longer qualify to make a large purchase (home, auto, business, etc.) without first making an 80 to 90% down-payment because of their modest incomes, yes, that should slow down the economy: When lending institutions can substantially reduce the number of loans they handle — but increase the interest rate on those they do make several-fold, again, this should help to "strengthen" them. (Didn't know they were anemic.) And as for the "small savers," yes, those who are still working and have something left over to deposit will be able to receive a higher rate of interest on their savings. But they might not have that much left over to save after paying the "butcher, the baker and the candlestick maker." That is, those super-large conglomerates that will be able to survive skyrocketing interest rates to ultimately pass on these costs to those who can afford their products.

But if Mr. Carter is that concerned about the welfare of the "little saver" — why is it that ordinary U.S. savings bonds (which may be purchased for as little as $25) must be held for at least 6 months before paying an annual rate of 4% — and at maturity (11 years) pay only 6½ percent?

While the **big savers** ($10,000 or more) in March of 1980 were earning an annual interest rate of 15.7% on six-months Treasury Bills. What a fraud!

No, there can be little hope of halting the runaway inflation until we get an honest government: one that doesn't tell us that "high interest rates" (like a kick in the head) are "good for us." When interest rates, both **offered** and **charged**, are gradually reduced to a sane level (including that charged by credit card companies), then we will have at least a "fighting chance" of bringing inflation under control. Such a move, automatically, should also re-kindle a willingness on the part of individuals to participate once again by direct investment in the productivity process. This last point is extremely important if we truly want the greatest number of our citizens to enjoy the better standard of living which is possible — and affordable — under the free enterprise system.

We know that the creation of new wealth in the United States is achieved principally by two forces: capital and labor. But as technology increases at an ever accelerating pace, it is obvious that the contribution of labor diminishes accordingly. With this knowledge in mind, it is absolutely essential that government promulgates policies which foster and encourage individual participation on the "capital" side of our wealth-producing economic sector. After all, isn't that what the "American dream" is all about? The alternative is a "class system" in which eventually perhaps one-tenth of one percent will be the super-rich, five to ten percent the moderately rich, and 90 percent the perennially poor.

But intelligent and responsible government policies alone are not the answer to this particular dilemma. How many children leaving school today truly understand how the free enterprise system operates? Even more important, how many have any conception of the multitude of ways in which they can become a part of that system? Unfortunately, any comprehensive knowledge of the subject of economics is generally limited to college-level courses, and often is even missing from that curriculum.

One of the great myths currently leading our youth to

general apathy and a resigned acceptance of the "status quo" is the belief by many of our younger people that "I'm too late in the scheme of things." To dispel this myth, however, we need only look at our Gross National Product. America's GNP now reaches well into the trillions of dollars annually. In other words: all **existing wealth** is really just a "drop in the bucket" when compared with the **new wealth** that is constantly being created by our forces of productivity.

But we must not confuse the idea of a much broader participation in the ownership of our productivity-process with so-called "share the wealth" programs. These two concepts are diametrically opposed, not only in principle, but also in results. Under the latter concept, existing wealth is divided and soon dissipated, the incentive to create and to excel is destroyed, and productivity stagnates as a direct result.

If there be any doubt regarding the effect of high interest rates on the inflationary process, we should consider the following. We know that the average middle class family usually has charge accounts at several department stores. Such families are also purchasing an automobile on time, seldom pay their credit card bills in full each month, and sooner or later are "on the hook" for at least one personal loan from a bank or finance company. In the aggregate, these interest payments, along with ancillary charges, may total well in excess of $2,000 annually. If there is a home mortgage to be added to the above assemblage of credit purchases, then such an estimate of interest payments would surely more than double.

The above interest payments, however, are merely the obvious ones which are paid directly by the individual. Like hidden taxes, there are also enormous "hidden interest" costs which must ultimately be paid by the consumer. Every time we buy a loaf of bread, a pair of socks or a hammer, **indirectly** we are also paying the interest on operating funds borrowed throughout the entire cycle of production, distribution, warehousing, merchandising and sales. Since the "mark-ups" at each stage in this process apply to the total and are cumulative, it's easy to see that even a mere one percent variation in interest rates at the lowest level in this chain of commerce must inevitably result in a significant difference in the cost of such items to the ultimate consumer. And of course, any state sales tax is always added to the **final** selling price — and thus in a sense is a tax-upon-interest charged at each level in the production cycle.

It would be almost comical — if it were not so grimly frightening — to watch our government "inflation fighters" as they repeatedly attack the evidence of inflation while completely ignoring the causes.

Why haven't Alfred Kahn and his boss, Jimmy Carter, noticed that the rise of inflation over the past 15 years has virtually parallelled (a) the rise in interest rates and the phenomenal growth of financial institutions, and (b) the soaring requirement for corporate borrowing, which, proportionately, greatly exceeds the increase in our GNP? These two factors alone spell INFLATION in capital letters.

This obviously abnormal trend has resulted in the creation of an artificial super "third power" (the money-changers) which now reigns supreme in the productivity process, standing above both original capital (the stockholders) and labor. The idea that it is necessary to offer high interest rates in order to attract the dormant capital of individuals is, of course, absurd. Repositories for excess cash (such as banks) are a convenience factor which would in any case be used by the general public, without regard to such incentives. That is their only legitimate purpose; they should not be considered as "investment houses."

To further illustrate the inflationary effect of this "new economic order," we might even consider the incredible sums of money now being spent each year on advertising by such institutions in order to attract new depositors. Does this advertising contribute directly to the process of baking a loaf of bread, producing a movie, or tailoring a suit of clothes? Indeed it does not. It is simply an expensive and highly competitive exercise by the "middle men" for control of the financial resources of the individual. We must somehow find a way to bring capital (investors) closer to the productivity process without first ballooning it through a third, fourth or fifth party.

We might also note that social programs that undermine self-reliance, and particularly, incentive, like high interest rates for the middle class, tend to be the "offering of a bone" in exchange for non-participation in the **ownership** of productivity. Monies lavished on such programs keep the recipients generally satisfied — they are extracted from the middle class — and ultimately gravitate to the very rich. Unfortunately, such programs are often difficult to challenge because they seem necessary and proper in the exigencies of the moment.

It is all too evident, however, that these exigencies, in most cases, are simply the result of basic political philosophies which "sell" extremely well at the polls but do not stand up in the crucible of practical application. Virtually every politician today campaigns on the promise that he (through the instrument of government), will remove our fears of hunger, poverty, illness, and lack of economic security in our old age. But what is "fear," and should this very human emotion be destroyed? Not to be confused with paranoia, it would seem that honest, normal, healthy fear serves a useful purpose. After all, it is not the sight of an onrushing automobile that keeps us from stepping into its path (that's merely knowledge), but rather the fear of being injured or killed. So we see that "fear" itself is perhaps the most necessary and practical of all our human emotions.

The obvious fallacy in government policies that assume the economic responsibilities of the individual is that in the long run they will virtually assure the recipients of a permanent place in the "status quo." When food, housing, recreation, legal services, transportation, higher education, entertainment, medical care and a limited amount of spending money are all available gratuitously from the government, where is the need for personal responsibility that is normally generated by the "fear" of being without?

3. Unreasonable Unionism: Contrary to popular belief, **higher wages** are not the reason behind **higher costs** — both of which are often assumed to be the **cause** of INFLATION. This is particularly true in the case of rising wages which tend to **trail behind** the rising cost of living.

Both of these items are the **evidence** rather than the **cause**, and this is why Wage and Price Controls will not halt IN-FLATION. It is not wages but unreasonable union practices which concerns us here.

When we see cases of "featherbedding" (the requirement to hire more employees than are actually needed for a job) and other ridiculous practices which lower productive out-put, then such labor "gains" are merely illusions in terms of the whole. To be specific; if management is required to hire three people to do the work of two — in the long run — the standard of living of all three is **reduced by one-third.** While it may be difficult to view it this way on an individual case level — across-the-board — that's the way it turns out. Money, per se, is just so many numbers printed on so many pieces of paper: It's what we produce in the way of goods or services that actually determines whether we enjoy a higher or lower standard of living.

If there ever was a case in which the maintenance of a "balance of power" structure is absolutely vital to the sur-vival of both parties, it is that which exists between labor and management. Too much power in the hands of labor "kills the goose" (as it did with our shipping industry) or fuels in-flation. The over-powerful labor factor has, for example, been the most significant single contributor to the decline of England as a world power.

But no power in the hands of labor is equally bad. It is an inherent fact that management will exploit whenever and wherever it can, depressing wages, which in turn reduces the overall purchasing power that is necessary to support a healthy economy. Unfortunately, that "balance" is not always easy either to find, or define. We do know, however, that government, per se (at every level), must remain neutral in this perennial conflict: It must not be controlled by management, nor managed by unions.

4. Extraneous Overhead Factors in Our Way of Life: Primarily, this category encompasses demands upon society which are the direct or indirect result of governmental laws, regulations, and policies. Since they do not normally show up under the "cost of government," however, they must be

considered as a separate — and perhaps the most important cause of inflation. Unlike the other three major categories — the insidiousness of this category — is that its impact is almost impossible to calculate in budget-like terms. Under this category we might find such items as: bilingualism, the cost of administering affirmative action programs, unnecessary record-keeping and reports, legal and judicial matters, the cost of crime from one branch of government countermanding the efforts of another, and the list is almost endless. Many of the items within this category are examined in greater detail in other chapters.

Finally — the solution to inflation is so simple that it is obvious that government wishes to **create** rather than halt this phenomenon:

1. A **federal** limitation of 12% interest that may be **charged** by all conventional lending institutions, with perhaps an additional 4% for personal finance companies which specialize in higher risk loans. This **national** restriction would also help to stabilize the present unhealthy situation of capital flowing out of states with lower to higher interest rates.

2. **If** it is necessary to "cool down" the economy, a system of flexible **down payment** requirements could be applied selectively **where** and **when** needed. As example; if the desire is to reduce small credit purchases (credit cards and charge accounts), raise the minimum monthly payment requirements from their present 4-5% to 15, 20, even 25%. In the case of new car purchases, in order to stimulate the sale of American made automobiles without imposing import-duties (which could backfire), again, simply require substantially higher down payments on foreign cars. Such a system could effectively stimulate or dampen certain aspects of the economic environment **without ripping-off** the general public with higher interest rates and more inflation.

CHAPTER 9
POPULATION VERSUS OUR ENVIRONMENT

In the building of this country, little thought was given to the idea that we might also be destroying our country. As frontiers moved westward, our requirements were plucked from the earth to satisfy our needs with little or no concern for the generations to follow. This was not a mean or callous attitude; it was simply practical for the day, a natural result of the natural abundance we enjoyed.

When one forest was stripped clean, we had merely to move the operation to the next hill. The horizons stretched without end in a land in which a person could literally hunt, fish, trap, mill or mine not only wherever, but however one pleased. There was no such thing as a license, a limit, a season, or even the thought of any form of regulation.

A great deal of irreparable damage occurred before we finally realized that conservation and concern for our natural environment are necessities for present as well as future generations. Fortunately, in our pre-awareness age the overall population was still fairly small, and our lifestyle was not nearly as punishing to the ecology as it is today. Detergents, smog, pesticides and most other pollutants were still unknown.

As the nation continued to grow in population, various government agencies came into being for the express purpose of preserving our natural resources and, in later years, the protection of the ecology as well. However, since government often bends, or is sometimes influenced by political considerations, a third "watch dog" force has come into being, in the form of private conservation and ecology organizations. As need brought on by rapid growth sometimes creates exigencies of the moment that over-power intelligent government decisions, there appears to be a three-handed chess game taking place between these forces.

Unlike the stripping of our natural resources, which is usually visible and apparent, damage to our ecology is most often of the latent variety. It happens long before we become aware of the fact, and we seldom have the ability to rectify the damage.

The largest body of fresh water on earth, the Great Lakes, contains vast areas of "dead water." This water, which has been killed by pollutants, is void of the oxygen necessary to support any kind of useful plant or animal life. Similar areas have also been found in our coastal ocean waters.

In the space of merely the last few decades, millions of acres of beautiful and productive land in this country have been desecrated in the process of making room for more people. Each time we add another 1500 people to our population (native born or immigrant), we take another 375 acres of usable land out of service.

While there are hundreds of similar examples throughout the nation, the Santa Clara Valley of California is particularly tragic. Less than 30 years ago this fertile area, whose growing season encompassed the entire calendar, was one of the most beautiful and productive agricultural regions on earth. Today this virtual Garden of Eden has been laid to rest under a concrete headstone of hundreds of square miles of super highways, housing developments, parking lots and shopping centers. In an area only a few short years ago prevaded by the fragrance of blossoms, residents suffering from respiratory diseases are now cautioned to wear some form of "gas mask" during periods of intense smog. The question might logically be asked, "How many more such periods of 'Thirty years of progress' can this nation survive?"

Beauty, however, is not the prime concern in the ecological battle. As we continue to ravage millions of acres of land in our growth process, we are also destroying much of the green plant life which produces sixty percent of our oxygen supply. With pollution of the oceans starting to whittle away at the plankton life which generates the other forty percent of our oxygen, we have ample reason for concern.

Recent reports by the EPA (Environmental Protection Agency) prompted a major television network to produce a special program titled "Caution - Drinking Water May Be Hazardous to Your Health." The subject dealt with the quality and safety of the nation's public water supplies.

Since a large percentage of our water comes from subterranean wells, the tracing of pesticides, chemicals and other pollutants is extremely difficult. Waste materials dumped in what appears to be a safe area seep into the ground and make their way through underground rivers to a water supply hundreds of miles away.

In a report made public on February 9, 1977, the Environmental Protection Agency noted that the practice of burying low-level radioactive waste in 20-foot-deep covered trenches at a nuclear waste disposal area near Buffalo, New York, had failed to prevent leakage. Even though the report concluded that the leakage posed no immediate health hazard, increased radioactivity has been noted by state and federal agencies in streams near this disposal area for several years.

But nuclear waste is not the only hazardous disposal problem of an industrialized nation with a high standard of living. From almost the beginning of our now gigantic chemical manufacturing industry, toxic chemical wastes have been simply buried and forgotten with little concern, and even less knowledge, of their potentially dangerous after effects. In 1947, the Hooker Chemical Company of Niagara Falls, New York, began burying toxic wastes in drums which were dumped into the Love Canal. This practice was continued until 1952, when the canal was sealed over and the property sold for one dollar to that city's Board of Education for a public school site.

After years of corrosive action by water, soil, and the contents within the drums, some 82 different chemical compounds (11 of them suspected carcinogens) began percolating noticeably to the surface in 1976. In addition to a nauseous stench, the following abnormlities were noted in the residential community surrounding the old canal:

Children and dogs playing around the canal site suffered burns on their arms and feet. Pets died at an unusually early age.Trees in areas where rain water had carried the wastes were literally eaten away. Basements in many of the nearby homes were permeated with noxious odors which monitors recorded as from 250 to 5,000 times the safe level. A preliminary evaluation of the human effects showed an abnormally high 29.4 miscarriage rate, while 4 out of 24 children born on one block suffered mental retardation. In one family alone, it is reported that a son has blisters on his eyes, one daughter's hair is falling out in chunks and another daughter was born with a cleft palate, slightly retarded, with an enlarged liver and a double row of bottom teeth. By Presidential order, this community was declared a disaster area in August of 1978. It will probably take several years of study, however, before the total effects of this tragedy are fully determined.

The Niagara Falls incident, while undoubtedly the worst to date, is but one of more than 400 known cases of damage caused by careless disposal of hazardous wastes. John Lehman, director of the hazardous waste management division of the Environmental Protection Agency, estimates that there could be as many as several thousand neglected dump sites around the nation, unknown and unmarked, capable of causing future trouble. Often, no one is even aware of their existence until a bulldozer rips into them in the process of new construction.

In 1976, Congress passed the Resource Conservation and Recovery Act, which is intended to provide public safeguards for future dump sites. It is anticipated that guidelines will include: a buffer zone around such areas; and a notation on the property deed to inform future owners that such land was a former "hazardous material" dump. With some 35 million tons of toxic chemical wastes being generated in the United States each year, it is indeed time to know exactly where, and how, these potential "time bombs" are being treated.

In a speech delivered on April 22, 1975, Russell W. Peterson, chairman of the Council on Environmental Quality, warned that the nation will be flirting with disaster if it allows water cleanup to be set back for economic reasons. This cabinet level officer noted that the waters which surround us are a *fragile, finite, life-sustaining environment which we are punishing at a rate wholly unprecedented in the three million year existence of man.*

Mr. Peterson was obviously concerned about our tendency to minimize the importance of protecting environmental quality when it conflicts with economic development. Secretary of Interior Rogers Morton, who had called the three-day meeting of the nation's top water experts, also warned, *"If we don't act, the next generation may well face a water crisis of even greater consequence than our current energy situation."*

Those more tolerant of water pollution — those who think we can always filter enough for a good drink of water — might ponder this thought: Tracing the product from beginning to end, agronomists calculate that it takes 120 gallons of water to produce a single egg, 300 gallons for a loaf of bread, and 3,500 for a pound of beef. It may seem incredible to us that we have to think, much less worry, about something as common as water. When we realize, however, that our average daily use amounts to 371 billion gallons, it obviously warrants considerable thought and meticulous planning for the future.

California, whose population is mushrooming under an avalanche of immigration and new domestic residents, is virtually assured its destiny will include a water crisis of catastrophic proportions. Had the drought in that area in 1976 and 1977 continued into a third year (and it might well have done so; dry cycles throughout the world often run 5 to 7 years), that state might well have resembled another Hiroshima. Many of California's normally bountiful reservoirs were as parched as the Sahara Desert. Completely discounting the requirements for agriculture, manufacturing, lawns and other foliage, it just isn't possible to *haul* even *drinking water*, much less, that needed for sanitation, to serve the needs of 23,000,000 people.

Water tables in California have been dropping for many years, which simply means that water in that state is being consumed at a faster rate than it is being replenished by nature. In a February 1, 1979 address to the State Board of Food and Agriculture, Director Ronald B. Robie of California's Department of Water Resources warned that California is *overdrafting* its groundwater supplies by more than two million acre-feet per year. Now the measure of an "acre-foot" of water is just what the term implies: an amount of water one acre in extent by one foot deep, which equals 325,850 gallons. So with a little simple math, we see that if California were to make up this deficiency by hauling water from out of state using giant 8,000 gallon tanker trucks, it would require a fleet of such vehicles capable of making 81,462,500 trips annually. Absurd, of course.

But the survival of California's population is not the only concern. The rest of our nation depends heavily on that state's agriculture for its subsistence. For example: California is the nation's largest producer of rice — and it requires 5 acre-feet of water for each acre of rice grown.

Other states, too, are facing inevitable water crises. Arizona, whose population has literally mushroomed in recent years, will be one of the first confronted with this problem. According to U.S. Geological Survey figures, groundwater tables in the Phoenix basin area have been dropping at the rate of 10 feet per year ever since 1950. But the continual overdrafting of groundwater supplies from any area poses two other hazards of potentially catastrophic proportions: First, it could result in a gradual sinking of the ground with considerable damage to the surface and any structures thereon; and second, and perhaps even more important, it could lead to the permanent loss of this natural underground storage capacity, which is by far our nation's largest source of fresh water.

Solid waste collection and disposal in the United States requires several billion dollars of tax monies each year, in addition to our individual monthly garbage bills. Individuals alone generate well over a hundred million tons of refuse annually, and what to do with this staggering quantity of garbage is not just a problem — it is almost a crisis in many communities. Since a great number of open dumps which serve as disposal areas for thousands of the nation's smaller cities and towns are in violation of many state and federal health standards, we may expect this problem to get considerably worse before it gets better.

We must bear in mind that a growing population not only consumes more resources, but in the process also creates vast amounts of waste for disposal, which in turn results in the devouring of other valuable land areas. How many hundreds of thousands of acres of arable land already lie irretrievably buried beneath the garbage dumps of our cities, towns, villages and hamlets is difficult to estimate. It is a negative survival factor, however, that will continue to grow with both time and population.

In spite of our general awareness and massive efforts to master the problem, the American lifestyle and industrialized economy are still extremely punishing to the ecology. Agricultural, mining, and industrial waste are being generated at the rate of several billion tons per year.

Air pollution is considerably more than just an eyesore and a human health hazard. Scientists at the University of California Air Pollution Research Center fear significant changes will occur in California's forests, gardens and crops as the result of increasingly polluted air. Even the stately ponderosa pine of the Sierra is not immune to these toxins and may be in permanent decline. A significant decrease of new growth in this species has been noted in the state's national forests. The Center also believes that air pollution is probably responsible for reducing by one-third in recent years, the valuable cotton crop of California's San Joaquin Valley.

Researchers at the Center express concern that some day (in the not too distant future) crops such as oranges, grapes, and lettuce will amount to little more than a memory anywhere near the state's two major metropolitan areas. In a 1976 newspaper interview, James Pitts, Jr., director of research at the Center, stated, "We've become more moderate about what to hope for in future years," and added that he believes that in another decade stationary sources such as factories and homes might be producing as much air pollution as cars.

Standards of the 1970 Environmental Act required auto exhaust emissions of three pollutants — hydrocarbons, carbon monoxide, and nitrogen oxide — to be reduced 90 percent by 1975. This deadline, which has already been extended three times, is still in the process of being amended, and due to the current energy crisis it will probably be extended indefinitely.

There is a tendency by many people to misinterpret reports in recent years about a declining American birth rate. As a result, individuals are often heard expressing the view that our population has stopped growing, and some persons even seem to think it is on the decline. They are wrong, of course. Increases or decreases in the "rate" indicate only a change of speed, not of direction. They must be coupled with the death rate, plus the immigration factor, in order to arrive at the only meaningful indicator: the growth rate. Unfortunately, massive illegal immigration of the past several years precludes an accurate assessment of the immigration factor. We can judge population growth, however, from other indicators, too. According to the Department of Transportation, in 1970 the United States had 108,407,306 registered motor vehicles. By 1975 this figure had risen to 132,950,410, an increase of 24,543,104 vehicles (22 percent) in just five years, and by 1977 had leaped another 15,814,424 to a new total of 148,764,834. (These figures do not include "off-highway" vehicles used for farming purposes only.)

From the above statistics we can draw one of two possible conclusions: Either American citizens, beginning in 1970, suddenly became affluent; or our population is actually growing at a much faster rate than the federal government cares, or even dares, to admit. Census figures are derived primarily from information submitted voluntarily by the residents of each community. (How many in the household, etc.?) Obviously, illegal aliens avoid this count completely, if they can, or minimize their numbers as much as possible.

Recent federal energy policies that are forcing a number of electric generating power plants to switch from oil to coal will cause considerable increases in air, water, noise, and solid waste pollution. If President Carter's July 1979 proposal to ultimately reduce the use of oil and natural gas in electric generating plants by 50 percent is realized (and those are relatively "clean" fuels), we may expect this problem to become severe in many areas. As a result of the anticipated dramatic increase in the use of coal for power generating plants, the EPA announced in August of 1979 that it would spend $900,000 on research projects relating to acid pollution of rain clouds by automobiles and industrial smokes. Rainfall east of the Mississippi is generally acidic, and the EPA estimates there are more than 300 lakes in New York State alone that cannot support fish life because of the acid problem.

But perhaps the most idiotic of all his proposals is represented by the billions of dollars he intends to pour into the development of synthetic fuels. Now "synthetic fuels" are not to be confused with "alternate sources" such as wind, solar, or gasohol. The synthetics are enormously expensive fuels which are to be derived from coal and tar sands in a process that even government environmental officials fear will require the "waiving" of so many environmental protection standards that the destruction caused could become a national disaster. And even then, it would take almost a decade to achieve any significant production.

It would seem, rather than spending ourselves into bankruptcy — it would seem, rather than acting like a moron who chops up the family furniture for firewood — that our Washington "Whiz Kids" could recognize that it is people who generate fuel-consumption. And the more people, the greater the consumption factor.

But no, instead of enforcing our immigration statutes and protecting the sovereign integrity of this nation, like the moron above, "America the beautiful" is now gearing itself to tear up this land and burn everything in sight — to meet what is essentially the energy demands of our mushrooming illegal alien population. In his July 1979 energy message to the American people, Mr. Carter decried the "crisis of confidence that is threatening American democracy." Indeed! Now how could that be?

CHAPTER 10
THE HAT AND THE RABBIT

As even a child will tell you, a good magician can always pull a rabbit out of a hat. We have grown so accustomed to marvels and miracles in our lifetime that the rabbit seldom appears as a surprise. With the real world presenting space walks and heart transplants almost as filler material on television, the miracle of show business is that the magician can still draw an audience.

In an age of incredible scientific and technological accomplishments, we are creating a dangerously sophisticated attitude in many people that, regardless of the magnitude of a problem or crisis, another "breakthrough" will come along in time to save us. When such confidence actually means betting one's life on the potential of future achievements, it must be regarded as blind faith — as meaningless as plain superstition.

Ecologists, with irrefutable evidence to back up their positions, claim that we have pushed our ecological boundaries to the limit, and perhaps beyond. Agronomists and demographers, equally concerned, publicly state that the world cannot tolerate its ever expanding population.

Surprisingly, quite a number of people actually believe that, as the world's population reaches the point where it exceeds the earth's capacity, colonies will be established on other planets, or simply in outer space. Others firmly believe that huge metropolises built on the floor of the oceans will be our salvation. While not even the technology necessary for such undertakings is presently available, the principal fallacy in such hope lies in the enormous material and energy resources that would be required for such projects. Indeed, if we had such resources, we might not have to look for another home.

More realistically, many are convinced that atomic energy will solve most of our problems. While at some future time it may be considered one of mankind's blessings, it is certainly not that today. In a single year (1974), there were more than 3,300 violations of safety regulations in atomic energy plants across the United States. In 1979 there was near panic and population evacuation caused by the radiation leaks and "melt down" threat at Pennsylvania's Three Mile Island nuclear facility. Since the gauges used there for monitoring radiation levels went completely "off scale" during that accident, no one can really say just how much radiation was actually released into the atmosphere.

Often thought of by the layman (and a sales pitch touted by the proponents of nuclear power) as an inexpensive source of energy (once the enormous installation costs were paid), nuclear power is not the "bargain" it is claimed to be. We have already accumulated millions of gallons and thousands of tons of radioactive wastes over the past thirty years without as yet being able to find a safe and permanent means of disposal. And one of the less-publicized cost factors regarding nuclear plants is that, unlike hydroelectric generating facilities, they are *not permanent installations:* The life span of a nuclear plant is only about 30 or 40 years, after which it is "worn out" (unsafe) and must be decommissioned. There is one "small problem," however, associated with the shut-down of an atomic power plant: as yet, no one knows for sure of any absolutely safe or economically feasible method to accomplish the "de-commissioning" of any of our gigantic nuclear power generating installations. Pennsylvania's Three Mile Island complex is now being referred to as a "billion dollar mausoleum," an inevitable epitaph for all such nuclear plants. How or why America managed to get itself so far out on the "nuclear limb" is indeed a mystery. We still don't know what to do with our present supply of radioactive "garbage," much of which will require thousands of years of "baby sitting," while we continue to generate and accumulate more.

Currently under study as potential means of disposal are: (1) Burial in the arctic masses. This, however, is thought too dangerous by many scientists, who fear that the heat given off by nuclear waste could trigger movement in the ice pack; (2) Disposal in space, which is economically prohibitive, and in addition carries with it the ever present danger of accidental fall back to earth; (3) Liquid injection into extremely deep holes in our land mass; and (4) Burial at sea, which at present seems to be favored by many as the most promising solution. This method would involve drilling holes a half mile deep in the areas of the ocean floor deemed safe from possible volcanic eruption.

Whatever the ultimate choice of means of nuclear waste disposal, it will not come cheaply. This is particularly true in the case of our huge "nukie" power generating plants, which involve tens of thousands of tons of highly contaminated equipment and material, which, in a few short years, will require some form of disposal. With these cost factors in mind (even assuming that no other liabilities are generated accidentally), it is difficult to see how anyone can accurately predict a *final* total cost figure for electricity generated by nuclear installations.

In the area of food production, we have made significant progress in recent years by vastly increasing the yield per acre of farmland, primarily through super-fertilization and the development of hybrid varieties of crops. Here, too, however, we are beginning to see evidence that our gains may not actually be as great as we had originally believed. In this push to attain greater yields per acre, we are finding it necessary to expend many more calories of energy in the very process. In the meantime, over-use of chemical insecticides has resulted in the evolution of pesticide-resistant insects. Even certain fattening agents used to increase beef production are now suspected of causing cancer in humans. In essence, therefore, we are beginning to reach the level of trade-offs, rather than achieving significant net gains in these areas.

In our frantic search to make the nation self-sufficient in terms of energy, we are exploring and exploiting every possible resource. The least offensive potential energy sources, such as wind and sun, are still many years away from economical and practical feasibility. In a December 1973 report to the President on the nation's energy future, Dr. Dixie Lee Ray, then chairman of the Atomic Energy Commission, identified the following as impediments to the early increased use of geothermal power: (1) the lack of economical ways to find and assess geothermal reservoirs and determine their nature; (2) the absence of recovery and use techniques for low-temperature or contaminated geothermal resources, and (3) *minimal understanding or control of potential environmental insults (earthquakes, tremors), and disposal of vast amounts of noxious gases, minerals, and salts that might result from substantial geothermal exploitation.*

Just as necessity was once the mother of invention, an accurate tracing of the lineage now finds exploitation, abuse, and risk to be the step-children of need. There is little doubt that we will attempt to squeeze the very bowels of the earth as the need arises.

If we don't soon take a breathing period from *forced growth,* but continue to place unreasonable demands upon our nation's problem-solvers, our magicians may some day look into the hat for their rabbit, only to find that the hat is empty.

CHAPTER 11
A VIEW FROM THE IVORY TOWER
. . . everything is beautiful, simply grand.

On May 29, 1975 Mayor Abraham Beame of New York City made an unprecedented live television braodcast from a city council meeting in which he bitterly assailed the major financial institutions of Wall Street for failing to come to the aid of his virtually bankrupt city government. The federal government had initially turned down New York City's plea for help, and it was certainly illogical to believe private banks would, or even could, lend money entrusted to them for safekeeping by depositors to bankroll a bad risk, one of already proven insolvency.

New York, like most of the nation's other large metropolitan cities, was in trouble — serious trouble. With unemployment soaring, crime at an all-time high, and the older parts of the city's physical structure rapidly degenerating, the city's financial plight was almost insoluble. On the other side of the continent, in San Francisco, a city at least outwardly affluent, the welfare rolls had grown by 64 percent during the preceding five years, to the point where almost one out of every four residents was on some form of the dole.

With the nation's relief rolls at an all-time high, and with 19.7 million persons then receiving food stamps or other free food assistance, the cost of local government certainly needed no artificial stimulus from the Congress. The cities didn't need it, they didn't want it, and they certainly couldn't use it — but . . .!

By a vote of 341 to 70, the House of Representatives in June of 1975 chose to ignore prudence and reason in passing a bill requiring that voter information, voter registration forms, and ballots be printed not only in English, but also in the alien language of every foreign-language group constituting more than five percent of the population of a particular area.

The Voting Rights Act of 1965 eliminated literacy tests as a prerequisite to voting for a period of ten years. The specific intent of the act was to prevent discrimination against Blacks in the South. The House bill referred to above was passed by the Senate in July of 1975, permanently suspending literacy tests, and expanding the provisions of the Voting Rights Act of 1965 to include the foreign language printing requirements.

This costly and burdensome demand upon municipalities means that, in cities such as San Francisco, election publications now must be printed in English, Chinese, Spanish, and soon Tagalog (Filipino) and possibly Korean and Vietnamese as well. Where the Congress thought funds for such an enormous project would come from is unknown. They could come from a reduction in other essential services, or they might come from an increase in taxes — but in any case, what is known is that they will not come gratis.

Since it takes a minimum of five years for an alien to become an American citizen (three years if married to an American), one might think that surely within that time, a person genuinely sincere about upholding and defending the Constitution of the United States, or interested in entering the mainstream of the American economy, would take the trouble to learn the language of this land.

Throughout the nation, millions of dollars are thus being constantly added to the cost of government by the necessity for the duplicating, triplicating, or even quadruplicating of printed matter to serve our growing alien population. This requirement, however, is minor in comparison with other foreign language requirements generated by the newer voting acts.

As we have witnessed, the seed, having taken root and sprouted, eventually flowered and branched into a multitude of other foreign language demands in addition to that of printing. Interpreters are needed in the voting places. Translators have to draft the propositions and arguments, as well as the ballots themselves. Mechanized voting equipment may have to be modified at considerable expense, and multilingual specialists are necessary to tally the votes. These are but a few of the more obvious aspects of the additional workload and increased financial burden imposed by the new voting laws.

If there is any single factor to which this nation's greatness might be attributed, it would be the personal initiative of its citizens. In the arts, sciences, and humanities, it is initiative that propagates both creativity and productivity. In too many ways, our government is discouraging personal initiative, with countless programs whose costs fall upon the already overburdened taxpayer.

Across the nation, many cities are facing the dilemma of impending bankruptcy. Before each election, politicians of every party and at every level of bureaucracy eloquently campaign on the "need to cut the cost of government." But despite dramatic technological developments of the last two decades which should result in efficiencies providing better government services at lower cost, in fact essential services are constantly being reduced while costly programs designed to de-emphasize personal initiative are being introduced and expanded.

It is the fondest hope of the citizens of this country (and not an unreasonable expectation) that their well paid administators and legislators serve them in a competent and loyal manner. The previously mentioned action by Congress of requiring voter information and ballots to be printed in foreign languages is an insult to the American people. It is also a fairly good indication that this act may be only the forerunner to removing even the prerequisite of citizenship to voter eligibility.

By such acts of irresponsible government, slowly but surely the productive elements of our society are being driven out of the big cities. The resulting effect is a continual reduction of the tax base necessary to support the municipal establishment, leading to the eventual collapse of the total structure — as is dramatically exemplified in the case of New York City.

The citizens of this nation, who have long prided themselves on being simply Americans, are currently being systematically segregated and categorized at every level, from the federal government down through the public schools, into specific racial, ethnic, cultural, or national groups. The cost of this massive effort, a diversion of dollars from otherwise productive pursuits, must indeed be no less than astronomical. Examples of such categorization are everywhere.

In a 1976 proposal by the San Francisco Superintendent of Schools ("an Educational Redesign for the San Francisco Unified School District"), we read under Section I: **"We must provide for the students who are non-English speaking continuous development in speaking, writing, and reading skills in their home language as we teach them English."** Why is this so? If these dollars were not sorely needed in fundamental instructional areas, such a proposal might be entertained. Furthermore, it is clear that students from non-English speaking homes already have adequate basic communicative skills in their native language, and that further development in that area will be at the expense of their English skills.

In Section V of the same proposal, we read: **"We must establish a goal that each school's certificated staff will be such that no ethnic or racial group will be in the majority.**

"We must establish a goal that each school's classified staff will be such that no ethnic or racial group will be the majority.

"We must establish a goal that the central office staff, classified and certificated, will be such that no ethnic or racial group will be the majority."

While no one should tolerate, much less promote, discrimination in employment, those who would accept government definition of which, where, when, and how persons shall be eligible for employment are naively following false prophets, and contributing directly to the decline of American education.

It is no secret that our nation's public school system, once the envy of the entire world, is now facing the greatest crisis in its history. The new teaching methods and curricula of the post-World War II era (along with a multitude of other factors) have resulted in a serious decline in educational standards. The growing number of high school graduates who can neither read nor write is constantly the subject of TV documentaries and magazine articles, as well as law suits by parents and students against their schools. With most educators in agreement that a return to basic instructional needs is essential to a reversal of this trend, the question must be asked whether such duties and responsibilities as those mentioned above are compatible with this profession — or are they, in essence, contradictory to the very concept of education? If there is no place for the "best qualified" in the school system, then where is the incentive for the student?

Each person by their own effort has the opportunity of advancing their own educational skills (in or out of school); it's a matter of choice and determination. But how many students would believe they could actually alter their racial or ethnic background in order to qualify for a job? Surely, not many. The most obvious point, however, is that if our public school systems are already failing in their primary duty, why do we insist on saddling our educators with such extraneous responsibilities that can only be counterproductive to the educational process?

According to an article in the February 22, 1976 issue of the **San Francisco Examiner & Chronicle,** titled "*Chicano power at work — Legislators to learn Spanish,*" a group of fifteen California lawmakers were to begin Spanish classes in the state capitol the following day. The stated purpose: "so they can solicit support and listen to problems of Chicano constituents." A logical progression in the current national policy of deAmericanizing the United States.

The 1976 Canadian election, in which the Separatist Party of Quebec won an overwhelming victory (a victory many observers see as signalling Quebec's eventual separation from Canada) should indicate the need for our taking a much deeper look into the ramifications of this subject. With perhaps the exception of Switzerland, throughout history and in every corner of this earth, a nation with more than one language eventually divides itself — people from people — along separate language borders. Language is the very nucleus of "difference' which inevitably leads to violence, turmoil, divisiveness, and never in any case toward cohesion.

Theodore Roosevelt, who was president of the United States during our peak period of legal immigration

(1901-1909), recognized the inherent dangers of a nation such as ours developing separate linguistic enclaves, and he expressed his concern in these words:

"We have room for one language here and that is the English language, for we intend to see that the crucible turns our people out as Americans of American nationality and not as dwellers in a polyglot boarding house."

The system worked beautifully, and America — the crucible — became a united nation, as was intended. Suddenly, for some unknown reason, we now find the government subsidizing the division of our country into separate linguistic and racial camps. A 180-degree contradiction of other enormously expensive government programs designed to eliminate racial and ethnic barriers.

The time has come for the American citizen to challenge those in public office who serve alien interests above and before those of our people. Their motives seem unmistakably clear: the support and control of huge and rapidly growing power blocs, which are deliberately being encouraged not to learn the English language.

The ability to manipulate such forces by those with a command of the foreign language, or indirectly through "puppet" entities, is manifesting itself in a new breed of political strategists. Patrick Henry, addressing the First Continental Congress, said: *"I am not a Virginian; I am an American."* The new political tactics of isolation, insulation, and manipulation, once established, will inevitably destroy our founding fathers' concept of democracy.

Almost from the day our new voting statutes went into effect, San Francisco's Registrar of Voters has been the target of harrassment by Oriental and Hispanic political groups demanding even greater emphasis (and costs) be placed on the bilingual voting process.

As the result of such agitation, on October 27, 1978, a suit was filed in federal court against the city of San Francisco by the U.S. Attorney General's office. In spite of the extravagant costs already expended by the city on multilingual voting, this suit alleges that San Francisco had deprived its non-English speaking citizens of their constitutional rights under the 14th and 15th Amendments. To be in compliance with the 1975 voting act (as interpreted by this suit), the U.S. government makes the following demands upon the taxpaying citizens of San Francisco:

Par. 17, b, of this legal action reads: ". . . to assure the full and fair exercise of their right to vote as required by the Constitution and statutes of the United States, such action to include, but not limited to:

1. Recruitment of bilingual poll officials on a year-round basis through assignment of regular staff in the office of the San Francisco Registrar of Voters. Said recruitment efforts to be conducted through and with the cooperation and assistance of community groups in language minority communities, and to include development and publication of public service messages via English and minority language press, radio and television for the recruitment of such bilingual poll officials;

2. Development of a training program to instruct poll officials, both bilingual and monolingual, in the bilingual voting requirements of federal law, bilingual registration and voting procedures undertaken by the City and County of San Francisco in compliance with federal law, and approved methods of rendering effective assistance to language minority voters;

3. Establishment and use of accurate assessment procedures to measure bilingual language ability of bilingual poll officials and of minimal standards of speaking in the relevant minority language for such officials;

4. Development of a glossary of key election-

related words in both English and the applicable minority languages and publication and distribution of said glossary to election officials prior to each election;

5. Establishment and advertisement of a telephone hotline for language minority citizens to provide information necessary to assist language minority citizens in registering and in exercising their right to vote;

6. Development of a voter registration outreach plan to actively register language minority voters which plan shall include: (1) establishment of a timetable for distribution and collection of registration forms, and related materials, and (2) a procedure for identifying specific places in the community where registration forms should be distributed to effectuate said plan;

7. Establishment of a cooperative working relationship between the office of the Registrar andcommunity groups in language minority communities for the development and implementation of voter outreach programs;

8. Provide community groups interested in voter registration, access to addresses of all unregistered residences;

9. Development of a comprehensive media campaign directed to language minority citizens to advertise all aspects of the voting process from registration to the casting of ballots which program emphasizes both the right to vote and the importance of voting;

10. Establishment of a task force under the supervision of the Chief Administrative Officer of the City and County of San Francisco to advise and assist the Registrar of Voters in complying with federal voting laws;

11. Establishment of effective measures for distribution of bilingual voting and registration materials to all language minority citizens of voting age;

12. Assignment of regular staff of the office of the Registrar of Voters to manage the development and implementation of tasks necessary to bring the City and County of San Francisco into compliance with 42 U.S.C. †1973aa-la;

13. Establishment of effective procedures to determine in advance of election day those language minority voters who require minority language assistance at polling places and establishment of procedures to insure that such assistance will be available when and where needed.

c. Authorize the appointment of Federal examiners pursuant to 42 U.S.C. 1973a(a) and 1973d to enforce the voting guarantees of the United States Constitution and Federal statutes in the City and County of San Francisco.

d. Grant such other and further relief as the Court deems appropriate together with the cost and disbursements of this action

Dated: October 27, 1978

Griffin B. Bell
Attorney General

(Note: Emphasis Added)

As we can note from the above list of demands (particularly, par. 7 and 8), the real motive behind bilingual voting seems to lie in giving unscrupulous politicians an inside tract to ethnic voting -bloc "clout." And to do so at the expense of the taxpaying public. That's "democracy at work?" With such costly special emphasis applied solely to the voting of our non-English speaking citizens, what happens to the "constitutional rights" of our other citizens? Those millions of English-speaking Americans who often fail to vote.

In a televised address to the nation on March 15, 1980, President Carter insinuated that it is the American people who are the cause of the inflation problem. Apparently they spend too much money on food, clothing, transportation, housing, etc. — and to break them of this habit — he would again raise interest rates. At the same time, however, the above referenced legal action is still dragging through the court, consuming thousands of hours of expensive litigation on the part of both the federal government and the city of San Francisco.

Proponents of bilingual voting often cite now-ancient treaties and practices (mid-1800's) between Mexico-Spain and the United States in support of their argument. In doing so, however, they conveniently ignore the obvious conclusion that such bilingual conventions were intended solely for the purpose of facilitating an orderly transition from Spanish, to an American (English-speaking) government. We cannot accept the premise that a hundred years later this transition is still going on, nor that we were ever in a transition period from Chinese, Filipino, Korean, Cambodian, Vietnamese — or whatever foreign language group happens to constitute 5% or more of a particular voting jurisdiction.

In the wake of Watergate, millions of words have been used to extol the virtues of honest government. Such virtues are indeed noble, but they do not guarantee that such a government is intelligent and tolerable.

Between the courts and the Congress, with their abstract decision untempered by reason or practicality, the American dream is well on its way to becoming a nightmare. Pure abstract justice, when practiced without logic or feasibility, is often less fair than injustice, for the consequential side effects fall unjustly on the general public, and in far greater proportion and severity than the original grievance.

Section 312, 8 USC 1423 of our immigration laws requires that applicants for American citizenship must demonstrate both a written and oral proficiency in the English language. The purpose and intent of this requirement is to assure that such new immigrants will become American citizens in **fact**, rather than merely in **documentation**. It would appear then, that those who now demand foreign language services (**if** they actually are American citizens) acquired their citizenship through fraudulent intent and therefore should be deported on the basis of that fraud. Wouldn't that make more sense than using taxpayer dollars to subsidize the setting up of foreign enclaves within our nation?

Typical of the contradictory and self-defeating management principles are the following extracts from a major newspaper. On the one, hand, a banner headline in the November 8, 1973 edition of the **San Francisco Chronicle** read:

**NIXON'S ENERGY PROGRAM —
HE ASKS EMERGENCY POWERS**
President Urges Nation to Lower
Car Speeds and Home Thermostats

Supporting news stories of that day detailed potential crisis conditions, including the possibility of an inadequate supply of even such basic requirements as heating fuel. With the advent of winter, such conservation measures seemed like the logical admonitions of a responsible government to its citizens.

Such an illusion was quickly dispelled, however, by careful scrutiny of the very same newspaper. Buried on the third page was a tiny article, reprinted here in its entirety:

"Cubans Entry
Washington
The Nixon administration has decided to

*waive immigration regulations to permit
the entry of 25,000 Cubans, it was
announced yesterday."*

In 1977 we found a new administration recognizing exactly the same energy problem and reacting with precisely the same mentality by ministering to the effects of this ailment — while totally ignoring one of the major cause factors. In a nation of finite natural resources, the elementary principles of supply, demand, and shortages is, briefly stated, simply a matter of total resources divided by the total number of consumers. While we may somewhat alter, amend, mitigate, or prolong the supply through a variety of options, we can in no way change the basic law that consumption is generated by people, and that when demand exceeds supply, the per capita availability is diminished accordingly.

Considering the fact that only a few short years ago the United States was a **net exporter** of energy, and that even our current petroleum production is staggering when compared with world averages, we can scarcely term the U.S. "oil-poor real estate." What then? Apparently the thought has never occurred to those advising Mr. Carter on his "Energy Plan" that to a very significant degree the problem itself is the result of the ever-increasing number of U.S. **energy consumers.**

At no time during the week long 1977 "Energy Symposium Spectacular" did Mr. Carter, Mr. Schlesinger, or any other member of the President's team of advisors make even a casual reference to the **energy impact** of what has become a mass migration of illegal aliens into our country. Or for that matter, the increasing number of refugees and other "special category" legal immigrants that are not chargeable against our statutory limitations on immigration. Certainly this is a factor worth mentioning, and one that we shall examine — for the benefit of the doubt, doing so using Mr. Carter's average per capita energy consumption figure as equal to 60 barrels of petroleum per year.

In 1976, the President admitted to a figure of some 8 million illegal aliens residing in the United States. Other estimates range closer to 16 million, and with a three year interim period of addition high illegal immigratiuin since those estimates were made, we are certainly justified in using a current median figure fo 12 million illegals. With simple mathematics, we find that our present illegal population is consuming the energy equivalent of some 720,000,000 barrels of petroleum annually — 2,000,000 barrrels daily — a sum equal to our **total energy deficiency.** Now that would seem to be an "energy impact" worth noting.

As a prelude to any program that extracts innumerable sacrifices from the citizens of this nation, one might have expected the number one goal in "conservation measures" to be the immediate and complete stoppage of this invasion. As incredible as it seems, however, quite the contrary took place: Just two weeks prior to his 1977 energy message, we found the President encouraging the invasion by stating that he favors amnesty for illegal aliens. A statement that could only be interpreted to mean "stick around" to those illegal aliens who might have considered returning home of their own volition; as an open invitation to the untold millions contemplating unlawful entrance; as a slap in the face to the honest applicants around the world, hopefully waiting for legal immigration into the United States; and last but not least, as a complete mockery of the sovereign integrity of our nation and of the laws passed by Congress.

Nothing changes but the calendar, and again, this time in July of 1979, we find the President ascending the mountain at Camp David for ten days of conferences with his top advisors concerning the nation's now-chronic energy problem. This time, however, his meditation paid off: He'll solve the dilemma by establishing two more huge federal bureaucracies.

In the mean time (just to make **sure** that we don't run out of energy crisis'), the administration is traveling half-way around the globe collecting hundreds-of-thousands of refugees, while continuing to allow the illegal entry of another million or so aliens annually. And that's how we solve all such problems in the Ivory Tower.

CHAPTER 12
HISTORY OF IMMIGRATION INTO THE UNITED STATES

In 1976 the United States of America celebrated its 200th anniversary as an independent nation. Since the earth is variously classified as being several million to perhaps billions of years old in the space of time, our entire national history comprises considerably less than the blink of an eyelid.

Immigration to these shores actually began in the early 1600's. The Dutch settled New York, the French along the Mississippi River and the territory of Louisiana. The Spanish established their colonies in Florida and the Southwest, the Swedes in Maryland and the English in Massachusetts and Virginia. By the year 1700 the colonial population was estimated to be approximately 275,000 people.

The first actual census was taken in the year 1790, and by that time the population had reached 3,929,214. A further breakdown of these figures showed that 75% of the inhabitants were of English extraction, 8% of German and the remaining 17% was fairly evenly divided among Swedish, French, Dutch and Spanish ancestries.

Each colony, in the early days, tended to set its own standards and requirements for allowing immigrants into its communities. This was later followed by the individual states passing laws relating to immigration, and it was not until the U.S. Supreme Court ruled these laws were unconstitutional that the federal government established a policy of national control over all immigration matters.

In 1875 Congress passed the first piece of permanent legislation relating to immigration with a law prohibiting the entry of prostitutes and convicts. This was followed by the Act of August 3, 1882 which placed a "head tax" of 50¢ on each immigrant and also excluded from entry convicts, mental incompetents and persons likely to become a public charge. The same year Congress passed the Chinese Exclusion Act, which barred from entry those of Chinese ancestry.

On February 26, 1885 the first contract labor law was enacted, designed to protect the pay scale of the American worker by preventing the importation of cheaper foreign labor.

In March of 1891 Congress passed another general immigration law, which required that immigrants be medically inspected. This act barred those suffering from certain diseases, as well as polygamists and paupers. Other provisions of this act called for the deportation of all aliens who had entered the country in an illegal manner.

During the period from 1881 to 1920, more than 23 million persons immigrated into the United States. While a number of lesser immigration acts had been passed in the interim, it was not until 1917 that the first comprehensive legislation which included all previous grounds for exclusion was enacted.

This act excluded from entry persons from the "Asiatic Barred Zone" which encompased not only Asia but most of the Pacific Islands as well. Another significant provision of this law was that it required immigrants to be able to read and write. In addition, the act provided for the deportation of aliens who had committed certain crimes or who had entered the country illegally.

In 1921 Congress passed a temporary quota act which was the first piece of legislation actually to limit the number of immigrants entering the country. This was followed in 1924 with a permanent quota act which tied immigration directly to a percentage of each nationality residing in the United States, according to the 1890 census. In 1929, the 1924 act was amended to use the 1920 census as the basis for determining quotas. It was the intent of Congress in establishing the percentage factor formula, that in this manner, further growth of the nation through immigration would not alter the traditional values and culture of the existing population.

Congress passed the first of a series of acts designed to eliminate racial barriers to immigration when the Chinese Exclusion policy was removed in 1943. This intent was broadened again in 1946 by the removal of additiional categories from the restricted list. Finally, complete abolishment of all racial barriers to immigration was accomplished by the Act of 1952.

Since 1945, numerous immigration acts have been enacted, allowing war brides, displaced persons, refugees, orphans, and certain other special categories to enter the country as permanent residents without regard to the usual immigration quotas.

The Act of October 3, 1965 eliminated the "national origins" system of eligibility for immigration, which had been the primary law regarding immigration for over 40 years. This law provided for a limitation of 170,000 immigrants per year from the Eastern Hemisphere, with no more than 20,000 visa numbers allotted to any one country, and no more than 200 visa numbers within that allocation to any dependent area of that country. A numerical limitation of 120,000 immigrants per year was established for the Western Hemisphere, with no allotment of visas per country. Visas were issued on a first-come first-served basis.

The Act of April 7, 1970 allows for the admission, in a non-immigrant (temporary visitor) status, of the alien fiancees and fiances of United States citizens for the purpose of marrying the citizen petitioner within 90 days of entry. Perons in this category, along with their children, are eligible to adjust to permanent resident status at a later date.

In 1978 Congress combined the allotments for both hemispheres into a single worldwide total of 290,000 immigrants annually, with no more than 20,000 per country.

The preceding paragraphs are but a very brief description of some of the more important aspects of our many immigration laws. A detailed account would take volumes rather than pages to chronicle.

While economic factors around the world have always figured prominently in our immigration picture, never has the issue been so volatile as today. With two-thirds of the nations in this world experiencing a growth-rate that will double their present populations within the next 19 to 36 years, their economic plight can only get worse.

Gross population figures by themselves, however, do not tell the entire story. The distribution of various age groups determines the number of people who will be entering the work force at any given time. In most of our neighboring countries to the south, nearly half of the inhabitants are under 15 years of age. This means that, regardless of any miraculous reductions in birth rates (which are among the highest in the world), the number of persons soon to be entering the work force in those countries is staggering.

Typical of these nations is Mexico, whose work force totalled 16 million in 1970. This force will swell to 28 million by 1985, and to 40 million by 1995. With serious current unemployment problems, their economic future is indeed bleak. Poor employment opportunities in their native lands will obviously motivate these people to seek jobs elsewhere, first to their own large cities and then to a foreign country.

Famine and the threat of famine will also play a vital role in the migratory process. The past decade has seen many nations which were formerly net exporters of food drop from that list because of their spiraling population problem. The world now has only four major exporters of food: the United States, Canada, Argentina and Australia.

Two thousand years ago Egypt was able to provide 13 million bushels of grain per year to the Roman Empire. Today, Egyptians cannot feed themselves. As one of the oldest civilizations on earth, at the turn of this century its population was still slightly under ten million inhabitants. By 1950, however, this figure had almost doubled to 19 million, and then doubled again to 38 million in 1976. A factor that has now reduced their ration of arable land to 1/5th acre per inhabitant (approximately 25% that of world average), and necessitated the importing of over 100 million bushels of grain in 1974. Already heavily in debt as a nation, their economic situation appears insoluble. How long they can continue to borrow from the rest of the world to feed a mushrooming population, is questionable.

Unfortunately, the ability of this earth to feed more people is rapidly reaching the saturation point. Virtually all of the world's economically usable farm and range lands are already in production. Further growth and output will be both slow and costly. It will take many years of expensive irrigation projects in order to bring additional acreage under the plow, and even then these sub-par soils will be marginal at best from an economic standpoint. With the soaring price of oil, the basic ingredient of most commercial fertilizer products, it is doubtful that the poorer nations will be able to compete for this essential requirement without huge subsidies.

While the world's population is growing at a rate of 2 percent per year, food consumption requirements are actually rising at an annual rate of $2\frac{1}{2}$ percent. This difference in growth percentages may be accounted for primarily by the upgrading of living conditions taking place in many of the world's developing nations, a factor which will gradually increase in importance as more countries enter the industrial age, and by the increased food consumption of the world's population as infants grow into adulthood. With the extemely high birth-rates in much of the world, this latter point will undoubtedly accelerate the disparity between population growth and food consumption, and in turn, the migratory process.

CHAPTER 13
FOOD FOR THOUGHT

Year after year the United States becomes more dependent upon other nations of the world for economic survival. Part of this predicament may be attributed to the high level of technology our society has achieved, the maintenance of which demands vast supplies of almost every commodity on earth. Another equally important part of the problem lies in poor planning and the inefficient utilization of our own natural resources, as well as the supplies we import.

Our recent confrontation with the oil-producing nations of the Middle East should provide us with at least two very important lessons. First and foremost among them is that under no circumstances can we afford to tie our economy and way of living to uncertain and unreliable energy sources. The fact that as of 1977 we have to import almost 50 percent of our petroleum requirement, is not just a matter of concern — it should be a matter of alarm.

Second, and perhaps equally important in many respects, is that we, too, have something the world needs: *food*. The United States now enjoys a very comfortable margin in food production over its consumption requirements. Lest we forget, however, we also enjoyed this margin in petroleum production not too long ago, and we could just as easily lose this cushion by failing to recognize in time what must be done to protect this asset. Unlike other problem areas which might respond to a "treatment" or "cure," there is no alternative to prevention in this case.

In many ways the American farmer is truly a genius in the rough. He has learned to combine hard work, innovation, technology, education and an inquisitive mind to reach incredible levels of productivity. As a result, where the African or Asian farmer must spend five days in the field to produce one-hundred pounds of grain, the American accomplishes this feat in but five minutes. Where the efforts of the Russian farmer feeds seven people, the American farmer through the same efforts feeds forty-seven.

The production of food, however, is dependent on more

than just ground, seed, water, and "know how." It takes the equivalent of eighty gallons of fuel to produce just one acre of corn. Stated in terms of a "trade-off" of resources, we get back four calories of food from corn for each calorie of energy expended in the process. Most other crops return significantly less. Again we find adequate reason for not allowing our population to over run our petroleum supplies.

The encroachment of civilization also poses an enormous economic threat to existing farm and range lands. This is dramatically evidenced anywhere near population centers. Where the land is in agrarian use, it's worth no more than $500 to perhaps $4,000 per acre; this same land, however, can "fall" to residential and industrial developers at prices ranging from $10,000 to $50,000 an acre. Many industrial uses devour land far in excess of their actual plant facilities. One atomic power station in Florida uses 168 miles of canals through fertile lands to recirculate water used in the process for cooling purposes.

Increasing population is a factor that whittles away at our food-producing land reserves in two major ways. In considering land requirements for habitation purposes only, we must include a proportional fraction of that required for every single business listed in the classified section of metropolitan telephone directories, plus city, county, state, and federal support activities, as well as recreational areas and roads. It is not a simple matter of just one more bedroom for one more person.

In addition to the above land requirements, it takes 2½ acres to produce the food required by each American. The portion devoted to feed-support and pasturing for livestock, poultry, and dairy products is already being challenged by certain world humanitarians as wasteful. Some claim, for example, that there is less nutrition in milk (as a by-product) than would be available directly from the feed required to produce it. If our country's population continues to grow, it is clear that we will be forced to adopt such an agrariar philosphy.

Even a casual survey of today's merchandise market provides ample evidence that we no longer occupy our once lofty position in the world of productivity and technology. Japan and Germany, in particular, have now taken over in fields in which we reigned supreme for many years. We can expect, however, to remain at least a solid contender in world trade, provided that we maintain adequate purchasing power for the acquisition of raw materials. There are hundreds of basic commodities such as cocoa, coffee, rubber, chromium, tin, and manganese which the United States will always have to import.

We must also recognize that, despite a number of temporary local problems, the United States has not suffered a major disaster in food production since the great drought of the 1930's. At that time, years of sub-normal rainfall turned millions of acres of Midwestern farming and range land into what was literally referred to as "the dust bowl." Many farmers were forced to abandon their properties, which were as parched and devoid of vegetation as the landscapes in the pictures we have seen of the moon.

There are other potentially catastrophic hazards to food production which are continually present. Livestock, poultry, or crop diseases or insect plagues could attack huge areas of our country at any time. With the nation's food reserve bins only recently empty, we are exhibiting more nonchalance in this matter than common sense warrants.

In assessing our productive land resources, we must also realize that land and soil, like the human body, need occasional periods of rest in order to remain prolific. Overworked or overgrazed lands which are not given a period in which to rejuvenate their productive vitality eventually become as barren of nutrients as sand or chalk.

With urban sprawl and highways eating away at the nation's productive land at the rate of 1,250,000 acres per year, we seem almost "hell bent" to join much of the rest of the world as a liability to survival of the human race. Just as an overloaded airplane will fail to get airborne at the end of the runway, so too, land has a limited human carrying capacity.

As we watched the disastrous floods which struck California and Arizona in February of 1980, one thought (never mentioned in official damage estimates) came to mind: Yes, there was millions of dollars in property damage from mudslides alone, the direct result of land excavation, deforestation, and the literally thousands of miles of paved surfaces which accelerate water run-off rather than seepage back into the earth's water storage tables. All this to keep up with the demands of our mushrooming population. But how about the mud, itself? After all, mud is actually *topsoil* that has taken the natural processes of nature thousands of years to create. And each year, throughout the United States, it is estimated that some *4 billion tons* of this *life sustaining* substance is washed out to sea; irretrievably lost to this and all future generations of Americans.

Our nation's ability to produce more food than our domestic consumption requirements is a national treasure that we cannot afford to lose. but with an immigration posture that allows over 500,000 legal immigrants, and another 1 to 3 million illegal aliens to enter this country annually; it is obvious that we are dissipating this asset far more rapidly than most Americans realize, and in doing so, literally inviting *inevitable* catastrophy.

For a sobering, even grim, picture of things to come, consider the following statement published in the Wall Street Journal in 1975 by The Environmental Fund, a non-profit organization which solicits neither memberships nor contributions, but which is gravely concerned — as we all should be — with the disastrous imbalance looming in our future.

THE REAL CRISIS BEHIND
THE "FOOD CRISIS"

The world as we know it will likely be ruined before the year 2,000 and the reason for this will be its inhabitants' failure to comprehend two facts. These facts are:

1. World food production cannot keep pace with the galloping growth of population.

2. "Family planning" cannot and will not, in the foreseeable future, check this runaway growth.

The momentum toward tragedy is at this moment so great that there is probably no way of halting it. The only hopeful possibility is to reduce the dimensions of the coming disaster.

We are being misled by those who say there is a serious food shortage. This is not true; world food production this decade is the greatest in history. The problem is too many people. The food shortage is simply evidence of the problem.

It makes no difference whatever how much food the world produces, if it produces people faster.

Some nations are now on the brink of famine because their populations have grown beyond the carrying capacity of their lands. Population growth has pushed the peoples of Africa, Asia and Latin America onto lands which are only marginally suitable for agriculture. No amount of scientific wizardry or improved weather will change this situation.

For a quarter of a century the United States has been generous with its food surpluses, now vanished. We have given at least 80 billion dollars worth of food and development aid since World War II. The result? Today, the developing world is less able to feed itself than it was before the massive U.S. aid program began. A generation ago, the population of poor countries was increasing by 16 million a year; now it increases by 67 million each year and the imbalance grows.

Furthermore, our past generosity has encouraged a do-nothing policy in the governments of some developing nations. At the 1974 United Nations meetings in Bucharest and Rome, spokesmen for these nations incredibly asserted that they had no population problem. They defended these twin policy statements:

1. The hungry nations have the right to produce

as many children as they please.

2. Others have the "responsibility" to feed them.

We believe that these statements are irresponsible and indefensible. Any nation that asserts the right to produce more babies must also assume the responsibility for taking care of them.

Some speak optimistically of progress within the hungry nations as evidenced by the modest acceptance of family planning programs in many countries. "Family planning will succeed," they tell us. But how is this possible? Family planning advocates, to gain acceptance, insist that parents everywhere may have as many children as they desire. If the number of children wanted had always been two (on the average) we would not now have a population problem. The crisis exists because parents want more than two children.

In Moslem countries, for example, the desired number of progeny per couple is "as many as God will send." This turns out, on the average, to be seven.

The country which has spent the most money on family planning over the longest period of time (India — 24 years) has accomplished virtually nothing. Its population in 1951 grew by 3.6 million. Now it grows 16.2 million each year. Mexico adopted family planning only three years ago and the birth rate there has abruptly risen.

Yet many people insist that it is our moral obligation not only to continue but to increase our aid, totally overlooking the fact that it is impossible, from a practical standpoint. Eighty percent of the world's grain is not grown in the United States. All that we can sell or give away amounts to only 6% of the world's production and less than three years' population increase, alone, would consume this.

There can be no moral obligation to do the impossible.

No one really likes triage — the selection of those nations most likely to survive and the concentration of our available food aid on them. The question can only arise if we should reach the point where the world population outruns food resources. When such a situation arises, some people will die no matter what the disposition of the inadequate food supply will be. In that event, some hard decisions will have to be made.

At some point, we in the United States are going to find that we cannot provide for the world any more than we can police it.

In summary, our position is this: The sovereign right of each nation to control its own reproduction creates the reciprocal responsibility to care for its own people. The U.S. can help and will — to the limits of our available resources.

The belief that the crisis results from a "shortage" of food leads to disaster. Attempting to deal with this by producing and distributing more food, **while doing nothing about population,** is incubating disaster.

We must not permit our aid to underwrite the failure of some nations to take care of their own. When aid-dependent nations undertand that there are limits to our food resources, there is hope that they will tackle their population problems in earnest.

We owe it to posterity — ours and that of the rest of the world — to promote policies that lead to solutions instead of catastrophe.

CHAPTER 14
ILLEGAL IMMIGRATION

In a February 7, 1975 address before the Commonwealth Club of California, the then Commissioner of Immigration and Naturalization, Leonard F. Chapman, stated that:

". . . the illegal immigrant problem in the United States is totally out of control."

To better understand Commissioner Chapman's alarming statement, we must first examine the normal mission and workload of this government agency.

The Immigration and Naturalization Service administers and enforces federal immigration and naturalization laws. (It does not make the laws or establish the policies; these are functions of the Congress.) The Service is responsible through every phase of the operation, from the time petitions are filed for immigrant visas, during entry formalities, and finally, through the naturalization process to citizenship. In addition, it handles the adjudication of requests for the various benefits accorded aliens once in the United States. It is also this agency which is responsible for preventing the illegal entry of aliens, and the investigation, apprehension, and removal of those who succeed in illegal entry.

By perusing the 1977 ANNUAL REPORT: IMMIGRATION AND NATURALIZATION SERVICE (the latest **Annual** Report available as of April 4, 1980), we can begin to understand why this vital agency has literally broken down under an avalanche of ever-increasing workload. In spite of repeated warnings from former Commissioner Chapman that our nation's immigration posture was crumbling — from the attention and concern given that fact by Congress and the administration — he might just as well have been talking to a group of penguins at the South Pole.

In the course of their normal duties during fiscal year 1977, the INS inspected more than 266 million people crossing our borders. These included our own citizens entering and leaving the country, as well as immigrant and nonimmigrant aliens (tourists, business people, diplomats, students, etc.) and others who cross the border daily for legally authorized purposes. Arrivals come by land, sea, and air, around the clock, at almost a thousand points of entry.

The purpose of inspection procedures is to assure that aliens who have no right to enter the United States, or whose entry would not be in our country's best interests (such as known terrorists and revolutionaries) do not, in fact, enter. A record high of 874,123 persons were refused entry in 1977. The importance of adequate inspection and exclusion before entry can be noted in other areas of the Immigration and Naturalization Service workload. In 1977 there was also a new high of 58,898 cases which had to be referred to immigration judges for deportation or exclusion — a procedure extremely costly to our nation, since the United States government must bear the expenses of the court, the judges, the INS attorneys who represent the government, and often the defendant's attorney as well, through government-subsidized legal assistance programs.

With a total work force of approximately 10,000 persons (administrative, clerical, border patrol, and field agents), it is evident that the INS is woefully understaffed to handle the steadily rising workload.

Illegal immigration started a dramatic climb with the end of the "Bracero" program in 1964. That year, immigration officials apprehended a total of 86,597 illegal immigrants. In 1968, this figure rose to 212,057. In 1972 they apprehended 505,949 persons, in 1976 the total was 875,915, and in 1977 reached 1,042,215. While these apprehension figures are correct, the totals are misleading if taken as the actual number of illegal immigrants. Particularly in recent years, the workload has risen so far beyond the capability of INS agents to cope with the problem that no one really knows the total number of illegal aliens presently residing in the United States. The problem is already acute in California, Texas, New York, Florida, Illinois, and Washington, D.C., and is rapidly spreading throughout the entire nation.

As might logically be expected, alien smuggling has also increased drastically in recent years. In 1964 the INS recorded 513 smuggling cases. This figure rose to 1,210 in 1968; to 4,564 in 1972; 9,600 in 1976, and reached 12,405 in 1977. This represents an increase of almost 2,400 percent in the short space of 13 years.

While we should give credit to the Immigration Service for their 12,405 seizures in 1977, it must also be recognized that this is only the tip of the smuggling iceberg. Smuggling is known to be a business, and for any business to be profitable, the chances of success must be reasonably good. If, then, there were 12,405 failures during that year, we can only guess at the number of successful smugglings.

Of the 1,042,215 deportable aliens located by INS agents in 1977, 92% of the total 954,778 were Mexican nationals, most of whom had entered the United States illegally at other than ports of entry. Of these surreptitious entries, 90% (934,787) were made across the Mexican border.

Although the apprehension of most illegal aliens is conducted in a peaceful, even cordial, manner, the operation often poses actual as well as potential danger to agents in many situations. Thousands of illegal aliens are found each year to have prior criminal records. Many are armed and actually involved in criminal acts (such as smuggling narcotics or weapons) at the time of their arrest. In 1977, Border Patrol agents arrested 241,108 aliens who had previously violated U.S. immigration laws, and of these, 12,333 had prior criminal records. On the southern border, 129,750 individuals were found to be armed at the time of their arrest.

The counterfeiting or altering of immigration documents has become a flourishing business in recent years. Although some 20,000 fraudulent cards are picked up each year by the INS, this number is estimated to be less than 10 percent of the fictitious documents actually in use.

The Border Patrol section of the Immigration Service usually has the first opportunity to deter illegal immigration. This unit, however, is so critically understaffed that at times it was able to respond to only one-third of the electric sensor alarms set off by illegal aliens. With only 2,400 persons assigned to Border Patrol duty, and literally thousands of miles of border requiring coverage 24 hours a day, seven days a week, this low level of response to alarms is understandable.

Certain technicalities of our immigration laws are widely used by organized criminal elements to accomplish the illegal entry of aliens into this country. Professional marriage brokers, operating with the efficiency of real estate or employment agencies, arrange marriages between aliens and Americans for a set fee. The parties, who have never heard of each other before the arrangements, seldom spend a night under the same roof. They sometimes do not even bother with the formality of a divorce before initiating the same process all over again. Usually the fee, which may run as high as $1,500 or more, is divided between the U.S citizen and the broker.

A classic example of this type of operation is that of a Flordia woman who has two daughters and a common-law husband. The woman had married six alien husbands; each of her two daughters had married three alien husbands; and her common-law husband had married two alien wives. In addition to thus effecting the entry of 14 aliens into the United States, this one enterprise was able to collect welfare under the names of the woman's six husbands, under each of the daughters' three husbands, and a separate check to the woman under the Aid to Dependent Children program for the two daughters. For a grand sweep of the welfare circuit, along with those 13 welfare checks, the woman was assigned a free Public Housing apartment — which she sublet, pocketing the rent.

In Washington, another woman was discovered to have married no less than 15 alien husbands before her marriage mill was exposed by the Immigration Service.

The incredible ease with which an alien can obtain employment in the United States must certainly astound the citizens of most other countries. The fact that illegal aliens are often found with as many as five different Social Security cards in their possession indicates that they have a better working knowledge of our immigration system and its weaknesses than do our own citizens. But all this is no surprise to those familiar with the magnitude of the illegal alien problem.

For a number of years, there has been a significant increase in the number and size of organizations whose purpose is to help illegal aliens avoid detection, apprehension, and deportation. They provide a multitude of services, including harboring, job placement, transportation, and even expert legal counseling.

After a lengthy investigation, in 1978, a naturalized American citizen from Chile was arrested in Houston by the INS's Anti-Smuggling unit. This culprit, an ordained priest, would advise his foreign customers to obtain a legal tourist visa, and once here, he would furnish them with fraudulent documentation (including baptismal certificates) which could then be used to obtain a Texas birth certificate. In certain cases, the Texas birth certificates were then used to obtain U.S. passports which later surfaced in the hands of terrorists in South America. His fee — $2,500.

In this vast and rapidly expanding subterranean climate, the illegal alien is furnished with the technical training and know-how to soundly defeat our immigration system and laws. Telephone numbers of people to contact in a nationwide network of individuals and organizations, with hideouts and even sources of bail, are part of the illegal alien's kit. The whole procedure is startlingly reminiscent of the infiltration of enemy agents in a wartime operation. The open manner in which many organizations conduct harrassment campaigns against the Immigration Service further testifies to a strange muteness, or apparent lack of awareness, on the part of the American public.

On the 21st of April, 1975, nine organizations representing alien interests were joined by the American Civil Liberties Union in a press conference denouncing the District Director of the San Francisco office of the INS. Former director Richard L. Williams had conducted an aggressive campaign to deport illegal aliens, especially those holding jobs. Since a large percentage of the illegal aliens apprehended were members of "minority" groups, the director's actions were labeled as "racist." Such a charge requires no foundation in logic or evidence in order to pervert the facts. San Francisco, beset with welfare and unemployment rates that were among the nation's highest, was decidedly being hurt by massive illegal immigration. Cries of "racism" only tend to confuse the issue and screen the facts.

Other evidence of well directed plans to discredit the INS in its effort to stem illegal immigration occur quite frequently in the TV program titled "La Raza" (The People). While the viewing public generally accepts such presentations as "documentary" or even "public interest" offerings by the network, that is not what they are. Every foot in those taped programs is shot, edited, and narrated by the La Raza organization itself, and can hardly qualify as unbiased or objective examination of the issue. In a July 1975 presentation of La Raza, INS agents were portrayed as Mafia-type hoods, whose primary occupation was graft, corruption, and extortion, and whose avocations were brutality and the forcible seduction of alien women.

In a subsequent offering by La Raza which was advertised in **TV Guide** as a "colorful, authoritative history and heritage of Mexico and the Southwest United States," viewers were treated to an hour long presentation that was almost entirely political in content and motivation. The program format involved skipping about among segments of interviews with professors of Mexican history and culture at a number of colleges in the Southwestern United States. In fairness to the participating educators, it must be recognized that such interviews probably lasted an hour or more when each was individually taped. After final editing (with sentences often cut off in the middle), the broadcast consisted of statements which were almost all derogatory to the United States and its people. Since those interviewed were of Mexican heritage, it is natural that they would have commented at some point (particularly if prompted in that direction by the interviewer) on what they consider examples of discrimination and injustice. Americans of other cultural heritages — Chinese, Irish, or Italian, for example — could doubtless provide similar remarks, if so prompted.

The obvious message promoted in this **"colorful and authoritative history and heritage of Mexico and the Southwest United States"** was that Arizona, California, Colorado, Nevada, New Mexico, Texas, and Utah were illegally taken by the United Sates, and that in the light of this consideration, the millions of illegal aliens pouring across the border have a perfect right to be here. If we were to accept any part of that argument, we would logically have to consider giving Alaska back to the Russians, the Louisiana Purchase to the French, and so on, to the point of complete national liquidation.

Once again, the role of television — a powerful medium with a "captive audience" — is in question. We are a nation of many national origins and diverse cultures, "indivisible" only in the belief in "one nation" by and for the benefit of all. Programming which fosters separatism or a feeling of unjust treatment by any group is certainly capable of spawning irrational and illegal acts, and it should not be considered as "broadcasting in the public interest."

Unfortunately, revisionist historians can always find a morsel of fact to support outlandish claims. In the case of militant Chicanos laying claim to the land lost by Mexico in the War of 1847, we often hear the cry "my forefathers were here before there was a United States." But let's review the facts: Mexico acquired the territory in the first place by **conquest** and later lost it in much the same fashion. However, America compensated Mexico in the amount of $15,000,000 immediately following that war, and five years later purchased a small strip underlying New Mexico and Arizona for another $10,000,000. So in essence, receiving $25,000,000 for land they never really owned wasn't too bad a deal. And of course, this does not include the literally hundreds of millions of dollars the United States has spent (and will probably go on indefinitely spending) through the Bureau of Indian Affairs, in compensating the original inhabitants of this land. So let's put that argument to rest once and for all time. Furthermore, under the Treaty of Guadelupe Hidalgo, ratified by both governments, Mexican nationals residing in the new U.S. territory and who wished to stay, were automatically offered American citizenship. End, finis, kaput.

The magnet which draws most illegal aliens to this country is, obviously, better employment opportunities than exist in their native lands. And somehow this magnet must be turned off if we are ever to get an effective handle on the problem. In the past decade numerous bills have been proposed in the Congress which would make it illegal for an American employer **knowingly** to employ an illegal alien. Perhaps the best known of such measures was the Rodino bill, authored by Representative Peter Rodino of New Jersey, which would have imposed escalating penalties ranging from a warning citation for the first offense, civil penalties of up to $500 for second offenders, up to a fine of $1,000 or one year in prison or both for subsequent violations. This bill passed the House of Representatives twice, only to die both times in the Senate due to strong, influential opposition. Since this bill applied only to employers who **knowingly** hired illegal aliens, it is inconceivable that the measure should have been defeated. But it was, twice.

On February 5, 1975, Senator Edward Kennedy introduced S.651, another bill which dealt with the issue of employers knowingly hiring illegal aliens. Unfortunately, this bill contained so many dangerous and impractical provisions, along with policy totally contrary to fundamental American ideals, that, had it become law, it would have done more harm than the grievance it was intended to correct.

Mr. Kennedy's measure would have granted blanket immunity to any alien residing in the United States for a period of three years (in practical reality, meaning every illegal alien, since affidavits of residency are easily obtained from underground sources), while at the same time **proportionately reducing the legal and lawful entry of immigrants from the illegal alien's country of origin.** It's not difficult to see the heartbreak and disillusionment such a policy would have handed to the honest applicants around the world, waiting patiently for legal immigration into the United States, only to find that their place and quota had been given to a sneak.

The ability of our nation to accomodate reasonable levels of legal immigration in the future — certainly a desirable goal — is totally dependent upon our will and determination to halt illegal entry **now.** Any talk of amnesty, particularly from a public official, can only be construed as an open invitation to illegal immigrants, aggravating the problem to the point of hopeless catastrophe.

From Table 11 in the INS Annual Report which encompasses historical data, we note that in the 52-year period from 1908 thru 1960, there was a discrepancy of only 29,557 between the number of "arrivals" and "departures" of Non-immigrant visitors. This includes such categories as foreign students, business persons, tourists and diplomats; but it does not include crewmen, immigrants, or those who cross our borders routinely on permits or other such documentation. From 1961 thru 1970, however, there were 4,829,890 fewer departures than arrivals in this category. But the next 5-year period from 1971 thru 1975 topped the previous decade with a total of 7,411,632 and the rate continues to increase: In the following 2-years, plus a transition-quarter (change-over to a new fiscal year), another 5,847,508 fewer departures over arrivals were recorded by the end of 1977.

While the above figures might be adjusted slightly to account for other categories of "non-immigrants" such as the alien fiance(e)s of U.S. citizens, who later converted to "permanent resident" status; such a revision would be almost negligible in comparison with the total.

The above statistics are particularly noteworthy as we peruse the federal budget for FY 1980. We see that in spite of inflation and the ever increasing workload of the INS, the operating budget for this critical function is being reduced by 4 million dollars. But even more important is the notation contained in that document that the Immigration Service is to **"deemphasize apprehensions in the interior."** Apparently, it is the intent of the current administration that any aliens, legal or illegal, who make it past the border can consider themselves "home free." This assumption is further reinforced by the utilization INS commissioner Castillo made of the modest personnel increases he inherited through the efforts of his predecessor. Former commissioner Leonard F. Chapman fought hard for additional **enforcement** personnel, only to have Castillo redirect these gains to augmenting the Washington headquarters staff by almost 40 percent —

by increasing his personal office force by some 400 percent (many being political appointees filling authorized positions belonging to other segments of the organization) — and in some cases, by reducing the number of investigators (field agents) at regional offices by almost 25 percent. (Castillo resigned Oct. 1, 1979.) It is the INS field agents who have the responsibility of apprehending illegal aliens within the interior of the United States. This includes not only person who have entered the country surreptitiously, but also those who have entered lawfully and subsequently violated the terms of their entry.

In the past decade alone, eight separate studies by the GAO (General Accounting Office) have all warned of the pontentially disastrous consequences of our nation's invasion by illegal aliens. In addition, there have been dozens of other government inquiries, (including both houses of Congress) numerous studies by independent organizations, literally hundreds of articles in magazines (including **U.S. News and World Report** and **TIME** magazine), all with the same conclusions. The American Legion, VFW (Veterans of Foreign Wars), and other patriotic organizations have expressed their opposition to our "toothless" immigration posture, and how were their concerns answered? In 1978 our courageous president sloughed off the issue with yet **another** congressional "study." The summary findings of this laborious "re-study" are not due until December 1, 1980, which by sheer **coincidence**, just happens to be the month **following** the Presidential election. The commission's final report is not due until March 1, 1981.

Could this possibly mean that on March 1, 1981, American citizens will once again be protected from an invasion of their homeland by aliens? Not so! This multi-milllion dollar "boondoggle" around the nation by the Select Commission, has almost nothing to do with enforcement of our existing laws: It is concerned primarily with administative procedures that apply to **legal** immigration such as: "How many immigrants?" — "By what criteria?" — and "Through what process?" And it could still take years for the "study" to result in legislation. This fact, however, has not prevented Mr. Carter from using this study as a crutch to ward off the

Invasion Issue. From the narrative portion of his 1981 proposed budget, we read the following:

". . . the administration's proposals do not provide for the full border patrol increase authorized in the last session of the Congress because the administration does not believe that this increase would, by itself, make a significant contribution to border enforcement." ". . . Until the Select Commission on Immigration and Refugee Policy issues its report, which should assist in developing agreement on statutory changes to remove the incentives for illegal immigration, large budget increases for enforcement would be unproductive."

What our president lacks in courage, he certainly makes up for in gall: Imagine! Telling the American people that it "would be unproductive" to keep illegal aliens out of our country in the first place, rather than chasing them down and trying to deport them afterwards. The approximately 3½% 1981 budget increase for the INS, after adjusting for a better than 13% inflation factor, represents a substantial reduction in its overall operating funds. And the incredible workload dumped on the INS by the Asian refugee program reduces its enforcement capabilities even further.

If there are still any American citizens skeptical of the fact that they and their posterity are being "sold out" by their politicians, consider this November 26, 1979 directive from Attorney General Benjamin Civiletti to Acting Commissioner of the INS, David Crosland: "Effective at once, immigration officers will not seek out undocumented aliens in places of residence." Now if we combine this, with court cases now in progress which would establish the requirement for INS agents to obtain search warrants **naming** each suspected **illegal** alien at a business establishment before conducting a search; then we can begin to get the point.

And how does all of this come about? Simple; our nation has become so "ethnic politics goofy" that we even have an Hispanic Working Group within the Attorney Generals office, that sits in judgement of everything the Immigration and Naturalization Service does. On November 7, 1979, Civiletti met with this group and discussed plans to convert the Hispanic Working Group into an Official Advisory committee to the Justice Department, the purpose: to advise him on Hispanic affairs and **immigration matters**. (The INS is a branch of the Attorney General's Office.)

With each passing day, it becomes a little harder for the average American citizen to determine who his real "Russians" are: Texas is the only state in the Union that actually has a law prohibiting the use of public money to educate the children of illegal aliens. And with its proximity to the border, this is quite understandable. However, 17 separate lawsuits against school districts, challenging the constitutionality of the Texas law, have been consolidated and brought before a U.S. District Court in Houston. And again on behalf of Mr. Civiletti, Assistant U.S. Attorney General Doris Meissner has filed an *"amicus curiae"* brief with the court, **against** the State of Texas. And of course, Texas feels that they have considerably more at stake in this case than merely the education issue: If they lose this case on constitutional grounds, it is almost certain that the precedent will eventually be applied to every form of welfare entitlement.

Meanwhile, out in California, a November 1979 ruling by U.S. District Judge Howard Turrentine decreed that aliens (even illegal) and citizens alike are protected by our civil rights laws. Assistant U.S. Attorney David Doyle described the ruling as historic, saying that it clears the way to prosecute U.S. law-enforcement officers who violate civil rights, even after the victims have left the country. And certainly (at least on the surface anyway) that seems to make sense: Why should anybody be mean to anyone else, regardless of their citizenship. However:

The above ruling came in a case involving 4 Border Patrolmen who were accused of using their fists and nightsticks to drive a group of illegal aliens back into Mexico. And somehow — somewhere along the way — our nation's abstract legal-minds are going to have to start mixing and equating "justice" with "reality." We see here a case in which 4 American law-enforcement officers are being tried as common criminals for using force to repel invaders. Illegal invaders that are **violating** the "civil rights" of every

American citizen. But apparently such "realities" are not to be considered.

The president of our nation has demonstrated that he is unwilling to take any action on the illegal alien problem that might cost him the Hispanic vote. But how about Congress? They, too, have had the power to act. Unfortunately (at least in this case), the primary responsibility for the various functions of government are divided among a multitude of congressional Sub-committees. Senator Edward M. Kennedy is **chairman** of the Senate's sub-committee on immigration, and surely, must have been aware of this incredibly dangerous situation for almost as long as he has been a senator. And over on the House side of Congress we have Representative Elizabeth Holtzman who **chairs** the House sub-committee on immigration; but views her responsibilities from a totally different angle.

Concerned about our nation's deplorable immigration posture, a letter was sent to Mr. Carter on February 8, 1980, signed by 13 members of both houses of Congress. *(Ernest Hollings, Robert Byrd, John Tower, Pete Domenici, Dennis DeConcini, Harrison Schmitt, Howell Heflin, Walter Huddleston, Quentin Burdick, Sam Nunn, Wendell Ford, S.I. Hayakawa, Malcolm Wallop, and Robert Dole.)* Apparently these gentlemen were unable to understand why the most critical post in our nation today (Commissioner of the INS), remained vacant. Extracts from this letter follow:

"Dear Mr. President:

We believe that the positions of Commissioner and Deputy Commissioner of the Immigration and Naturalization Service must be filled as soon as possible with individuals of proven managerial and leadership competence.

These positions have been vacant since Commissioner Castillo departed on October 1, 1979 after giving substantial notice of his intention to leave. While an Acting Commissioner has been appointed, no Deputy Commissioner is in place.

As you know, the burdens of the INS are increasing dramatically. The agency must carry out an extensive enforcement program as well as fulfill substantial administrative duties . . .

. . .*It is also imperative that the new commissioner represent the broadest spectrum of the American people and be devoid of the appearance of leaning toward any special interest group.* (Emphasis added.)

We urge you to act immediately to fill these vacant positions with the most qualified appointees. We stand ready to work with you on these appointments."

Sincerely,

It is also apparent from the above text, that this letter was in response to the administrations decision to again play "ethnic politics" with this vital post. At the president's suggestion, Mr. Civiletti has recommended Matt Garcia, another Hispanic Texan, for the job. An appointment that would indeed smack of "hiring the fox to guard the chicken coop."

Mr. Carter's previous choice of INS Commissioner's, Lionel J. Castillo (a big-wheel in the Houston Democratic party), was a pure example of political-patronage mixed with "ethnic overtones:"

Interviewed on the May 13, 1977 "MacNeil/Lehrer Report" on the Public Television Network, Mr. Castillo showed only a minimal knowledge of the immigration problem, and indicated he was more concerned about the **rights** of aliens. There is no argument against the premise that the **rights of all persons** should be respected. However, let us distinguish between **rights**, and **assumed rights**. There is a difference. And certainly, whenever a conflicting interest is so obvious as it is in the basic immigration question, shouldn't that sensitive post have been filled with a commissioner whose first commitment is to the American interest?

Castillo further expressed his belief that enforcement measures capable of totally halting the migration across our 2,000 mile southern border would be both impractical and impossible, citing the fact that the Border Patrol had but one

(1) helicopter assigned to that sector. A valid observation, but one that was not followed with a statement of intent to ask Congress for enough additional equipment and manpower to do the job. His predecessor, Commissioner Chapman, never stopped "bugging" Congress for additional aid (which he seldom received), and therein may lie the answer to Mr. Castillo's selection for the post: a commissioner that the administration could feel "right at home with."

If we consider the fact that the United States shipped some 25,000 helicopters **9 thousand miles away** to protect American interest in Vietnam (not to mention additional thousands throughout the rest of the world), but could provide only one (1) helicopter to help stop what has become literally an invasion across our southern border, then we have certainly answered the question "why" it hasn't been stopped.

But our president is not alone in using the power of his office to play the ethnic-politics game for **personal** — not national — interests. As **chairwoman** of the House sub-committee on immigration, Representative Holtsman has used her powerful position to literally force the INS (against their wishes) to set up a **special task force** within that agency whose **sole duty** is to track down some 200 suspected Nazis; believed to have entered this country as immigrants following WW II. The INS had given up any further **special** attention to this matter years ago on the ground that it was totally unwarranted **priority-wise.**

Ms. Holtzman has taken this action as a "gimmick" designed to endear her with her large New York Jewish constituency? But are her aims **really** in the **interest** of that constituency? New York city has been inundated by well over a million illegal aliens that constitute not only an enormous financial burden, but a serious threat to the security of every citizen in that city. And yet, Holtsman has seen fit to divert millions of dollars (and a sizeable portion of manpower) from the INS's already pitifully small budget to conduct what is now (35 years after the fact); a totally useless "witch hunt." And it is "useless" for a multitude of obvious reasons: At this late date, the chances of finding the suspects and then **proving anything**, border on the impossible. But

133

assuming that it could be done with an enormously extravagant effort, what then? A **second**, and again, complicated and expensive process of **de-naturalization** would have to take place before such individuals (if they are still alive) could be meted out the maximum punishment available to them in this country - **deportation.**

With such cheap "political hucksters" as those mentioned above running this country; can there be any wonder at "why" this nation of ours is "going down the tube?"

CHAPTER 15
ALIEN INFRINGEMENT UPON THE RIGHTS OF UNITED STATES CITIZENS

As an immigrant to any other nation in the world, the individual agrees to certain conditions upon entry. Since immigration is a voluntary act, it seems a little incongruous to negotiate the terms after the fact of entry. That is the way it used to be in the United States: immigrants accepted our country the way it was and adapted themselves to their new environment. In recent years, however, we have watched this concept gradually but definitely fade into oblivion.

In January 1974 the U.S. Supreme Court ruled unanimously (Chan vs. United States) that the San Francisco public schools must provide special language classes for non-English speaking students. This ruling opened the door and laid the groundwork for multilingual educational programs throughout the nation, programs now costing the taxpayers hundreds of millions of dollars annually.

The alien infringement upon the rights of citizens in this case is not so much an infringement upon the rights of taxpayers as it is upon the rest of the nation's children, many of whom are already receiving inadequate schooling even without this additional burden upon the public school systems. Budgetary limitations have forced many of our schools to drop significant programs in art, music, drama and sports.

Also in January 1974, the U.S. Court of Appeals for the Ninth Circuit District ruled that "resident aliens of the United States have the right to apply for and hold federal jobs." This ruling, if upheld and applied nationally, means that several million permanent resident aliens in the United States have the same rights as American citizens to federal jobs. Needless to say, this ruling could also pose some very dangerous possibilities for our national security. (This ruling was later reversed by the U.S. Supreme Court.)

Case after case is being brought against schools and universities, against city, county and state governments, as well as against public utilities and even private industries, in which ethnic groups are demanding hiring, not according to the tradition of qualification for employment, but rather by percentage quotas.

In states such as California, which has 28.3 (1977) percent of the **registered** aliens in the United States, mass marches, rallies, and picketing by alien groups of both public and private facilities are fairly common occurrences. One organization demanded at a public press conference that President Ford fire Attorney General William Saxbe for suggesting that illegal aliens be deported from this country. Saxbe had made the suggestion in a speech at Brownsville, Texas, in October 1974 in which he cited the tremendous impact of illegal aliens upon our rising unemployment and welfare costs. The group gave an alternative to firing Saxbe: that the President himself apologize for remarks, or that he make Saxbe do so.

In February of 1980, Thomas Kearny, a 29-year veteran civil servant of the City of San Francisco, was removed from his post as Registrar of Voters for **allegedly** being overheard casting a racial slur (damn Chinks). Kearny had been under attack for several years from foreign language groups, particularly, the Chinese community, which felt that the Registrar was not providing them with enough bilingual services. And when Henry Der, head of the Chinese for Affirmative Action group presented the Mayor's office a petition with 5,000 signatures, that was all it took for the city's Chief Administration Officer to remove Mr. Kearny. While this indeed indicates the "muscle power" of San Francisco's mushrooming Chinese population, it also brings into focus not ony an important point, but an equally serious **question:**

One of the basic requirements for **naturalization** is that the applicant (immigrant) have a knowledge of the government and history of the United States and be **literate in English.** By law, the Immigration and Naturalization Service must assist candidates in preparing for this examination. This includes free textbooks and study materials, as well as a host of other educational activities. With this in mind, it is possible that San Francisco's Chinese community of **voters** might be composed of **more** than **citizens?** When Congress passed our new bilingual voting statutes, it failed to make —

proof of citizenship a prerequisite to voting.

From 1976 through 1979, mobs of so-called Iranian "students" rampaged the streets of our cities, disrupting traffic, often engaging in pitched battles with American police forces, as they "demonstrated" against a foreign ruler who at that time lived and reigned in a foreign land. On January 2, 1979, the citizens (many of them elderly) of a quiet residential area in Beverly Hills, California, were terrified as hordes of screeming Iranians stormed their streets overturning and burning automobiles, battering down their gates and fences, and setting fire to the woods surrounding their homes. And again, on November 5, 1979, an Iranian mob determined to "show its muscle," forcefully **captured** the Statue of Liberty in New York harbor.

And why not! The United States government has repeatedly illustrated that it is more inclined to defend foreign lands and foreign interests, than it is to defend American citizens, American lands, and American interests. So, is it any wonder that the thousands of Iranians who originally entered this country as temporary "guests" — have long over-stayed their visas to become "illegal aliens" — and act accordingly. After all, they are well aware of the fact that they outnumber our Immigration agents no less than 100 to 1, and have every reason to be completely contemptuous of our spineless administration.

Faced with mounting unemployment in February 1975, the mayor of San Jose, California, announced on television that the city would undertake a survey to determine the number of jobs in the San Jose area held by illegal aliens. At the time of the announcement, the mayor was confronted by numerous protestors. One week later, the mayor again appeared on television, this time to announce that San Jose would discontinue the project immediately. While the reason she gave was that the city was not equipped to conduct such a survey, the official announcement was made directly from the mayor's office, which was filled at the time with witnesses representing the community's various alien groups. Whether intimidation was responsible or merely coincidental is of little importance.

Some four months earlier, a San Francisco non-profit organization, concerned about the growing flood of immigration, had cautioned in a letter to the public: *"Although California citizens do presently have the numerical sufficiency to guide their own destiny, the present trend, if unaltered, will reverse this position in less than a decade."* Apparently the prediction of ten years was far too optimistic.

Even in states as far inland as Colorado, we find pronounced evidence of the infringement by aliens upon the rights and entitlements of our own citizens. Dr. Clifford Govan of the Colorado Health Department, in testimony before a subcommittee of the House of Representatives, 92nd Congress, made the point that illegal aliens in Colorado compete unfairly with our own migrant workers, the rural poor, small farmers, and other rural residents, for an already inadequate health system.

The 1974 unemployment crisis, which resulted in many Americans losing their company-affiliated health benefits, forced a number of these people to seek public health assistance for the first time in their lives. Even though they have supported these public health programs through a lifetime of taxpaying, it was necessary for them to compete for the limited service available along with foreign nationals who may have arrived in this country only the previous night.

There is no requirement under federal law (Social Security Act of 1935, as amended) that an individual be a U.S. citizen or even a legally resident alien in order to receive many forms of public assistance. This was further established in a 1971 decision (**Graham** vs. **Richardson**, 403 U.S. 365) in which the Supreme Court ruled that a permanent resident alien could not be denied a particular benefit because of non-citizenship. The significant and abiding fact here is that the court, in rendering its decision, failed to distinguish between legal and illegal aliens, thereby leaving the entitlement open to all.

The legality of this entitlement was again reaffirmed by the December 1974 decision of a superior court judge in California who ruled that aliens may receive welfare in the state without proving that they are in this country legally.

The Supplemental Security Income Act of 1972 (SSI) was specifically intended by Congress to aid the elderly and disabled of our country whose ability to survive has been seriously jeopardized in recent years by inflation. This program provides for payments of up to $356 per month for an individual, and up to $600 for a couple. Although operated by the Social Security Administration, the SSI program derives its budget directly from the general tax fund. Newspaper columnist Guy Wright in February 1977 filed the first of a series of articles in the **San Francisco Examiner** in which he exposed the "rip-off" of this program by newly arrived aliens.

Typical examples of the abuse cited by Mr. Wright were: aliens who voluntarily remove themselves from the SSI list jut long enough to **sponsor** the entry of other aliens, and then reapply for SSI assistance as soon as the new immigrant arrives; immigrants who have hidden assets in other countries that would normally make them ineligible for SSI benefits; aliens who stay in this country only long enough (30 days) to qualify for SSI assistance, then return to their native lands, having friends or relatives cash their checks in this country. The list and variety of ruses used to defraud the SSI program, particularly by aliens who can rely on language technicalities and the virtual impossibility of tracing legitimate assets in their native lands, plus the almost paranoid fear of most bureaucratic agencies of a charge of "discrimination," all combine to simplify the fraudulent process enormously.

The Supplemental Security Income program is expected to cost the taxpayers of the United States 6.3 billion dollars for some 4.2 million persons during the year 1980 — and this does not include the cost of their entitlement to medical care, which often goes hand in hand with the alien's "instant pension." It should be fairly obvious that if we are having trouble (and we are) in adequately providing assistance to our own elderly, blind and disabled, continuing to take on such obligations from the outside world can only be at the expense of diminishing support for our present inhabitants, or bankruptcy for the nation.

In March 1975, Joseph L. Alioto, then mayor of San

Francisco and president of the U.S. Conference of Mayors, while in Washington, D.C. arguing in favor of special federal appropriations for cities, told a press conference that San Francisco had a unique problem because of Chinese immigration. **"It has brought in a lot of those without jobs,"** he said. **"We certainly don't argue with the immigration policy, but there has been no federal program to compensate for it."**

Why Mr. Alioto singled out one particular group is not known. San Francisco is being literally swamped by immigrants (both legal and illegal) from all parts of the world. As to his statement that **"there has been no federal program to compensate for it,"** there has — and it's called welfare. Federal monies fund 50.3 percent of the Aid to Families with Dependent Children (AFDC) program and 100 percent of the Supplemental Security Income (SSI) program.

While the SSI assistance is available only to citizens and legally resident aliens, AFDC is less restrictve, requiring only the furnishing of a Social Security number to receive the aid. However, aid may not be denied an applicant, or delayed, pending the issuance or verification of a Social Security number. And there are also other federally funded programs which provide such services as medical, dental, legal, maternal care, and free school lunches to needy aliens, regardless of their legal status. Although our immigration laws specifically prohibit an alien from becoming a public charge within five years of date of entry, such restrictions have no practical means of enforcement. Welfare agencies do not maintain a separate listing of aliens. There is no coordination between such agencies and the Immigration and Naturalization Service, and even if there were, the Right to Privacy Act would preclude welfare agencies from divulging this information.

Just how well the "public charge" restriction works can be found in a sampling of case loads from the San Francisco office of AFDC. A family of five from Burma signed up for AFDC seven days after arriving in this country, and received $459 per month. A family of four from Russia signed up two days after arrival and received $402 per month. A family of seven from the Philippines took advantage of the program a month after arriving and received $555 a month, while a family of six from Israel started collecting $516 per month less than two months after their arrival.

These particular incidents reported by columnist Guy Wright in the **San Francisco Examiner** are typical of what is happening in welfare offices all over the United States. (Those monthly payment figures, however, reflect the 1977 rates for AFDC, rates which are doubtless higher now.) According to Mr. Wright, it is even believed that some aliens travel to the United States on a "fly now pay later" plan, using their AFDC checks to pay for their transportation.

Edwin Sarsfield, head of the San Francisco Social Services Department, estimates that more than 20 percent of those signing up for AFDC locally are aliens. There is little, however, that any single agency can do to correct the problem in view of the multitude of rules, regulations, laws, court decisions, and governmental departments whose policies affect entitlements.

While many of the foregoing examples go back several years, it is not because there are no current examples. On the contrary, it is simply to illustrate that these are not **new problems.**

Far too often, government fails to recognize the "domino effect" of its well meaning gestures. This is particularly true in the case of those who advocate amnesty (legalization) for the 12 to 20 million illegal aliens presently in the United States. Such a move would immediately entitle those who could qualify for the benefits of the SSI program. A much greater disaster, however, is that it would then furnish many in this enormous group with the entitlement to legally sponsor the entry of their entire families, which in some cases may run as high as another 15 persons. Unfortunately, a large percentage of these (as we have already witnessed) would be the aging parents of both spouses, who would then start collecting a lifetime of U.S. government benefits without having contributed a single day's effort to the American economy.

The evacuation and acceptance of some 200,000 Vietnamese refugees following the capitulation of South Vietnam was both understandable and necessary. America's current policy of accepting another 14,000 "boat people" each month is neither. While their plight is indeed pitiful, their putting to sea is entirely a matter of voluntary choice on their part. Many are doing so to evade military service, others are trying to get their wealth out of the country, large numbers seek to avoid oppression, and others are simply looking for a better way of life. And who can blame them?

Unfortunately, life is not exactly a "bowl of cherries" for anyone in that part of the world, and it's going to get a lot worse before it gets any better. The point is that as long as there is a place to go, as long as there are places that will accept the refugees, such crises will continue to occur with **increasing frequency**, not only there but in other parts of the world as well.

In a 1977 address to the National War College in Washington, D.C., former Ambassador Marshall Green offered the following anecdote relating to population problems plaguing Southeast Asia:

"Shortly after the downfall of Sukarno, the new emerging leader, General Suharto, called me to his office and his first request was for half a billion dollars in U.S. aid to help transfer the excess population of Java to the relatively underpopulated Indonesian islands of Borneo, Sumatra and the Celebes. I had to point out diplomatically to Suharto that, even if the **Queen Mary** *left the port of Djakarta every day loaded down with Javanese, it would not take care of the natural increase of the population on the island of Java."*

So whether the next exodus of "boat people" comes from Vietnam or somewhere else, whether the reason for the exodus is attributed to political, social, economic, racial or ethnic friction, the root cause will still be "too many people, for too little resources" — and there is nothing the United States or any combination of Western nations can do to solve **their problems.**

In the meantime, we are taking on additional liabilities to our own survival that may be of far greater consequence than we presently envision. Dr. Tran Van May, assistant director of the Indochina Social Services Project in Los Angeles, noted in an August 1979 interview with the **San**

Francisco Examiner that a spot screening for tuberculosis of 270 recent arrivals revealed 156 to be positive. While only 49 of the cases were serious enough to warrant treatment, nevertheless the disease is present and will inevitably surface in the others if not followed up with medical care in the future. Dr. May also feels that some 80 percent of the refugees are depressed due to such factors as guilt and remorse at leaving loved ones behind, the trauma of losing their homeland and roots, and marked cultural differences in their new environment. These are conditions which Dr. May feels could emerge as neurotic and psychotic problems long after their resettlement and material needs are met.

In San Francisco, a family of nine refugees from rural Cambodia are now being cared for by a church group. They speak no English and are illiterate in their native language. Until their arrival in the United States, they had never ridden in an automobile, much less been exposed to the clamor of a metropolitan existence. In fact, this family had never experienced life with electricity, even a single simple light bulb. Indeed, this will be a traumatic transition that may never actually bridge the gap between their two worlds.

As we watched this family of nine on TV being resettled into a large home in a residential district of San Francisco, several idiotic aspects of this operation began emerging: First, their housing, which undoubtedly is being subsidized by HUD (Department of Housing and Urban Development), is probably at a monthly rate several times larger than their previous total annual income. Second, since the job market for primitive Cambodian farm skills is rather limited in metropolitan San Francisco, and since they will first have to acquire at least some knowledge of English merely to move around in their new environment, it is obvious they will remain a "ward of the state" (HUD, AFDC, Food Stamps, Medicare, etc.) for some time to come. All of which raises the ultimate question:

Since most of the refugees from Southeast Asia are ethnic Chinese, and since Mr. Carter is on such fine terms with Beijing, why aren't these people being returned to the land of their ethnic and cultural roots? Surely a few hundred thousand more people wouldn't even be noticed on the mainland, and the cultural adjustment required would be almost nil.

But as previously noted, it is not always a "life or death" situation that is behind refugee movements such as the "boat people." On February 8, 1979, Honk Kong authorities announced finding more than $1,000,000 in gold aboard one of the refugee boats from Vietnam. In September of that same year, 733 Vietnamese who were given refuge on the Chinese mainland, were expelled from Hong Kong where they had later fled. It is a fair assumption that the U.S. was the intended destination of these people when they left Vietnam, and that Red China was simply an unexpected detour in the road.

While the decision to accept 14,000 refugees monthly was made in Washington, the responsibility for health planning has been left largely to volunteer organizations. Judith Hodgens, head of the Catholic Resettlement Organization in San Francisco, has complained bitterly in both television and newspaper interviews that the federal government has not responded financially to their needs. Other spot screenings by county health departments in California have found many cases of TB, venereal diseases, parasites, and severe skin problems. While most officials believe that there is no cause for alarm on the part of Americans regarding "rare exotic diseases," or even epidemics of common medical problems, they also seem in agreement that we are inheriting a problem of long-term medical follow-ups.

But medical and readjustment problems are only part of the concerns Americans will be faced with as a result of this sudden, unplanned, and unexpected deluge of new immigrants. Somewhere between one-third and one-half of the new refugees are expected to settle in California, a state already suffering from a severe housing shortage and skyrocketing rents. And again, this is still only another of the many facets of the impact. California is also experiencing extremely high rates of immigration (legal and illegal) by persons of Spanish surnames and by other nationalities of Oriental ancestry. This means that for American citizens with the "wrong" surname or racial lineage, the future outlook for employment is indeed bleak, since they do not qualify as a "minority" entitled to "Protected Group" status under Title VII of the Civil Rights Act of 1964. While such preferential statutes also adversely affect their opportunities for higher education, the impact of massive minority immigration will be particularly acute in employment, as we can note from the following:

The Fair Employment Practices Commission of California (the local Civil Rights Act enforcement agency) spells out in its booklet, "Affirmative Action Guidelines," its intention of achieving a perfectly balanced state-wide profile of employment by ethnic group and sex, by EEOC job categories in the total workforce, and also in each division and department, as well as within **"narrow income ranges."**

At present, the Affirmative Action Program is applicable to governmental agencies, and is enforceable only upon those private enterprises receiving a certain number of dollars in state or federal business. However, to quote again from the California "Affirmative Action Guidelines" booklet: **"The trend is clear; few employers will be exempted from the affirmative action requirements."** Many firms presently operating under the AAP policies are finding these additional requirements extremely burdensome and costly, and the incredible "juggling act" required in matching and mating percentages capable of giving a migraine headache to a computer.

The significant factor here is that, as more and more "minority" qualified immigrants arrive and compete for jobs, fewer and fewer job opportunities will be available to residents without a "minority" classification. Even the advancement possibilities for those already working is being hampered by the "Affirmative Action Plan." It is not at all unusual today for the person who would logically be chosen on the basis of qualifications, experience and seniority to be bypassed because of affirmative action policies. Initiative, hard work, self-sacrifice, ambition, and the desire to succeed are of little avail if the individual's quota "percentage number" is out of phase with the "big picture." It might be appropriate to observe at this point that the "programming" of our people for "1984" is proceeding right on schedule.

To understand more fully the impact of massive "minority qualified" immigration into California, we need only to consult a few recent court actions. The case of **Tostado** vs. **State Board of Education** resulted in the enactment of California legislation requiring bilingual education in all **districts** having ten or more limited-English speaking children in **any** school.

A settlement in the case of **Waco** vs. **Alioto** commits the San Francisco fire department to a goal of 40 percent hiring of minorities, and to increasing the advancement opportunities of minorities by limiting the importance of seniority as a factor in promotions.

In the case of **Officers for Justice** vs. **Civil Service Commission,** the city of San Francisco agreed to the following: To hire a minimum of 50 percent minorities and women; to eliminate seniority as a promotion factor; and to promote women and minorities on parity with the more senior non-minority members of the police department. The city is also required under the settlement to establish a special fund for unique programs to attract and retain minorities and women in all ranks of the police department.

A suit brought by Black and Chicano plaintiffs against the J.C. Penney company resulted in a settlement in which 25 percent of the management trainees at their California stores must be Chicano, and 15 percent Black. And the list of similar suits and settlements against public utilities, schools, municipal governments, and private businesses is almost endless.

Under California's Affirmative Action Plan, aptitude tests for employment are an exercise in futility. Mandatory guidelines for such tests spell out that where tests are used and insufficient numbers of minorities manage to qualify, such tests must be redesigned — and if necessary, re-, re- and re-designed until they do qualify. It's entirely conceivable under this concept that in some instances a passing grade for the position of "Head of the Brain Surgery Department" might be achieved by naming the main thoroughfares in Guadalajara or Kowloon. That is, of course, in the event the government's master plan for race, sex, and ethnic "parity" dictated the need for an Oriental or Spanish surnamed person in such top management position.

Constantly increasing demands upon government, industry, and public utilities for multilingual services has, in many parts of the country, become a significant factor in the "cost of doing business." That cost is ultimately passed on to the general public through higher taxes and prices, or by a reduction in the amount or quality of service provided.

For many years, particularly since World War II, the United States has made a sincere effort to upgrade the status of its disadvantaged citizens. As we continue to take on more burdens from the outside world, we will see severe retrogression in the progress already made, and **absolutely no hope for future achievements.** Depressed employment opportunities, along with the necessity of competing with alien groups for potential training programs and dollars, will again isolate and coccoon our own disadvantaged people into more and larger ghettos and Appalachias.

The greatest impact that immigration has on our economy is, unfortunately, also the least perceptible. It is the effect that more people have, and will increasingly have on the inflationary process. Simple inflation — if there is such a thing — would mean that wages, prices, and incomes all increase at approximately the same time and rate. The necessary condition for such hypothetical inflation, however, is that there be a totally adequate supply of both goods and services.

It is clear that we are well into the era when we no longer have a totally adequate supply of material goods in this country, and we must, accordingly, pay more as availability decreases. Competition among more people for an inadequate supply has tripled gasoline prices in recent years, and has quadrupled the cost of many other commodities.

Let us examine the effects of "more people" on our basic need for housing. In 1930, the proportionate cost of the land in a new home amounted to approximately 4 percent of the total cost. Now, with suitable building land becoming scarcer every day, the proportionate cost of the land in a new dwelling has risen to approximately 21 percent of overall price. In areas of high immigration this factor is even more dramatic. The cost of residential property (homes) in

San Francisco has risen 25 percent in just the preceding 12 months.

As might be expected, as our usable land continues to shrink, governmental control over land usage continues to increase. All 30 states with a coastal area participate in the federal coastal zone management program. Others have the authority to designate "environmentally fragile" areas. And this does not include local governments, with their capability of zoning restrictions. All of these will continue to aggravate the cost of housing as more and more land is removed from potential use. In essence, we are facing a situation where continued growth will make home ownership, as we have always known it in the United States, a thing of the past for the person of average means.

As more and more items and basic supplies are added to the not-so-plentiful list, we may expect this competition factor of inflation to increase. The advanced stage of short supply is very limited supply, at which time even legitimate suppliers cannot compete for such items and the commodity becomes eligible for the black market.

Except for very brief periods in our history, the United States, this "land of plenty," has been free of the large scale black market activities that are so prevalent in other parts of the world. Isn't it obvious that only the ability to establish and maintain a relatively stable balance between population and supply will enable our nation to escape this fate?

Unfortunately, Mr. Carter, his advisors and his Cabinet, along with the Congress of the United States seem totally incapable of comprehending this very elementary principle: And as we enter the year 1980 it now seems almost certain that we will see some form of gasoline rationing before this year is out. But **how** will it be rationed? Will it be issued on the basis of "how many cars" in the family — or will it be on the basis of "so many coupons **per person**? Whatever the final determination of "modus operandi" in the rationing process, we may be sure that upwards of 20 million illegal aliens in this country will be cutting deeply into the rations of the American citizen.

Then, too, massive immigration into this country presents other serious ramifications to the world's petroleum supply and problems: Due to our nation's extremely high standard of living, America already consumes **one-third** of the world's **total** petroleum production. With this fact in mind, it would seem more logical (at least to the rest of the world) that we should be **exporting** people rather than **importing** them. Needless to say, as our population and consumption of oil has mushroomed beyond our own domestic supplies, we, more than any other nation on earth, have been responsible for driving the price of foreign oil right through the roof. And as we continue to do so; we will further alienate not only our adversaries but eventually, our friends as well.

And certainly not the least of infringements upon the legitimate rights of American citizens will be the consequences associated with the coming 1980 federal census. Those who drafted our constitution couldn't possibly have foreseen that someday this nation would be overrun with illegal aliens, used the term "persons" rather than "citizens" throughout that entire document. Article I of our Constitution established the requirement of a national census every 10 years for the purpose of apportioning congressional seats in the House of Representatives. But the preamble to the Constitution leaves absolutely no doubt as to **who** they were referring to in using the term "persons." It reads:

> "**We** the **People** of the **United States,** in order to form a more perfect Union, establish Justice, insure domestic Tranquility, provide for the common defense, promote the general Welfare, and secure the Blessings of Liberty, **to ourselves** and **our Posterity,** do ordain and establish this Constitution **for the United States of America.**" (Emphasis added.)

With the exception of foreign diplomats and foreign tourists, the Census Bureau traditionally has counted all of the residents in our country. However, even the **specific exclusion** of **foreign diplomats** and **foreign tourists** would again seem to indicate that the intent of the census is to count **American citizens.** Unfortunately, since few in Washington are willing to admit that our nation has been invaded by millions upon millions of illegal aliens, they too (wherever possible), will be considered as "persons" in the overall totals. This means that those states that have been inundated by massive amounts of illegal immigrants (California, Texas, Illinois, Florida, as example), will gain seats in the House of Representatives, which of course, must be **taken away** from our lesser populated states. In other words, our huge illegal alien population, in many cases, will literally **disenfranchise** many American citizens of their rights to representation in Congress.

And it is also on the basis of this total "head count" that some **50 billion** dollars in federal funds will be allocated among the various states. Which is undoubtedly why, as quoted by The New York Times, Representative Robert Garcia of the Bronx, chairman of the House subcommittee on Census and Population prefers to use the technicality of the term "persons" as written in the Constitution, rather than citizens, as must surely have been intended. Those favoring the inclusion of aliens in our census believe that such states need these extra funds to provide services to their alien population.

Fortunatley, not all of our legislators put "ethnic politics" above the good of our nation: In December of 1979, five Representatives in Congress (Paul Findley, Henry Hyde, Edwad Derwinski, Clair Burgener, and Walter Huddleston), joined in a suit with the non-profit organization FAIR (Federation for American Immigration Reform) seeking a preliminary injunction to delay the census until this matter of interpretation is resolved by the court.

FAIR is a recently formed Washington, D.C. based organization which is **solely** concerned with shoring up our nation's shattered immigration posture. With literally dozens of powerful ethnic groups constantly pressuring Congress for everyting from amnesty for illegal aliens, to unlimited legal immigration; those citizens who feel otherwise and would like representation in Washington might wish to contact this organization: The address is: FAIR, 1330 New Hampshire Ave., N.W., Washington, D.C. 20036.

CHAPTER 16
ENERGY FROM "BANANA OIL"

There is a popular misconception held by many of our citizens that it was the United States that "invented" democracy — and that as a result of this *new* form of government, America became a strong and affluent nation. The Greeks practiced the concept of democracy over 2,000 years ago. The very word "democracy" is derived from the Greek words *demos,* meaning "the people," and *kratein,* meaning "rule." In essence, however, the only true democracy — rule by the people — would be that (such as a Town Hall meeting) in which *all* of the citizens vote *directly* on *each and every issue.*

America is thus not really a democracy, but is, instead, a Republic, a form of government in which the people elect legislators and public officials to serve as their delegates or representatives and do whatever is deemed necessary for the "running" of the country. We can even note this fact in our Pledge of Allegiance, which is to the "Republic," not to the "Democracy." But perhaps this is more a matter of semantics than of substance. What is important is that we recognize that America's greatness and affluence did not come about so much from its government as it did from its *lack* of government. After all, the primary reason the Colonies broke away from England in the first place was that King George II was providing this country with just *too damned much* government. This fact is evidence and spelled out in detail in our Declaration of Independence. Too much government!

It has been said that of everything produced in the world during the last 2,000 years, over half has been produced by the United States in the past 200 years. Whether this statement is a hundred percent accurate is immaterial: we do know that by comparative standards, even our so-called "poor" would be viewed by over 80 percent of the world's population as living in utter luxury. And Americans owe this high standard of living not to our government, which produces nothing, but to our economic sector, which produces everything.

Next, we should point out that the reason our economic sector produces everything from apples to zippers, baby carriages to x-ray machines, is that in doing so it hopes to make a profit on the transaction. This concept of production and business is what we commonly refer to as "the free enterprise system," and the "system" has been extremely good to us. It is as simple as A, B, C in many aspects, and as complex as the human brain in others. There is no overall "master plan" to the system. Nobody decides "what" is to be produced; this is determined by "demand" in the marketplace. But the decision to "supply" is fraught with risk, and unless there is at least a reasonable expectation (incentive) of making a profit from supplying what is wanted or needed, the supply will not be forthcoming.

Visitors returning from Russia almost invariably remark about the lack of choice, quality, and variety of goods that are available to Russian consumers. In terms of "what's to be had," Moscow's department stores generally resemble one of ours on the *last day* of a "going out of business" sale. Primarily, this is because under the system of the state planning and providing "everything for the people," even after 60 years of practice, "everything" turns out to be "not very much." And so it is everywhere else on this earth where bureaucrats have a "grand plan" for the economy. It just doesn't work out as well as leaving these things to the only two persons who have a legitimate interest in such matters: the one who wants; and the one who is willing to provide. Put them together in the marketplace and amazing things begin to happen.

As a result of this interplay between demand in the marketplace and the incentive of profits to suppliers, Americans have always been provided with not only their needs, but their wants as well. Whether bread or baubles, mixers or mattresses, the American free enterprise system has always come through where it has been left at least relatively uninhibited by government. While prices on a specific commodity may vary greatly according to the supply and demand factors, such fluctuations are generally only temporary in duration. A greater demand than supply leads to higher prices and higher profits — and higher profits invariably lead to greater production, if not from the same sources, then from new and competing sources that will enter the field seeking those profits. As supply meets demand, competition for the market automatically drives prices downward again. In this very decade we have watched this cyclic phenomenon drastically affect the price of such important products as sugar, flour, and paper, along with perhaps thousands of less noticeable items. The important point here, however, is that at no time during these cyclic upswings in price did we hear cries for the government to nationalize our farms, take over the Kleenex business, or begin the manufacture of skateboards. But we are hearing these demands now regarding the petroleum industry, and we must ask why.

A part of the answer lies in the fact that Americans have literally become "energy junkies," and when we can't get our next "fix" of gasoline easily and cheaply, as we have always been able to do in the past, we simply "blow our cool." But this is by far the lesser part of the rationale underlying this movement. Most of the impetus stems from a lack of understanding of the basic problem by the public. This is further compounded by deliberate misportrayal of the factors involved by the government itself. Mr. Carter wants to jump from peanuts to petroleum, and if he has to slander the oil industry or even tell a few fibs along the way, so be it.

First of all, we know that the so-called "exorbitant prices" Americans are now paying for gasoline were being paid by motorists in Europe and other parts of the world 20 years ago. Today they are paying double such costs. But this is history, and we will not concern ourselves with that. What is important is that we make the right decisions now, decisions that will assure our nation an adequate supply of oil and energy in the future.

Next, we know that the shortage of natural gas in many parts of the United States was brought about primarily by the artificially low prices mandated upon this industry by our government. Those price controls generated an abnormal dependence on this form of energy, while at the same time inhibiting suppliers and potential investors from exploration and development of new wells. We must bear in mind that all of the easy-to-find and inexpensive-to-develop oil and natural gas fields in the United States were found many years ago. There is more oil and gas to be had, but future sources will be much more difficult to find, considerably more expensive to develop, and will involve far greater risk to investors. This last point is particularly cogent as we listen to Mr. Carter harangue the major oil companies: 75 percent of all new wells are not drilled by the "biggies" of the oil industry, but by the independents and by "wildcatters," at costs that often exceed $250,000 per well — and with results that too often produce liquid only in the form of tears of the investors. Ninety percent of the holes sunk are "dry wells." But in spite of these perils, entrepreneurs and investors will continue to "take their lumps" and bounce back again for yet another crack at the supply problem, providing the incentive of potential profit remains reasonable, and governmental interference minimal. They will do so because this is the free enterprise system, the most productive system devised by mankind in our 3,000,000 years on this planet. It is productive not only because those engaged in it have the expertise and imagination to create ping pong balls or petroleum and its thousands of by-products, but also because of the incentive of profits, intelligently tempered by the fear of personal losses. Now this last point is extremely important and cannot be overemphasized. It is the one factor that is missing in every enterprise government dabbles in, and is the sole reason for government incompetence and irresponsibility.

But government's misportrayal of the energy situation and its causes is greatly surpassed by Mr. Carter's deliberate falsification of the factors involved in his $140 (plus) billion energy plan. He has told us that this enormous amount of money will cost the American citizen absolutely nothing, that it will all come gratis, by levying a "windfall" profits tax on the big oil companies. Which of course brings to mind that he also told us that our paying Panama to steal our canal would cost us nothing. (Payments to Panama would come from ship tolls, revenues that otherwise would go to the American people.) Next, Mr. Carter has failed to define what is a "windfall profit." How does it differ from an unusually successful year of profit-making in the financial, electronic, or communications industries? Or, for that matter, how does it differ from the profit an individual might make on the sale of a house purchased 20 years ago? There's an awful lot of "shell game" in Mr. Carter, so let's examine the way he is using this tactic in regard to the oil industry.

First, in speaking of the major oil companies, he has a bad habit of suggesting that he is talking about a "Mr. Mobil," a "Mr. Exxon," and so on, rather than the millions of stockholding entitties which comprise just our major oil companies alone. This particular point needs further examination in the light of Mr. Carter's claim that his 140 billion dollar "pipe dream" won't come *out of the pockets of the American people*.

America's seven major oil companies are comprised of several million stockholding *accounts*. While most of these "accounts" are individuals, there are thousands of them which represent only a *single account* that are not: almost every endowment fund for orphanages, hospitals, universities, libraries, private medical research facilities, retirement homes for widows and the aged, union pension funds, etc., all have in their portfolios *oil company stocks*. One such private employee pension fund alone holds 15,000,000 shares of Standard Oil of California stock, which provides dividends to fund the retirement of some 26,000 past and present employees. So it wouldn't be too farfetched to assume that 99 percent of our population are the direct or indirect recipients of oil company profits. Even the "hophead" who stops by a drug treatment clinic for a methadone shot, or the viewer of Public Broadcasting programs, in all probability share in these profits. But what about government? Is it getting a "fair share" of the revenues generated by the *investment* of private citizens in this particular segment of our free enterprise system?

Out of every gallon of gasoline sold, the major oil companies net between 3 and 4 cents per gallon, which goes toward paying the dividends to the stockholding accounts mentioned above. But with no investment of capital — and with no risk of loss, even if the oil companies themselves were to suffer a net loss — the federal government takes 4 cents right off the top from the sale of each gallon. Next, the major oil companies being in the top bracket for "corporate income tax," they are hit with a 52 percent tax bill before there are any dividends available for payment to stockholders. In addition to a host of miscellaneous other taxes for the companies, those "dividends" are taxed *again* at the appropriate rate for each individual stockholder, all this combining to give the federal government another 6 to 8 cents from each gallon. Added to the initial 4 cents "off the top," we see that the federal government is already making 10 to 12 cents on every gallon of gasoline, while those who produce it make only three or four. And we haven't even mentioned the tax bite taken at the state and local levels. California, for example, takes another 12 cents per gallon "right off the top" of gasoline sales. So we see that government is already doing considerably better in terms of profit-making from the petroleum industry than it is from any other source.

But Mr. Carter is not the only one playing on the ignorance and base emotions of the public. In 1979, Ralph Nader and an assortment of union officials and public advocates called for the establishment of a government corporation to take over development and production of energy resources on public lands. The rationale behind this idea is that the private companies (lessees) are "ripping off" the public by making a profit from such ventures. Apparently Mr. Nader is more concerned with keeping in the public eye than he actually is with the public interest. If the latter were his real concern, then surely he would have done a little more "homework" on the subject: First of all, leases to *explore* for oil on public lands are not *given* to anyone; they are *sold*. But the right to "explore" carries with it no *guarantee* to "find." As example, several years ago the federal government sold exploration rights on the Atlantic Shelf for approximately one billion dollars. Since then, the lessees have poured hundreds of millions more into drilling operations, and so far have failed to find even enough oil to lubricate a Swiss watch.

Contrary to popular opinion, the petroleum industry is far less of a monopoly than almost any of our other major industries. While their profits which soar into the billions of dollars annually seem enormous when viewed by themselves, so are the investments which made those profits possible. Traditionally, from the standpoint of return *per dollar invested*, oil company stocks have been well below those of many other industries. Now if Mr. Nader and his cohorts feel they can do a better job than "the pros" are doing (and they would certainly do so *without* "ripping off" the public, as Mr. Nader puts it), then let them put *their money* where their innuendos are. Let them form their own syndicate or combine — and since they are going to give the "public" a better deal, it is assumed they would outbid those in the established industry, including independents and wildcatters — and let them obtain leases for energy development from public lands and thus solve the energy problem, while at the same time driving out all of the "evil spirits" which now inhibit this industry. And if "Mr. Clean" isn't prepared to do this with *private capital" rather than tax monies,* then let him go back to his seat belts and air bags, and stop adding to the confusion of an already thoroughly misinformed public.

If we were to follow the rationale of such advocates, the government should also enter the trucking industry to compete with truckers who are using "public highways"; sell advertising on PBS stations to compete with private broadcasters who use the "public airwaves via assigned and granted frequencies; and so on, ad infinitum. While we might overlook such silly utterances from the private sector, we can hardly be so forgiving of a president who knows better and yet uses the prestige of his office as a podium from which to slander the free enterprise system and promote the "cancer" of "nationalization."

Like all political hucksters, Mr. Carter has been wise enough to put a little "candy coating" on his $142 billion energy package. To sweeten this "pill" he has included a $2.4 billion item in the form of subsidies over the next 10 years which are intended to cushion low-income Americans against the effects of inevitably higher energy prices. And indeed, "inevitably higher energy prices" is a masterpiece of understatement if the American people are gullible enough to allow the creation of yet another multi-billion dollar bureaucratic monstrosity. We already have the Department of Energy (thanks to Mr. Carter) with its 19,000 employees budgeted for $10.2 billion in FY 1980, and what has it produced?

It seems a little insane to condone even the thought that a government so utterly incompetent at *everything* it does now contemplates raping a successful industry under the guise that "it can do a better job." We may be sure, however, that if JC & Co. get their way, that $2.4 billion "energy subsidy" for low income Americans, once it has been adjusted for the inflationary impact of this proposal, will scarcely pay the operating costs of the light bulb in their refrigerator.

In no way is this discourse on our nation's energy dilemma intended to "white wash," or to absolve the major oil companies, if, when, and where, they are guilty of improprieties. If guilty they should be "hit" and hit hard. But the very idea of turning over any part of such a complex and critical requirement to government, seems absurd.

Imagine! A government whose budget for FY 1980 is already larger than the combined budgets of all administrations from George Washington through the end of World War II, a government that is financing both sides of most world conflicts, a government that lends out billions of dollars of *our* money with almost no hope of ever getting it back again, a government that sold off its gold reserves to help pay for its irresponsible spending habits, and a government that has actually created the present energy crunch by allowing millions of illegal "energy consumers" to make a mockery of the nation's sovereign integrity — now tells us that all it needs to solve the energy problem is some real "folding money" (not peanuts).

Pulleeezze, Mr. Carter!

CHAPTER 17
CRIME AND PUNISHMENT?

Democracy breakdown

I am coming to the unhappy conclusion that democracy as a form of government no longer works.

As I look about me and see the crime, the corruption, the lack of patriotism, the breakdown of moral principles, I cannot help but feel that we desperately need a stronger form of government. What that might be I am in no position to say.

But the future looks bleak, Democracy cannot function unless we have an informed and intelligent electorate and from what I see about the kind of education being offered to our young people, I am afraid that instead of becoming more informed, more intelligent, the reverse will be true.

An uninformed, illiterate electorate may continue to show poor judgment in their selection of government leaders; they may fall ready victim to the charlatans and mediocrities who will seek public office to satisfy their lust for personal power rather than well-equipped and experienced patriots who will put the good of our country ahead of all else.

> R.H.
> San Francisco

So wrote a concerned American in a letter to the San Francisco **Examiner**. Any well-informed person who keeps abreast of events in our country knows that "R.H." indeed has reason for concern. Each day's news, it seems, brings us yet another and new catechism of corruption, mismanagement, and violence, all chipping away at the fundamental underpinnings of our nation. The picture is, indeed, a bleak one.

The increasing number of people who now find it necessary to put bars in their windows and entrance ways, making small "prisons" of their homes for safety, have in many residential areas created the impression of a caged society. No street in any of our big cities can be termed "absolutely safe" for walking, even in daylight, and increasingly in recent years we find violent crime moving into the once-safe suburbs. Often the elderly must be escorted to and from the corner grocery — or stay locked inside their homes. Even persons in groups, traveling on public transportation — bus and subway — have not been immune from attack by thugs. A pall of fear seemingly freezes observers into inaction. A reluctance to "get involved" permits a scandalous New York situation in which a Kitty Genovese is repeatedly stabbed and dies an agonized death over a period of many minutes, all under the eyes of more than a score of persons watching from nearby darkened windows, not one of whom offered to help, or even called the police.

Something is wrong, something has happened with our society. This is not the America that most middle-aged and elderly Americans grew up in. Somewhere along the way we obviously have taken the "wrong road." Indeed, it is time we paused in our journey for a little serious "soul searching." To ask questions, such as: "Where are we? How did we get here? Where should we like to go?" or most important of all: "Is our present course leading us toward or away from our desired goals?"

The "Where are we?" in the area of crime almost defies comprehension. The latest Uniform Crime Report for the United States (released in October 1979) presents a grim picture. Viewed in comparison with the statistics of 1969 (not exactly a "good year" either), we note that murder was up 23.3 percent, forcible rape up 66.5 percent, aggravated assault up 65.6 percent, robbery up 29 percent, and burglary up 44.7 percent. The overall crime **rate** (the number of crimes per 100,000 inhabitants) was up 38.8 percent from a decade ago.

To achieve these noteworthy statistics required 19,555 murders, 67,131 forcible rapes, some 400,000 robberies, in excess of half a million aggravated assaults, along with another nine million burglaries, thefts and larcenies. We must bear in mind, however, that the above were **reported** crimes. How many other muggings, rapes (attempted or completed), and "rip-offs" of property went unreported is unknown, but the total of such unreported crimes is believed to be high. The total of rapes, for example, is known from many sociological studies to be far greater than the total of reported rapes. In August 1979, several passengers on the city's transit system were assaulted by thugs on San Francisco's notorious "blood alley" (the Number 22 line), and not even one of them bothered to report the incident. Why should they? In terms of law and order, and the protection of society, the "system" has become little more than an exercise in futility.

Addressing a crime prevention conference in Indianapolis on September 21, 1978, Dr. Nicholas N. Kittrie, dean of the American University Law School, stated the problem most succinctly when he said, "Crime does pay." Dr. Kittrie cited the fact that "crime requires **no education, very little capital investment,** and the **odds of failure are minimal.**" To better understand the "odds of failure" factor, we need only to look at a few specific incidents;

In February 1978 a Coast Guard cutter operating in the San Francisco Bay area stopped and searched a boat that was out in weather and circumstances which the Coast Guard commander regarded as highly unusual for a pleasure craft. The commander's judgment was correct: 6,500 pounds of dangerous drugs were found aboard this craft, and the crew was apprehended for drug smuggling. The court, however, decided that the experienced judgment of this officer was insufficient basis upon which to justify a search of the vessel. Case dismissed.

In 1976, the Second District Court of Appeal in Los Angeles ruled that a suspect caught in the act could not be convicted of burglary if the arresting officer had failed to knock first (Section 844 of the California State Penal Code).

An October 1978 ruling by the California State Supreme Court held that a traffic officer had no right to perform a routine check for outstanding warrants on a traffic violator unless *"the circumstances known or apparent to the officer included specific and articulable facts"* sufficient to arouse suspicion of such possibility. The case which brought on this decision was that of a motorist stopped for a traffic violation. A routine radio check by the officer disclosed that the driver was wanted on a burglary charge in another town, and he accordingly was arrested, tried, and convicted of the charge.

But Justice for society is indeed blind, while for the criminal it works overtime: Not only was the citizen victimized by this burglar in the first instance, but he was victimized again, as a taxpayer, suffering the indignity of having his taxes pay for the burglar's attorney. It was a Public Defender who took the case all the way to the California Supreme Court in a successful effort to negate the conviction on a "technicality."

On February 27, 1979, California's Third District Court of Appeal overturned the murder conviction of "soldier" Russell Little of the "Symbionese Liberation Army" terrorist organization. Little and his co-conspirator Joseph Ramiro were convicted in separate trials in 1975 of the senseless slaying in 1973 of Oakland's school superintendent, Dr. Marcus Foster, and the serious wounding of Foster's top aide. The original 1975 trail allowed a "change of venue" from Oakland to Sacramento for the benefit of the accused, required 500 exhibits, heard 137 witnesses, took 46 days, and cost the taxpayers $281,702. The basis on which Little's conviction was overturned was a 1977 ruling by the California Supreme Court (People vs. Gainer) in which the court invalidated a procedure of law that had been in use since 1896, known as the "Allen Charge." The purpose of the Allen Charge was to allow judges to help "deadlocked" jurors to arrive at a unanimous decision. In this particular example we note two glaring violations of the fundamental principle that "justice" should be "interpreted in the interest of society":

First, once again it was a Public Defender (paid by the taxpayers, not by the accused) who continued to pursue this case long after the initial trial. And to fully appreciate this point, remember that the accused was not some hapless indigent who had taken a life in a fit of passion. No, this was Russell Little, who, with his co-defendant Ramiro, is one of the four surviving members of the psychopathic terrorist organization that kidnapped Patricia Hearst and for many months continued to taunt and torment lawful society. A felon who, even after being in custody on the original charge, had added another "five years to life" stretch to his original sentence for participating in an attempted jailbreak, in the course of which two deputy sheriffs were injured.

But the second point is an even more absurd miscarriage of justice: The judicial ruling upon which Little's conviction was set aside was not even in existence at the time of his trial. It was made two years later, but was also made applicable to all cases that were currently under appeal. So we see that while the prosecution had won its case by all of "the rules of the day," the California Supreme Court — retroactively — ruled otherwise.

In March 1976, a California Highway Patrolman stopped a motorist for speeding. When the driver was unable to produce either personal identification or a vehicle registration, a radio check by the officer revealed that the auto had been stolen. The driver and his female companion were taken into custody, where upon **the woman requested** that her luggage be taken from the trunk. In removing the luggage the officer noted two shoulder-holsters and a pistol. This led to the inspection of a box below the luggage, which was found to contain a sawed-off shotgun along with an assortment of illegal drugs. Another box found in the trunk also contained a cache of amphetamines and heroin.

The driver plead guilty to all charges and was sentenced to state prison. He later appealed his conviction, however, on the ground that officers did not have a warrant to search the vehicle's trunk. When a lower court upheld the guilty verdict, the case was taken to the California Supreme Court (again by a Public Defender using taxpayer money) which in 1979 reversed the conviction, claiming the evidence used was taken in an illegal search. Even though the occupants were riding in a stolen car, their right to privacy still superceded the officer's right to a prudent inspection of the vehicle in the interest of protecting his own life. In allowing the felon to withdraw his guilty plea, the court said that if the state wished to try him again, they could do so only with admissible evidence. California's Attorney General appealed the ruling to the U.S. Supreme Court which in March of 1980, denied the appeal. Once again, two of our nation's highest tribunals have illustrated their utter contempt for the "rights" of society.

The 5th Amendment to our Constitution prohibits a person who has been acquitted of a crime from being tried again for the same offense. A provision of law which is popularly known as the "double jeopardy clause." The 5th Amendment, ratified by congress in 1791, was certainly a reasonable safeguard for the rights of the individual: After all, until recent years, the prosecution was also accorded a fair chance to prove its case. But now, perhaps it is lawful society (which is comprised of individuals) that really needs the protection from "double jeopardy." When an obviously guilty person is allowed to appeal their conviction almost endlessly, on what are often ridiculous "technicalities;" and when such criminals are thereby released to prey upon society again — wouldn't that seem to constitute double, triple — even "quadruple jeopardy" for the law-abiding **individuals** of society?

It is apparent that many of our feeble-minded jurists conduct themselves as though they were dispensing justice among the Angels in Heaven. They are not. We are living in a jungle, one that is largely populated by cannibals of every size, shape, race, color, and creed. It is time the courts recognize this fact, and that our judicial system faced-up to its obligations to the public.

From the foregoing examples we may draw three fairly evident conclusions:

First, no matter how much money we lavish upon the system, we cannot "buy," nor are we getting, a better brand of justice. On the contrary, our present concept and practice far surpasses in silliness the old cliche about frontier justice: "He looks guilty; hang the varmint." Unfortunately, it is lawful society that is being "lynched" today by the utter stupidities of our system.

Second, this abnormal preoccupation with the rights of the criminal-element, completely invalidates the fundamental premise that the "majority" (that is, society) also has "rights." The right of peaceful, law abiding citizens to walk our streets unmolested, and the right to feel secure in their homes without having to virtually "cage themselves in" behind a latticework of steel bars.

Third, and most important of the three conclusions, is

recognition of **purpose.** What is the ultimate purpose of our legal and judicial system? Is it, as many erroneously believe, a civilized mechanism for exploring and uncovering the **truth** in disputes regarding "right or wrong," "guilt or innocence"? Or, for that matter, does it have anything at all to do with the protection of lawful society against predators? Unfortunately, the answer in both cases is an emphatic **no.** Our legal system as it functions today has degenerated into what has become, literally, a "playground" for the legal profession. An arena in which lawyers engage in their own special brand of "chess" — jousting with each other, with technicalities their weapons, until one is finally declared the winner. "Final," that is, until the rematch — or the re-rematch — which has become the norm rather than the exception. The plaintiff or the defendant, the accused or the accuser, and even society itself, are all little more than helpless bystanders who must suffer the consequences of this "theatre" in which the fantasies of "legal par excellence" are played out by the legal profession. And they are played out according to a script of laws, rulings, and technicalities which they themselves have written and imposed upon an all too trusting public, and which often defeat the ends of justice.

If the above assessment seems unduly critical, consider the facts: When 12 (tried and true) members of the jury are denied access to meaningful evidence, how can they possibly arrive at a just verdict? And when, on the basis of evidence withheld, an acquittal results in a violent criminal being permitted to commit such acts again, what happens to the conscience of those jurors who acted in good faith? It is indeed obvious that our rules-of-evidence operate, not to provide, but to deny juries as much evidence as possible. Justice is either interpreted in the interest of society, or it is not. It can't be **both.** From such examples as those presented above (and there are thousands of similar cases that could be cited), we note that justice invariably has been interpreted in favor of the criminal element. And when so interpreted in favor of anti-society, in that very same instant it becomes a ruling and an infringement upon the rights of every peaceful and law abiding person in the nation. That's not "justice," that's "injustice," and we shall see who **profits** from this almost unbelievable situation in a later chapter.

But there are others, too, who profit (or hope to) politically from undermining the credibility of all our nation's law enforcement agencies. They do so, not by simple administrative actions which basically are their assigned functions and responsibilities, but rather in highly publicized allegations, charges, and trials which are designed to endear them to certain segments of our voting population. Unfortunately, any organization with the incredibly heavy responsibilities of our major law enforcement agencies will eventually make a "boo boo.' It is **inevitable**, if they are really trying to do their job. The only way to avoid making errors indefinitely is to do **nothing**, or at least as little as possible.

A prime example of "headline hunting" political opportunists at work was the 1977 criminal indictment filed against John J. Kearny, supervisor of Squad 47 of the New York office of the FBI, charging unlawful mail interception and wiretapping activities. It is extremely important that we understand the facts and circumstances surrounding these incidents, which are alleged to have occurred between 1970 and 1972. During that period, the nation was literally under attack by an organization of terrorists who called themselves the Weather Underground. This particular organization had "cells" known to be operating at various locations across the country from New York to California. There had been seventy bombings in New York City alone during that period, and the FBI had every reason to believe that this was just the beginning of a nationwide wave of terrorism.

In the course of the FBI surveillance activity, **all of which was centered on suspected Weathermen and their contacts**, wires were tapped and mail opened without first obtaining court orders to do so. There was, however, **no evidence or even inference** that the agent-in-charge had taken these measures for any reasons other than **to protect the life, limb and property** of our nation and its citizens.

After months of costly "top secret" investigations, Attorney General Griffin Bell in April 1978 caused criminal indictments to be filed againt former Acting Director of the FBI L. Patrick Gray and his two top assistants, Mark Felt and Edward S. Miller. These three were alleged to have authorized the emergency surveillance measures taken against the Weather Underground. Commenting on this disgraceful attempt to emasculate our nation's top law enforcement agency, John Wasylik, then National Commander of the Veterans of Foreign Wars, called upon Mr. Bell to "knock off the hypocrisy for which the Civil Rights Division of the Department of Justice is becoming infamous." The VFW commander further noted that "The indictments of former FBI leaders, Acting Director L. Patrick Gray, Mark Felt and Edward S. Miller, are as cynical as they are politically motivated.

Now let's pause here long enough to put this pathetic farce into perspective. First of all, we are not talking about a couple of bully-cops "shaking down" a prostitute. We are talking about the most highly screened, best trained, most dedicated senior veterans of our nation's "first line of defense" against the very real terror of sabotage, terrorism, kidnapping and espionage: the Federal Bureau of Investigation.

Furthermore, these officers were being charged for conducting their operations (always in the public interest) according to the accepted pre-Watergate policies, almost ten years retroactively, by the post-Watergate mentalities **two administrations** "down the line." Think about this for a moment: Where does this leave all law enforcement agencies and their personnel, in terms of dedication and willingness to defend the public interest? What officer in any branch of law enforcement can afford or would be willing to jeopardize a lifetime career (maybe even go to jail) for "stretching a point of law" (which is just a point of law) under what he assumed to be an emergency situation? And to know that even though his actions were motivated solely by considerations of public safety, this condemnation could occur many years later from a hostile administration that placed a greater emphasis on technicalities than on life itself.

It is apparent that Mr. Bell spent a major part of his career as Attorney General in persecuting dedicated officers of the FBI for actions which, while perhaps technically **incorrect**, were nevertheless motivated by extreme concern for the public safety. Meaning, apparently, that the "letter of the law" is more important than its "spirit or intent." At the same time, as we noted from other examples cited above, those criminals — even **professional** criminals with prior records of criminal activity — who are obviously and indisputably "guilty of criminal **intent and actions**," often are freed by practitioners with that same legalist mentality. Why is it that dedicated officers who put their lives on the line to protect society are not given at least an equal "break" with that given the dedicated professional criminal? Is there any reason for us to wonder that crime in the United States continues to increase?

But the real purpose of this observation lies not so much in the substance of the facts, as it does in the illusions of the inferences. Our present "holier than thou" administration would have us believe that only by crucifying some noble public servants can we assure the nation that the public's phones will not be tapped in the future. The more gullible might accept such an absurd idea, assuming of course that they didn't take the time to consider the odds: Even if every FBI agent in the United States forsook all other duties and concentrated full time on tappng the telephones of our citizens, it might take some 10,000 years before any of us could be relatively sure that the FBI had listened to even a **single minute** of our private conversations. And it's fairly safe to assume that some fifty percent of our population wouldn't give a damn if the FBI learned that "Aunt Nellie is coming to spend the Fourth of July with us," anyway.

While there is no argument that "invasion of privacy" should be held to a minimum consistent with the safety of the nation, let us not confuse this premise with "at all costs." We live in a world of accelerating dangers, where almost every act is a calculated risk. Consequently, we must decide whether to put our trust in the judicious use of authority by established law enforcement agencies, or simply let the fates determine our lot. Given the choice, it's doubtful that the eleven dead and 75 innocent bystanders wounded in the 1975 holocaust bombing of New York's La Guardia Airport would have much trouble making that determination.

Almost every law enforcement authority in the world

predicts that "extortion by terrorism" will be the crime of the future. But we don't have to look to the future: it is already a terrorist "way of life" in South America, in Italy, and in many other parts of the world. Even the threat of extortion by "mini nuclear bombs" is now a reality. The technology and materials for such devices are readily available. All that is lacking is the necessary plutonium fuel — and we know from press reports that certain quantities of nuclear fuels are "missing" and unaccounted for. Here, of course, **prevention** by use of every possible means of surveillance that might lead to early discovery of such plots is our **only hope**.

The analogy is inescapable: The recent kidnapping and execution of Italy's former premier, Aldo Moro, by terrorists was the result of Italy traveling essentially the same path America seems to be choosing for itself: the continued erosion of the capabilities of law enforcement agencies to protect the law abiding citizenry, along with ever increasing legislative and judicial measures which result in fortifying the position and defending the membership of the criminal establishment. Needless to say, serious crime will continue to increase until we stop electing to office those feeble mentalities who encourage crime by unreasonably handicapping law enforcement activities, and all too often completely negating their accomplishments in the courts and on the parole boards of our nation.

One of the least publicized secondary aspects of flourishing crime is its incredible impact on the inflationary situation. The losses to industry and to private individuals from crime run into the billions of dollars annually. But still, that is only a minor part of the cost of "learning to live with crime" instead of "stamping it out." Where security guards in commercial buildings were a rarity a couple of decades ago, they have become almost a part of the structure today. The private security business is now the fastest growing industry in the United States. If we were to lump together the costs of all law enforcement and protective agencies (government and commercial), the courts and legal services, correction, penal and probation departments, along with the host of social services that are directly related to crime or protection from crime, the aggregate financial burden would be seen to be truly astronomical.

What we must understand is that while most of these costs show up under the heading of our "Gross National Product," they are not a **useful** product or service. They are simply a necessary item of "overhead" expense, in which we pay out **something**, and get **nothing** usable in return. And that's **inflation**.

How does our current administration view this deplorable situation? We can get an inkling of their "order of priorities" by consulting the FY 1980 federal budget. In that document, we note that the FBI is slated for a $3 million cut in funds and the loss of some 500 positions, while the Bureau of Alcohol, Tobacco and Firearms will lose 122 positions. Among BATF responsibilities is the monitoring of illegal use of explosives. In 1977, according to BATF acting director John Krogman, terrorist bombings killed 127 persons, injured hundreds, and caused over $11 million in property damage in the United States. On the other hand, the budget document tells us, under the heading "Federal litigative and judicial activities," that there is to be a "a 17 percent increase in assistant U.S. attorneys and support staff" . . . and that "Outlays for litigation and court support are expected to rise from $1,189 million in 1979 to $1,328 in 1980."

From the above we can begin to understand the commentary under "Federal correctional activities" which reads: "The Bureau of Prisons plans to close 3 antiquated penitentiaries at McNeil Island, Leavenworth, and Atlanta within the next decade. These closings will be made possible by a declining prison population, reclassification of prisoners to identify those who can be reassigned to lower security institutions, and increased use of community half-way houses." And of course, who needs a prison for criminals that are still walking the streets? Further reductions in the FBI and other such agencies could even lessen that need.

A society that refuses to protect itself from predators is a society condemned to extinction by its own hand. And still, even in the light of failure to master the problem, we continue to court the same misbegotten theories of cause, effect, and solutions. Certainly the most erroneous and popular notion about the "cause" of crime has been that it stems from poverty. An absurd conclusion, when we consider that three-fourths of the world's population lives in conditions of poverty far below that experienced by **any** American, and yet relatively few of them are criminals. Envy, laziness, and a host of other factors, yes, but not poverty. The cry of poverty is a "cop out."

The solution to this monumental problem can only be found by "returning to Square One." We have tried every possible humanitarian approach in rehabilitation, including job-training, conjugal visits, half-way houses, and work-furlough programs, and found them unworkable. Organized groups (many with members who have neither friends nor relatives in prison) have lavished TV and radio equipment, entertainment, and a host of other services, all intended to make prison life more palatable. (It would be nice to see them lavish the same compassion on autistic children, or on the mentally handicapped in our institutions who have committed no crimes.)

Only when we provide an environment in which any person even remotely contemplating a serious crime **knows** ahead of time that he is almost certain to be caught, will be brought swiftly to trial; is likely to be convicted if guilty, and will be sentenced to punishment befitting the crime — only then will serious crime dramatically decline. While there were over 19,000 murders committed in the United States last year alone (many too heinous to describe), there have been only two executions in the past 15 years. If we can kill as an "act of war" (and we know we must), then we must also accept the necessity of such action in what has literally become a "civil war."

Most important of all, we had better rid ourselves of any and all notions that punishment should reflect sociological experimentation in "compassionate rehabilitation." That is utter nonsense. The primary purpose of punishment should be acknowledged as **retribution**, reflecting the outrage of a victimized society.

Then, and only then, may the elderly once again walk our streets with dignity and pleasure, rather than fear and foreboding, at the sight of an oncoming stranger.

CHAPTER 18
"THE LAW IS A NOBLE PROFESSION"

Somehow, somewhere along the way, America has lost the concept of our country as a nation of the people, by the people, and for the people. It is not any longer — and the "people" are sadly deluded if they think themselves still in control of virtually any facet of their lives. What we as citizens may or may not do is simply by proxy of the legal profession. Since laws are made by legislators who are predominantly lawyers, and interpreted by judges who are all lawyers, the question might logically be asked: "Are lawyers more intelligent than other people?" or, "Are they any better than other people?" If the answer to such questions is, "No, not necessarily," then why is it that whether one be architect, doctor, educator, scientist, housewife, or business person, increasingly the American public is becoming little more than a milking-herd for the legal profession.

Indeed, the law is a noble profession, but all lawyers are not "noble" people. Until we recognize this fact, American individual freedoms will continue to erode until ultimately we reach the perfect "1984" society. As noted earlier in this text, each year some 200,000 new laws and regulations are added to the already mountains of rules which now govern our lives. And for each new restriction, we must consult a lawyer to interpret its meaning or run the risk of whatever consequences may attach to being at variance with its dictum. The American way of life has become so mired in a legal jungle of red tape, quicksand, booby traps, and spider webs that the meaning of "right" or "wrong" seems to have lost all significance.

While there is no denying that a legal establishment is not only a necessary, but also a vital part of civilized society, we must nevertheless question its dimensions. According to the Washington, D.C. non-profit organization HALT (Help Abolish Legal Tyranny), the average American today supports, on a per capita basis, **4 times** as many lawyers as the average Englishman, **5 times** as many as the German, **10 times** as many as the Frenchman, and **20 times** as many as the average Japanese. In fact, says HALT, Americans support **two-thirds** of all the lawyers in the **entire world.** Rather alarming statistics for a nation that is supposedly concerned about inflation. After all, in spite of the vital function it serves, the legal profession, per se, still comes under the category of "overhead" rather than being a productive part of our society.

There was a time in this country when most Americans managed to live out their lives without ever having to consult a lawyer. Even wills were often simply recorded in the back of the family Bible. Although such simplicity is hardly applicable to our present lifestyle, just how complicated must such legal matters be? Again according to HALT, it costs **100 times more** and takes **17 times longer** to probate a will in the United States than it does in England. And how many times have we heard of legacies being dragged through the courts for years, until finally consumed by attorney fees? But the real point of this observation is not the money. It is the fact that, ever so subtly, the average American citizen is being disenfranchised of his rights to life, liberty, and the pursuit of happiness through laws written in legal jargon that only lawyers can understand. In every real sense, the legal profession has evolved into not only a monopoly, but a conspiracy as well. While the individual has the choice of declining medical assistance, or even hospitalization, there is no way of declining — sooner or later — becoming involved in the judicial process. And who sits in judgment of the legal profession? Why, the legal profession, of course.

While the purpose of this chapter is not indiscriminately to castigate the thousands of honorable people practicing law, the foregoing is intended to lay the groundwork for understanding the question: Why has our nation's legal environment changed so much over the past few decades, and who are the real beneficiaries of those changes?

We know, for instance, that government bureaucracies employ hordes of lawyers. Those lawyers have a hand in writing the regulations that tell business what it must do, what reports it must submit to remain in compliance, and what penalities (civil and criminal) may be assessed for noncompliance. Similarly, businesses, too (regardless of how innocuous) must maintain a "standing army" of lawyers in order to stay out of the "pokey." It is reliably estimated that useless reports and paperwork forced upon businesses add well over 100 billion dollars annually to our cost of living. Again, this is a matter of getting "nothing" for "something" — a situation that seems to be expanding exponentially. But we cannot really blame the legal profession for this particular mess, as much as the bureaucrats, who apparently need the work.

Of far greater importance than any other consideration is the insidious manner in which American ideals, beliefs, heritage, and even our culture, are constantly being taken away on the pretext that it is necessary in order to protect the "rights" of some minority "race," "opinion," or "belief." For example, 1978 was a "big year" in the offensive of the ACLU (American Civil Liberties Union) and similar groups in their attempts to displace Christianity as a visible part of our culture. We know, as a fact, that America's heritage is steeped in Christianity, and in one form or another, most Americans are Christians. This does not mean that all Americans must be Christians; certainly, they need not be. The freedom to choose whatever form of religion, or none at all, is a part of our founders' concept of the separation of church and state. The First Amendment to our Constitution states: "Congress shall make no law respecting an establishment of religion, or prohibiting the free exercise thereof." The purpose and intent of this clause must obviously be interpreted in context with the time of its writing, a period during which it was common practice for other governments specifically to ban certain forms of religion, while demanding adherence to others. But Americans have never been faced with that problem, and those purist minds that are now pursuing this matter in the name of "separation of church and state" are simply attacking our fundamental cultural heritage.

In a 1978 suit brought by the ACLU in the U.S. District Court in Sioux Falls, South Dakota, that organization sought to prohibit the singing of "Silent Night" and other religious songs in public schools and public places. In December of that same year, a similar group forced the superintendent of public schools in Novato, California to carefully edit out all such songs and religous connotations from Novato school Christmas programs.

In the case of Fox vs. the City of Los Angeles (1978), the California Supreme Court ruled that it was illegal for that city to allow certain lights to be left burning in the city hall at Christmas time for the purpose of forming a lighted cross. California's Chief Justice Rose Bird, along with Justices Mosk, Tobriner, Manuel and Newman, felt that this act violated Article I, Section 4, of their State Constitution, which reads simply: "The free exercise and enjoyment of religious profession and worship, without discrimination or preference, shall forever be guaranteed in this State." Needless to say, such practices have been going on ever since there has been a state of California (and perhaps long before), but it is now considered such a public menace that it must be eradicated.

Justice Frank Richardson, in a dissenting opinion, noted: "The influence of relgion on the American consciousness is, at once, pervasive, historic, and beneficent. Were we to attempt on misguided constitutional grounds to effect a total and complete insulation of government from all religious influence and symbolism, we would have commenced no small undertaking." And Justice Richardson's comments might well be termed a masterpiece of understatement.

Consider, for instance, some of the ramifications inherent in complete "insulation." It would mean removing religious mottoes from all government seals, buildings, and coins. It would require changing the names of all cities, streets, parks, playgrounds, schools and beaches with names such as Santa Barbara, San Francisco, Santa Monica, San Jose, Sacramento, Santa Cruz, San Angelo, San Antonio, St. Paul and St. Louis — to mention but a very few. Towns would no longer be allowed to decorate their streets at Christmas time (regardless of the absence of religious symbolism) because the root of this celebration is still religious. And such prohibitions would also apply to Christmas vacation for school children, along with a host of other customs that have long been cherished as a part of America's culture, tradition, and heritage. But the real point of this observation goes well beyond the "Grinches that are trying to steal Christmas from our children." It lies in recognition that we have allowed our courts to become packed with jurists whose liberal ideologies border on outright subversion.

California's Supreme Court Justice William Clark wrote a separate even more stinging rebuttal to this ruling in his dissenting opinion. Taking the majority ruling point by point, Justice Clark clearly establishes that the majority in its decision failed to provide any justification for its decision. Since the evidence presented in this case showed that no other relgious body has ever requested a display of their symbol, and therefore had never been denied such by the city, even the connotation of "preference" could not be applied in this matter. Furthermore, while it was alleged by the plaintiff that the symbol of the cross "might be offensive" to certain segments of the population, that segment, however small, had not been inclined to register a complaint. The only complainant of record was a Los Angeles attorney named S. Dorothy Fox who had brought the suit, and thereby deprived some 3,000,000 residents of the City of Los Angeles of a bit of custom and tradition which the city had enjoyed for the past 30 years. In his concluding paragraph, Justice Clark wrote: "In sum, the majority opinion fails to reveal that removal of the offending symbol is constitutionally required. In truth, it is required only by today's decree from four judges." (Chief Justice Rose Bird wrote a separate concurring opinion.)

And certainly of equal significance in this matter is the issue of "priorities." The Supreme Court is offered far more cases for review than it can possibly adjudicate. Consequently, after a brief scanning for meaningful substance, the justices vote on which cases to consider. Neither Clark nor Richardson felt that a "nit-picker" warranted the court's precious time, but again, the liberal majority prevailed.

But unfortunately, justices such as Clark and Richardson constitute only a minority opinion on California's Supreme Court. It is the liberal majority that controls the awesome power of this court and has consistently favored the rights of criminals over those of society. It is also this "majority" that can generally be found voting in favor of any ruling designed to further complicate the legal and judicial process.

It is such behavior by our courts which has many — even within the legal profession — wondering just how long it will be before our entire judicial system finally grinds to a halt, entrapped in a maze of technicalities from which there is no escape. If such a dilemma were to occur, it could result in a return to a system of law as basic and simple as the Ten Commandments, augmented by a few dozen "rules of thumb" based upon common sense. Come to think of it, that might not be such a catastrophe after all.

While there is certainly an analogy to be found in the cancerous growth of government and the equally cancerous growth of the legal establishment, it is not easy to determine which is being "fed" and which is "doing the feeding." A case in point might be the 1976 Civil Rights Attorneys Fee Act. Under this new provision of law, public advocate law firms may bring suit (supposedly in the public interest) against anyone, including any branch of government, and be awarded legal fees for their services by the courts.

The discrimination suits mentioned earlier in this text against San Francisco's police and fire departments resulted in legal fee awards of $225,000 and $385,000 respectively, to the firm of Public Advocates, Inc. of San Francisco. This same firm, in a joint suit with the Western Center for Law and Poverty, was awarded joint attorney fees of $800,000 in the case of Serrano vs. Pirest, the landmark case challenging the constitutionality of California's method of public school financing. In this last case, the fee amounted to approximately $300 an hour for these "public spirited" attorneys. The concept certainly sounds "high principled" enough, but we must bear in mind that it is the taxpayers, the citizens of San Francisco and of California, who are paying these fees, and it is the court, which is but another branch of the same profession, that is making the award.

While it would seem that all laws tend to favor, discriminate, or reverse-discriminate against some faction, it is difficult to conceive of any law being unfavorable to the legal profession. Representing the plaintiff, the defendant, or judging, the legal professionals remain immune to the casualties of the action, while being amply, often magnificently rewarded for their participation.

The Civil Rights Act of 1964, which in essence divided Americans into different categories of citizenship rights, opened a whole new frontier of opportunity for the legal profession: a veritable "candy store" for lawyers and a "nightmare alley" of uncertainty for the general public. Contrary to popular opinion, there is not a great deal of latitude available in the business world (particularly in smaller businesses) for the practice of either favoritism or discrimination. Far too often, management decisions, which are composed of a number of different factors (many of which are not apparent to the casual observer), are mistakenly taken for bias. A typical example of this type of situation was a 1977 joint suit filed by an employee and the State Fair Employment Practices Commission, which charged discriminatory promotion practices against a San Francisco automobile dealer. Although the court found the charges baseless and exonerated the dealer, the defendant in this case was an "automatic loser" from the time the charges were filed. The subsequent trial was merely an exercise to determine the extent of the loss. In spite of "winning," it still cost this defendant $12,000 to defend himself.

And so it goes in case after case across the nation, many of which are settled "out of court" by defendants who recognize that the "deck is stacked" and simply wish to minimize their losses. As we have seen so often in the past, in many instances new laws are simply the result of failure to enforce existing statutes. The Civil Rights Act of 1964 was obviously the result of failure to enforce Section I of the Fifteenth Amendment to our Constitution, which as "been on the books" since March 30, 1870, and which reads: "The right of citizens of the United States to vote shall not be denied or abridged by the United States or by any State on account of race, color or previous condition of servitude."

It would be pointless as well as inaccurate to deny the existence of senseless discrimination in our country — or in any other nation on earth, for that matter. Unfortunately, "discrimination" is identified as such only when it is levied against a "protected" segment of our population (a list that keeps growing) by a non-protected entity. When it happens between Jack and Harry, and neither happens to enjoy a "protected" status, we simply write it off as **"c'est la vie."** But a point that we must never overlook is the fact that perfect **fairness** and perfect **justice** are often like the "perfect mate": they exist in the mind of the beholder. And that another 10,000 laws are not likely to make life any more equitable for us.

Of particular concern in this examination is how the term "rights" has been so perverted over the past few decades that it now bears little resemblance to its original meaning. We banter this term around as though it were some kind of divine endowment rather than something stemming from a logical root. If we pay our rent in timely fashion, and do nothing to abrogate the terms of our rental agreement, then indeed we have established a "right to occupy" which is based on logical, traceable roots. That is the kind of basic right that most people can understand without the aid of a lawyer. In this particular case, neither party is impinging his or her will upon the other. But it is apparent that "rights" (at least to the legal establishment) is no longer a two-sided coin with "responsibilities" on the flip-side.

To illustrate a more complicated form of rights, those in which lawyers and politicians seem to revel, we will refer to an information brochure from the law offices of Public Advocates, Inc. Outlining some of their projects and goals, this booklet states: "A lawsuit to expand dramatically childcare facilities throughout the State, forcing government to acknowledge that childcare is a right rather than a luxury." Surely no one but an ogre could challenge such a well meaning, high principled concern for children. We might, however, look at how this "principle" works out in "practice." In 1977, a year in which the per capita income of Americans was only slightly over $6,000 per year, it cost an average of $5,100 annually for each child in San Francisco's Child Day-care Centers. That's $10,200 for a family with two children enrolled, or $20,400 for a family with four enrollments.

Now, supposing we could remove the anonymity from this particular situation, and that each month (or annually) the parents of children in day-care centers would have to go to their neighbors and present them with the bill for this service. Would they still say, "It's my right to have children and your responsibility to pay for them"? Or might they be more inclined to say, "Thank you so very much. I certainly appreciate your generosity"? But with the anonymity of taxation, they don't have to face their benefactors, and consequently, are never called upon to face themselves. The point here is not to single out child day-care centers for any specific criticism. It is, however, to illustrate the complete perversion of the term "rights."

The U.S. government has become so involved in the issue of rights in recent years that it is doubtful they could recognize a "wrong" if they were to stumble over it. In spite of the fact that many black leaders who originally supported the idea of school busing as a means of ending segregation now vehemently oppose the idea, busing is still being expanded. In Boston this issue has spawned racial friction far beyond any previously experienced by that city, pitting children against children, parents against parents, and the city in general against the courts. Cleveland, which began its court-ordered busing this year, will be sending many of its children on a 17-mile bus trip every day. But, of course, such children, and their parents, have no "rights." Los Angeles, which began its court-ordered busing in 1978, lost 40,000 public school enrollments the first year and another 20,000 in 1979. The citizens of this nation are apparently getting fed up with government telling them to "drink their Koolade," and in spite of the obvious burden of private school tuition, are thus expressing their indignation.

In 1978, the Civil Rights Division of the Department of Justice ordered Brigham Young University in Utah to stop the practice of having separate male and female dormitories and living accomodations for **single** college students. While this particular action may be of little interest to the people of Albany, Atlanta, or Albuquerque, it does carry with it some ominous implications of a government that is trying to play God. BYU is a privately owned and operated university, and it's difficult to understand whither the role or the authority of the Justice Department in this matter. Attendance at BYU is by choice, and aside from the wishes and policies of the school, it is quite possible that parents and students felt that separate living accomodations provide better academic surroundings, or at least help in reducing the number of unwanted pregnancies. But whatever their reasons, such people are not to be allowed this choice. Surely, it must be evident that a government that can get away with such mischief is certainly capable of going a step further and assigning roommates — and ultimately "bed partners" — in the interest of social goals, if that's what their warped little heads decide.

But the benevolent hand of government in bestowing "rights" is not limited to children. On April 29, 1978, U.S. District Court Judge William Orrick ordered 75-year old Cecelia Puccinelli of San Mateo, California to pay a black couple $32,000 in damages, and $11,000 to their attorneys, for refusing to rent them her single-family bungalow. Mrs. Puccinelli apparently didn't realize that the days when even a 75-year old woman was allowed to be selective in choosing her tenants is past. That privilege has been outlawed in the name of "higher rights." Although she has changed attorneys and appealed her case, regardless of the outcome, Mrs. Puccinelli will still suffer a financial disaster from the costs of defending herself. And on this, as on all other such battlefields between plaintiffs and defendants, it is unlikely that we shall find the corpse of a lawyer.

CHAPTER 19
GOVERNMENT BY WHOM?

There is an old military axiom which cautions: "Read the problem." The crux of this sage admonition lies in being able to distinguish between the "root" and "symptom" of an adverse situation before seeking solutions. Since it is obvious that our nation's leaders have made little or no progress in solving any of our major problems, we might now ask: Are those in government so illiterate that they can't "read the problem." Or from the evidence, might we rightly conclude that every action taken, every promise made, every failure to act upon critical matters which may offend some sizeable constituency, is in reality; a carefully calculated move that is measured solely in terms of **votes**. If so, then government itself is the real **problem**.

Consider this example: In spite of ample evidence over a long period of time that the Reverend Jim Jones was a fraud and a dangerous man, politicians ranging from the Mayor and District Attorney of San Francisco — to White House officials in Washington, D.C. — continued to court this man with appointments and glowing testimonials. And they did so almost to the eve of his infamous Jonestown "party to end all parties." Why? It was simply because Jonesy was a man with frightening political-clout.

If there was a need for a few thousand votes at the right time, and the right place, Jones could deliver. Often it was a matter of hundreds of people demonstrating in what appeared to be the public's approval or disapproval of a particular issue. Whatever the requirements, the good old "Rev" could provide these "spontaneous" outpourings of the public-will (for, or against a politician) at the snap of a finger.

On a more national scale, but with the same implications of "favor" or "intimidation", we might consult an article titled "The NEA: A Washington Lobby Run Rampant" by Eugene H. Methvin, which appeared in the November 1978 issue of *Reader's Digest* magazine. The NEA (National Education Association) is the largest teachers union in the nation, with a membership of 1.8 million of our total 2.2 million public school teachers.

Mr. Methvin writes: ". . . A succession of NEA presidents have proclaimed its aims:

* *'We are the biggest potential political striking force in this country.'* said Catharine Barrett in 1972. *'And we are determined to control the direction of education.'*

* *'We must reorder Congressional priorities by reordering Congress,'* Helen Wise told NEA political fund raisers in 1974. *'We must defeat those who oppose our goals.'*

* Promised current NEA president John Rynor: *'We will become the foremost political power in the nation.'"*

Mr. Methvin's article continues: ". . . Senator Claiborne Pell (D., R.I.), chairman of the Senate Education, Arts and Humanities Subcommittee, candidly admits that he owes his 1972 reelection to "teacher power." *"Before they arrived, I was a two-to-one underdog. Then an army of teachers began knocking on thousands of doors and making thousands of phone calls, and I won by 33,000 votes. You can be sure,'"* he concludes, *"that I will continue to fight in Washington for a better deal for education."*

Surely we must ask: Just what did the Senator mean by a *better deal* for education? According to a Rand Corporation study released in 1978, the U.S. government has poured 80 billion dollars into public education over the past dozen years without significantly improving either the schools or their end product. We know that while elementary and secondary public school enrollments have declined by some 2.7 million students over the past decade, the system now employs over 170,000 more teachers than it did in 1970. And that the per capita cost of educating the students has skyrocketed well beyond the rise in the cost of living index.

Yes, it is apparent that this organization, whose members, by virtue of their occupation, are provided with ample time for political activism, have been able to *"reorder Congress"* and to *"defeat those who oppose our goals."*

But senators are not the only ones who "march to the beat of teacher union drums." On July 2, 1979, Vice President Walter Mondale, addressing the American Federation of Teachers union convention in San Francisco, acknowledged that it was the support of both the AFT and the NEA which provided the Carter-Mondale ticket with its margin of victory in 1976. Mr. Mondale also reminded the delegates that the Carter administration has delivered unto the teachers that part of the American treasury which he had promised — and expects this cozy arrangement to be continued in the coming election. (The law creating the cabinet level **Department of Education** was proposed by President Carter, passed both houses of Congress in 1979, and on his signature the new DOE became our 13th full-fledged department. The **second** new one added since his inauguration, and he is proposing more. Not bad for a politician who campaigned for office on the platform that "government is too big; we must reduce the size of government.")

For a truly shocking account of the "unholy alliance" of teacher unions and politicians, every citizen should read Mr. Methvin's complete article.

It is evident from other sources, too, that teacher unions are not only "getting the ear" of Congress, but are twisting it until it turns blood-red. From the document THE BUDGET OF THE UNITED STATES GOVERNMENT FY-1981, we note that while government estimates there will be 5 million fewer enrollments in elementary and secondary schools in 1981 than there were in 1975, budgeting for the new Department of Education skyrockets to $16.5 billion. For those who have to pay this bill and who might not readily understand such astronomical figures, look at it this way; that's 16,500 X's $1,000,000. But still bear in mind that 75% of the costs for higher education come from private sources such as, endowments, gifts, investments, and tuitions. And that almost 90% of the funding for elementary and secondary schooling is borne, not by the Feds, but by state and local governments.

Yes indeed, teacher unions are doing one "hell of a job" of

educating. — (Congress, that is.) But again, it is really the narrative portion of our budget documents, rather than the figures, which provide a better insight into the rampant-lunacy of our "big spenders." On page 214 of the 1980 budget document, we read:

"**Higher education.** — The primary mission of Federal higher education programs is to assure that students are not denied the opportunity to receive post-secondary education because of inadequate financial resources." A fairly in-nocuous statement, but let's examine its meaning in terms of reality:

First, we know that 90% (or more) of the **knowledge part** of a college education can be obtained by those who want it badly enough, in their spare time, **free of charge**, at almost any public library. Admittedly, it may take a little longer. It might not include the traditional "sheepskin," and it certain-ly wouldn't encompass the niceties of campus life, but it is available **without** government assistance.

Second, if the United States were a nation like Kuwait that literally has money to burn, we might facetiously add references to Cadillacs, Riviera villas, even "tall blondes" and "handsome princes." But we are not! Our nation is plunging ever closer toward bankruptcy.

And third, can there be any reason why a truck driver, machinist, tailor, or sales clerk (non-college occupations) should be forced to pay for the college education of another person who will reap the benefits of that education for the rest of his or her life?

Even the claim that "higher educated" people indirectly benefit the whole community is too often at variance with the facts. It is a fact that millions of students attend college for little more than the social aspects. It is a fact that millions more do so for the monetary incentives, which in some cases, for some students, are more appealing than the thought of working for a living. And, of course, there are millions more who pursue courses of instruction which return to the general community virtually no tangible benefits. Many of our Liberal Arts and Alternative Education institutions conduct their classes under the trees, or alongside the swimming pool, have no written assignments, give no grades — only "sheepskins." One Northern California university even has a credit course in **frisbee throwing!** But they still cost the "chump" taxpayer who is breaking his back in a coal mine, or working up a case of varicose veins behind a sales counter, plenty of hard earned dollars.

The idea that the so-called "economically disadvantaged" (which in the case of higher education now extends to families with annual incomes of $25,000) shouldn't have to pay for a college education seems just as absurd. After all, if a college education isn't going to enable such persons to earn a living commensurate with the cost of that education, then indeed, such fact is prima facie evidence that the expenditure was unwarranted in the first place. But there are so many individually tailored programs within the category of "higher education" which run into hundreds of millions of dollars annually, that it is obvious they have been designed to **miss no one**; not even the "Rockefeller kids." This availability of federal funds runs the gamut from outright grants to funding of part-time jobs to picking up the interest tab on student loans, and, of course, picking up the entire tab when such loans go "sour," as they so often do.

And in considering the higher education picture, we still haven't touched on federal grants made directly to the institutions, nor have we mentioned funds from other sources, such as food stamps, or housing subsidies from HUD, which are often part of the "higher education process."

While the foregoing may sound like a "bum rap" aimed at our kids, it is not! They didn't design these programs, nor are they the real reason behind the programs: They are simply the excuse. And if we had no kids to send, in all probability we would still be sending something — dogs, cats, chickens, or jackasses — because the **primary** mission of these programs is to keep these institutions **and their staffs** as fully occupied as possible. If we can learn to recognize and accept that fact, it might be the beginning of a sound, sane, fair, equitable — and financially affordable — system of higher education.

As the cornerstone of such a program, we might lay down

the guiding principle that higher education is neither a right, nor a privilege. Neither is it the responsibility of government to furnish it, nor the obligation of the population to receive it. There must be a reason for people going to college which is completely separate from either government's desire to send them, or the institution's desire to have them. And from the ratio of "start and stops," radical changes in program, complete drop-outs — or even those who have acquired the "sheepskin" only to **choose** an unrelated profession such as bartending or truck driving — then we see that a sound reason far too often is missing.

To eliminate the "lack of reason" factor, let's put higher education on the same basis with everything else in life — not only do "you get what you pay for," but in which we also "pay for what we get." With the exception of programs for the physically handicapped (which a **productive** society could afford and easily absorb), and veteran-associated eligibility right (which have been earned), the costs of virtually all other higher education programs should be returned to the general public from whence it came, by its recipients. And such a concept would certainly be no more difficult to administer than the present "bucket of worms."

Such a concept would not necessarily lessen the "opportunity" of anyone for higher education. After all, if we can "charge" an automobile for five years, a home for 30 years, then certainly we should be able to "charge" a higher education. And those charges should be just as collectible in the last instance as they are in the first two. By the use of the Social Security number and automatic payroll deductions, all such charges associated with the process (including food stamps and HUD subsidies) could be collected, whether it took 10, 15, or even 20 years to do so.

Remember, we are not talking about the aged or the infirm who have no future earning potential. We are talking about young adults, who after graduating from high school have reached what should be a point of serious "decision making." Faced with a decision that is based on "obligations" as well as "druthers," it is highly probable that many students might delay their entrance into the college system until they know precisely **why** they are entering college. In such a case, the drop-out rate would plunge, — and the academic achievement rate undoubtedly soar — and it is even conceivable — in the long run college enrollments would actually increase.

But the purpose of the foregoing is not to single out federal mismanagement of education as a particular oddity. We know that there are hundreds of thousands of people who literally "milk" the unemployment compensation system by working only long enough to accrue eligibility, and then sit back and collect the benefits. And we know that the guiding principle behind all forms of insurance is that "premiums" should correspond to "risk." And yet, those who **always take** from the system pay no more in premiums than those who **never take** from it. Why?

In view of the foregoing, it is indeed appropriate that we offer sincere and genuine apologies to the tens of thousands of our public school teachers who are just as dedicated to the well being and the education of our children today as were their revered predecessors. But they, too, and perhaps even more acutely, recognize that their once honorable profession has been pirated away by a new breed of opportunists and bureaucrats who bear little resemblance to the "school marms" and school masters of the past.

The plight of education is a typical case history of how government (at every level) has been taken away from the people by powerful pressure groups that now wield the real power of government. Each year it becomes more and more evident that the process we go through in electing public officials is simply an exercise in futility. Over the past decade citizens have watched helplessly as function by function, city, state and federal government has literally been "captured" by unions which have taken over the ultimate exercise of top management decision making. Their power of decision ranges from what type of services shall be provided by public employees — right up to "no services at all." The point, of course, is how can we look to elected officials for better management of the public house when in reality they **no longer manage** the public house?

The belief that unions can provide public employees with greater benefits than a well managed government, without destroying the structure itself, is preposterous. And needless to say, this factor alone presents an enormous, almost insurmountable barrier to any sane attempt by citizens to limit or reduce the size of government. Even the very idea of unions in government would seem to border on treason, since in **practice** it not only sanctions, but even advocates periods of **anarchy.** True, to date no American city has burned to the ground, although individual structures have, as fire departments "fiddled." Nor has any community yet suffered the equivalent experience of the "rape of Nanking" as the result of a police strike. But such catastrophes can and almost inevitably must happen as we continue to accomodate and encourage the means for such an occurrence.

In considering the concept of "unions in government," there are several cogent points that seem to have been overlooked by politicians who have allowed this intrusion:

First, that public employees occupy a special position of trust with the public they serve. No one is either drafted or forced to accept employment in the public sector; it's a matter of voluntary choice. This matter of trust stems from the fact that in delegating responsibility for such vital services to public employees, we as citizens relinquish not only the ability, but also the **authority** to perform them ourselves. That's really what government is all about. And this fact is the guiding principle based on which most permanent public employees take an "oath of office" to serve the public in a **loyal, competent, and trustworthy manner.**

Second, that unlike private enterprise, government is not a "profit oriented" business whose competitive stance would automatically tend to limit unions to reasonable and practical demands. On the contrary, by virtue of the critical nature of their services (and most often the sole source), government unions can "tap" directly into the treasury for a bigger "take" for the employees, regardless of how unjust their demands. Hence we keep getting higher taxes and a reduction in services. Faced with the same sort of dilemma, a private business would simply go broke.

Third, as administrators of the "public estate," our elected officials are guilty of gross misconduct of office: They have re-delegated much of their official responsibilities to "union bosses" without first obtaining permission of their employer, the citizens. Have any citizens of this nation, at any time, been given the opportunity of voting "yea or nay" on the issue of "unions in government?" A concept of "legalized extortion" (blackmail), in which the lives and property of the public are held hostage under the threat of withholding vital services, such as police and fire protection.

Fourth, we have watched an over-powerful union element virtually destroy Great Britian as a world power. Have we learned nothing in the process, or must we emulate their example, only to conclude later in shocked surprise: "Gee, it happened here, too!"

Certainly the concept of unions in government violates some very basic principles upon which this nation was founded. One of these is that in time of strife, regardless of its source, the citizens of this country should be able to find in government a "neutral ground" in which to take solace and refuge. Government, as composed of public employees, should never become the adversary of the public it serves.

While many will doubtless read into the above "anti-union diatribe" — is it really? Or is it the case that in their lust for ever more power, the union "bosses" have actually broken faith with the labor movement — a movement that was never intended to extend beyond the perennial confrontation between capital and labor? It must be evident to a great many union members in the private sector that their achievements in the past half-century are now being mitigated and diluted unmercifully, by being forced to support a union establishment in government that does not have to live within the same limiting factors as they do.

"Step by step and stone by stone," over the last couple of decades politicians seeking fat constituencies in "big labor" have done more to destroy this nation than have all of our foreign adversaries combined. They have done so by pandering control of the government function into union hands, in exchange for campaign contributions and political support at the polls. But let us not be overly simplistic about the problem or the solution. We didn't get into this mess just yesterday, nor is it possible — or advisable — to adopt radical "reverse gear" policies designed to extract us from this quagmire by tomorrow. We can, however, and without upsetting anyone's "apple cart," establish a firm policy of "divestiture" of union-control of government; to be carried out over a four year period.

We already have the precedent of anti-trust laws which are designed to prevent the practice of "strangulation" of an industry by a particular business. Is it any less reasonable to prohibit such practices against our sole mechanism for the maintenance of a safe and orderly society, government? Surely, within such a four year "grace period," experienced personnel managers (not political-hacks) should be able to work out an equitable program of public employment that is both; fair to the employee and to the taxpayer.

We seem to have forgotten that for some 180 years (before the advent of unions into the public sector), our cities, counties, states, and the federal government, had little trouble finding adequate numbers of dedicated personnel; and that such jobs were eagerly sought after. Nor should we ever forget — that in those pre-unionization days — with only half the number of employees, less than a third the present automation, and at somewhere around one-fourth of the cost — taxpayers were receiving more than twice the amount of reasonable and necessary services than they receive today. And it must be obvious, the "rank and file" members of unions in private industry (like every other citizen), must also bear the burden of this inflationary factor.

Admittedly, blame for the inverse ratio of cost-to-services trend cannot be laid entirely at the doorstep of unionization. Such an allegation would be as ridiculous as it is untrue. It is, however, of unique importance in that de-unionization is virtually a prerequisite to any hope of again achieving an affordable government structure. One in which elected public officials can be held solely accountable for their actions. But if they are to be held accountable, they must also hold the full range of prerogatives in managerial decision making. There can be no — "other way."

CHAPTER 20
AMERICA'S DECLINING DEFENSE POSTURE

SALT II — the second round in the talks for a Strategic Arms Limitation Treaty — deals only with the balance-of-nuclear weapons between the United States and the Soviet Union. At best, however, in a total evaluation which takes into account the multitude and variety of potential conflicts in which America might become embroiled, nuclear capability represents no more than 50 percent of our realistic overall security requirements. That is, provided our nation maintains a respectable deterent in sophisticated weaponry. In such case, hopefully, the world will never have to suffer the devastation of a nuclear conflict between the two super powers. But what assurance then does this give our nation of enduring peace?

A world rapidly becoming too small for its mushrooming population is a world heading toward **inevitable** conflicts. With such knowledge in mind, two logical questions arise: First, just how strong is the United States in terms of conventional military power; and second, do we have the necessary **will** of a unified people to exercise that power in defense of our vital national interests? The one without the other is virtually a useless commodity. For example, during World War II, there is no way that Great Britian, despite massive American "lend-lease" aid, could have survived the devastation of incessant bombings and the V-1 and V-2 rocket attacks without the indomitable courage and **will** of its people.

Referring again to that period of history, America then enjoyed a sense of belonging and powerful common purpose, which, combined with our industrial might, made us the most formidable military force the world has ever seen. Not Hannibal, Caesar, Alexander the Great, nor even the mighty Kublai Khan had the logistical capabilities necessary to conquer the entire world. In 1945 America possessed that capability.

Our troops were combat-hardened, seasoned for any occasion. American air power controlled the skies over the entire globe. Our navy dominated the seven seas and all the world's shipping lanes. Our ground forces had fought on the frozen arctic wastes, through steaming jungles, over parched deserts, across seemingly impassable mountain ranges, and had engaged in guerrilla operations as well as conventional tactical warfare. Nothing was missing, nothing had been overlooked, in putting together America's incredible war machine.

For England, France, Italy, Germany, Russia, Japan and China, their logistical capabilities for waging war had been decimated by five to seven years of continuous direct warfare — 14 years in the case of China and Japan. Only the United States stood physically unscathed. And by the end of World War II, there was virtually no limit in sight to our accelerating capacity to turn out ships, tanks, planes, guns, bombs, transport vehicles, food supplies, and all the other paraphenalia for war.

Not only were our military forces well trained and seasoned, they were also highly disciplined and possessed outstanding morale. There were no "fraggings" or mutinies such as occurred in Vietnam, and our forces enjoyed total support on the home front by a responsible, dedicated and patriotic civilian population with an indomitable will to win. But then things began to change. With the end of hostilities came the beginning of the psychological and ideological war between Communism and the Western World. This new confrontation was preceded, perhaps even precipitated, by our wartime administration's "sell out" of the Eastern European nations into the hands of the Russians, where they now languish as Soviet satellites.

In 1948's crisis over Berlin, despite our obvious military and logistical superiority, Russia managed to "out-psych" us, and the result was the West's docile acceptance of the appeasement alternative: the Berlin Airlift.

In the Korean conflict, our politicians (not our military leaders) made the decision to fight a "no-win" war, and our troops had to settle for a "tie" or a "stand off." This, in spite of America's enormous psychological advantage resulting from its massive superiority in atomic weapons. But it was the Vietnam War which literally destroyed our armed forces

— more from within than from direct enemy action.

The issue of whether or not America should have been engaged in that conflict is an entirely separate matter. (It is also a matter, and a lesson, that should not be forgotten.) The fact was, however, that we **were** in this fracas, and there is no such thing as "a little bit of war" — any more than there is in becoming "just a little bit pregnant." The number of American lives lost in that conflict as the direct result of diviseness on the home front and indecisive policies at the top is, at best, incalculable. When a soldier can't be sure whether the **real enemy** is in front of him — behind him at home — or perhaps even sitting alongside him — then what usually is a very unpleasant duty degenerates into a truly terrifying experience. And such was the case in Vietnam.

In retrospect, there is no denying that Hitler's notorious "fifth column" of saboteurs were not nearly as successful and productive as is Communism's "fifth column" on the ideological front. Unfortunately the House UnAmerican Activities Committee investigations into subversive activities in the 1950's backfired miserably, and resulted in accomplishing the opposite of their purported goals. Admittedly, the hearings held by Senator Joe McCarthy often were improperly conducted, poorly thought out, and seemingly at times more vindictive than objective in nature.

Now, some twenty years later, re-runs of the McCarthy hearings have become a popular item of TV programming. Commentators point out to us the often heavy-handed McCarthy approach, but no one bothers to ask: Was the basic premise of the senator's concern correct? After all, it is our news media, the entertainment world (primarily movies and TV), and our public school system which do not merely **influence,** but over a given period of years literally **dictate** public opinion and public conduct. While each may be a separate entity, they are all integrated parts of the overall educational system, and, whether we like it or not, have a share in the on-going indoctrination process. The fact that 98 percent (or more) of the individuals engaged in these fields are loyal American citizens is no justification for so vehemently denying the existence of clever, subtle and deliberately subversive elements within these industries. The record of their long-term influence and effect speaks for itself.

We certainly cannot be so naive as to believe that the disintegration of moral principles, the glorification of drug use, the ridicule of parental authority and family unity, or our constant exposure to perversion and violence have all come about by happenstance rather than through subtle "programming." But these "key" elements of influence and control are not the only elements of society open to subversion.

The Soviet Union, better than anyone else on earth, knows and understands the special vulnerability of a democracy to subversion. It is the easiest of all forms of government to pervert, even to the point of **self-destruction.** The very same institutions which make democracy such a desirable form of government also serve the purpose of promulgating and furthering the goals of those who would seek to destroy democracy. Our courts and our legislative processes have provided ample evidence demonstrating the truth of this hypothesis. We need only look at the number of legislative bills that are designed specifically to foster divisiveness in our society, or the number of court decisions that have resulted in encouraging the criminal element and punishing society. Even our economic policies, which completely violate principles of sound management, operate to destroy our nation's economic equilibrium, and thereby demonstrate the subtle hand of subversives at work within the hallowed institutions of our government.

But what is the answer to this dilemma? Patrick Henry said it best over 200 years ago: *"Eternal vigilance is the price of liberty."* Unfortunately, not enough Americans have heeded that sage advice, and consequently our nation is well along the path to self-destruction. Hopefully, we can reverse this trend — as we must, if there is to be an America tomorrow. The very first step in that direction lies in acknowledging the fact that our form of government is particularly susceptible to destruction from within, and then resolving to weigh all future actions on a simple scale: "Is this decision in the interests of our society, or is it in the best interests of those who **oppose** lawful society?" Such a determination shouldn't be at all difficult to make. Similarly, legislative and administrative actions will tend either to strengthen or to weaken our national posture. If they don't do the **former,** then obviously they accomplish the **latter.**

It has been well known for years that student-riots around the world have been orchestrated largely by Moscow. This is not to say that in many instances there were not legitimate reasons for the basic unrest: Often there is, which conveniently provides subversives with the cover they need. But this is not always the case. In January of 1980, the Soviet ambassador to New Zealand was expelled for funneling money to radical elements within that country. Surely, if Moscow would take the trouble of stirring-up unrest in a peaceful little nation like New Zealand (which lies almost in the shadow of the South Pole); can there be any doubt that the Soviets are extremely active here in the United States?

The Vietnam years brought "out of the closet" a number of avowed communist faculty members, who soon became "folk heroes" on many of our campuses. Even now, in 1980, communist radicals like Stokeley Carmichael are routinely invited (often at taxpayer expense to lecture at our universities on the evils of our form of government, and on the blessings of communism. (Mr. Carmichael renounced America long ago, to live in communist Guinea.) Daniel Ellsburg, another campus "folk hero" who can always be counted upon to be at the forefront of any movement designed to weaken America's defense posture, is often the star attraction of "No Draft" rallys. So again in retrospect, if we want to exhibit even a shred of objectivity regarding Senator McCarthy's concern about communist subversive activities (not his methods in pursuing this issue), then we must admit that "Joe was right on."

We can also find evidence of this fact in the number of students and faculty members of the University of California who are currently demonstrating against the continued use of the Lawrence Radiation Laboratories in Livermore, California for military research and development programs. In essence, they challenge the idea of colleges being in such a gruesome business. (The LRL is an extension of the

University of California, a taxpayer-supported institution.)

At first glance, their agitation seems to convey the idea of high moral purpose: After all, no reasonable person could believe that the carnage and sufferings of war are either delightful or desirable. In the main, however, most of these movements are initiated by "liberal intellectuals" who take immense pride in their own super-sophistication — the kind of people who consider that only "peasant mentalities" believe patriotism to be an integral and essential part of responsible citizenship.

Invariably, the central theme of their argument is that it is the "imperialist American war-mongers" who are perpetuating the nuclear arms race through insistence on "preparedness." A theory that might carry some weight if it were accompanied by even the least amount of **objectivity.** But with 35 years of historical evidence to draw upon, why should anyone have to resort to abstract theory? Why not simply examine the **facts** and see who **actually initiated** the arms race, and who has been solely responsible for **perpetuating** it ever since?

We might begin such an enquiry with the evidence that dispels the myth that America has "imperialist" designs of conquest against any nation. **The very existence today of our ideological arch-adversary, Soviet Russia, is by the sufferance and efforts of the United States and its Western Allies of World War II.**

Throughout that war, Russia painstakingly removed every shred of evidence of American markings from the enormous quantities of military hardware and supplies we sent them. In denying their people the knowledge of this support, the Soviet hierarchy demonstrated that it had no intention of continuing a "buddy-buddy" relationship with the United States after the cessation of our mutual hostilities with the Axis powers. In other words, the "die had been cast" **by Russia** for future confrontations with the West long before the war ended. With this knowledge at hand, the Western powers had two simple options available, either of which could have almost "instanteously" eliminated this bastion of communist ideology from future world concern:

(1) Just prior to the German collapse, Germany had eagerly sought a negotiated peace with the West on any terms that would have spared her people the dreaded Soviet occupation. It would have taken no greater concessions than those we ultimately gave them anyway, to have turned the German war machine around and sent it east. With Allied logistical support (but no loss of Allied lives), it could have completely destroyed Soviet Russia as a world power and - more important - as the "hatchery" for world communism.

)2) With or without German military assistance, if we had withdrawn our logistical support from Russia, the Western Allied forces were powerful enough to have sliced through that country easier and faster than Sherman marched to the sea.

In reiveving the record of history, it becomes starkly evident that the "imperialist" mantle fits the Soviet Union and its communist cohorts far better than it does the United States. One has only to consider the record of territorial aggrandizement by Russia at the expense of its neighbors: Finland, Latvia, Lithuania, Estonia, Poland, Rumania, Tannu Tuva and Afghanistan have all either suffered loss of territory or been swallowed up entirely by the Soviet Union.

At the end of World War II, the United States undertook the peaceful (but enormously expensive) task of rehabilitating virtually the entire war-damaged world. Now just consider what **might** have happened:

* Had there been no Soviet blockade of Berlin, no communist invasion of South Korea, no build-up of Russian missiles just off our coast in Cuba, no communist infiltration and subversion leading to almost incessant hostilities throughout much of the world;

* And had Soviet Russia at the close of World War II accepted this incredible opportunity (the first in her history) of bringing a decent standard of living to the millions of Russian peasants and workers through peaceful enterprise;

* Then in all probability a **third** A-Bomb would **never have been built.** Nuclear research would have dwindled to a trickle, to be sustained only by a cautious inquiry into the

peaceful applications of the atom. Instead of this rational approach to their future well-being, however, Soviet Russia immediately launched the massive build-up of its military forces and equipment to a level that far outstripped even its wartime commitments. And the Russians have continued ever since to pour a far greater proportion of their GNP (gross national product) into "tools of destruction" than any other nation on earth.

No, communism is not, as claimed, a movement whose sole aim is that of helping the working class. Indeed, quite the contrary. It is purely and simply the greatest ideological hoax ever perpetrated on a "too eager to trust" world. If we need more evidence of this fact, it is necessary to look no farther away than Cuba.

Fidel Castro's revolution against the oppressive and corrupt dictatorship of Juan Batista was a popular movement that was widely supported throughout the United States. It was largely (and perhaps only) because of the unofficial but tacit approval of our government, along with financial aid and volunteer military manpower from America, that his revolution was able to succeed in the first place. But what happened next?

Cuba, like Russia, is a country rich in natural resources. Nature and providence have provided that island with all of the essential elements needed to build a peaceful and prosperous nation. Under the Monroe Doctrine, Cuba is even assured protection by the United States against invasion by any European nation. With Castro's successful revolution, it appeared — for a brief moment — that the opportunity for a peaceful and happy lifestyle had at long last "knocked at Cuba's door." Unfortunately — and this is a fact that must now be considered **obvious** — the dogma of communism cannot survive in conditions of **peace.**

The salt water had hardly dried upon his sandals before ths pipsqueak Caesar turned upon and denounced the United States, and launched his revolutionary expeditions against the other nations of Central and South America. His 1962 importation of Russian missiles came close — God alone knows how close — to getting his whole nation (island included) blown off the face of the earth.

Castro's forays in the Western Hemisphere have failed badly, and he has since redirected his army to undertake a communist conquest of Africa. On May Day, with Cuba's annual parade of tanks, missiles and troops, Havana now looks more like Red Square than its model in Moscow.

Think about it! Is this what Cuban workers and peasants thought they were fighting and dying for in their revolutionary effort? Did they know that the resources of their beloved island, and even the lives of their children, would later be committed to world conflict? In all probability, the answer to that question would be an emphatic NO.

In spite of their placards which read "Workers arise" — "Workers demand" — "Workers unite," communism is not a movement whose true motive is to benefit the working class. That is, unless such people are looking for a short cut into the next world: they have been slaughtered by the millions, and for whose benefit? Certainly not theirs.

We can no longer ignore the realities of **all** communist-inspired revolutionary activities. In ascending order of rewards, the "profiteers" benefitting from such movements are: (a) The small ruling cliques whose lust for power is paramount, above all other considerations; and (b) The "arms merchants" who reap enormous fortunes supplying all sides in these conflicts. Since we know that the arms merchant is the very epitome of communism's alleged arch-enemy, the "capitalist pig," we must ask: Just how long can this stupid hoax be perpetuated?

In the meantime, let those who would weaken America's defensive posture in the name of "stopping the arms race" direct their efforts at the aggressor, rather than at those who for sheer safety must adopt adequate defensive measures. Certainly, the arms race is a case of "insanity on the loose," but it is Russia, not the United States, that needs to be made aware of that fact.

America has spent the last several decades (and literally billions of dollars) trying to establish and maintain peaceful relations between often relatively insignificant nations throughout the world. Maybe — just maybe — we ought to be spending a great deal more effort on direct negotiations (particularly, commerical and cultural programs) with the Soviets, to convince **them** to stop this lunacy before somebody "really gets hurt." Surely, we must have some common interests upon which we can build.

The world on which Lenin predicated his ideals and beliefs in "world communism" is as dead as Lenin himself. It no longer exists. Nations whose populations have doubled, tripled, quadrupled — or even more — since Lenin's day, have put the stamp of obsolescence on whatever theories he once held dear. At the present time (1980), Third World nations comprise approximately 70 percent of the world's population. By the turn of the century (assuming no cataclysmic events), this disparity in percentages will be approaching the 80-20 mark. In fact, it would not be too surprising that the U.S. and the U.S.S.R. actually share more realistic common fears of the future than we do adversary positions. This doesn't mean that we should suddenly become "pals" with a regime whose ideology includes the routine practice of treachery. But it certainly indicates an approach that we ought to explore thoroughly (and carefully) in our attempts to reduce the nuclear arms race.

Along with the above approach, we might also point out to our own radical elements that "world peace through world communism" is an idea that just "won't fly." Soviet influence was responsible for converting China into a communist state, and what happened? China in turn succeeded in establishing a communist government in Vietnam; Vietnam and China jointly supported the communist take-over of Cambodia; and if it were possible to put all of these "communist comrades" into the same ring, we would undoubtedly see the "damnedest dog-fight" of all times take place.

President Carter's request for a Draft Registration which followed the Soviet invasion of Afghanistan, at first widely accepted, is beginning to run into opposition. (His including of women in this request is too absurd to dignify with a comment.)

First, he called for the registration for the **wrong reasons:** If it is needed to protect our vital interests in the Middle East — it is already "a day and a half late — and two dollars short." With the Russians now in Afghanistan, should they choose, their forces could easily be somewhere south of the equator before our first new recruit even entered boot-camp.

Indeed we do need a much stronger military force, but solely for other reasons. There wouldn't be a great deal of sense in an aggressor leveling America's missile-sites with nuclear weapons, if they could not then physically occupy our nation. And while not entirely; it is primarily such considerations which should dictate our defense posture. We should have began recognizing the need long ago to stop allowing our nation to get into the position of having **war-potential vital interests** outside of our own bailiwick.

Second, the growing opposition (that which is genuine, as opposed to the obviously subversive) stems from an increasing distrust of the administration and its purposes: At the same time the president called for registration, he also proposed another $400 million in aid to Pakistan. And Mr. Carter's January 20th pronouncement that America is prepared to use *"military force if necessary"* to defend Pakistan — bordered on "crazy house" talk: What, and who, would we defend it with? And next, why? The very idea that such an untrustworthy "ally" would in turn, assist America in defending our interests in the Middle East; is a totally unwarranted assumption.

American foreign policy seems to have an affinity for booby-traps. Pakistan's leader, General Zia, immediately labeled our president's $400 million offer as "peanuts" — saying, "talk to us in terms of at least a billion dollars." We have already seen how a number of nations in that region of the world (India and Morocco, to name just two) have learned to play the foreign-aid game from both sides of the fence. Is there any reason to believe that in the event of a serious crisis, Pakistan, which borders on the Soviet Union, and whose loyalties at best are dubious, would not throw in with its neighbor and use that aid against us?

Admittedly, Russia's invasion of Afghanistan is wrong and should not be taken lightly. But neither should our president have started "shooting from the hip" with statements that our military forces couldn't back-up, nor with policies that in the long run are not in our best interests. As example, he immediately cut off the shipment of wheat to Russia, while the curtailment of high-technology came only as an afterthought. And while the Russians have proven themselves quite adept at "belt-tightening" in the past, it probably won't be all that necessary since South America has taken up much of the slack in their wheat requirements. However, in terms of "detente" — wouldn't an even greater Russian dependency on American wheat fields serve that purpose better?

But it is Mr. Carter's demand for a boycott of the summer Olympic games in Moscow that will backfire most of all, if it is intended as means of punishing Russia's leaders: The presumption being, that if nobody shows up (or at least the Western powers) for the games, those responsible for the Afghan invasion would be deeply humiliated in the eyes of their own people. Now what kind of **realistic logic** is that? We know that the Russian people live in a totally managed society in which the media (radio, television and newspapers) present only the official government version of the news. Several months after the invasion began, a poll of public opinion taken on the streets of Moscow by ABC television correspondents, revealed the following: Those who had any serious thoughts on the matter; (a) believed the invasion was justified, and (b) were equally assured that it had been brought on by **American** interference in Afghanistan. In other words, if the Western nations fail to show up for the Olympic games, again, it will be America and not Russia's leaders that are castigated for the incident. If Soviet citizens are to learn anything at all adverse about their invasion of Afghanistan, it will have to come on a "person to person" level. And the summer Olympics will provide the West with what may be its last opportunity for such a massive people-to-people dialog.

Even more disastrous than the single issue of the Olympics, is this attempt to again isolate the Russian people from contact with the outside world. If we persist in that policy — sooner or latter, but inevitably — "puff" — and that will be it.

As part of Mr. Carter's "get tough" policy with the Russians, he also approved the MX Missile project. A concept of strategic defense that is so stupendous that it boggles the imagination. It involves taking 50 of the largest valleys which encompass the entire states of Utah and Nevada, and undermining them with thousands of miles of tracks interconnecting silos from which missiles might be fired. The concept is that there will be so many silo's — and with the missiles traveling between them on a totally erratic schedule — it would be almost impossible for the Russians to know which ones actually held the missiles. Could be! But there are some rather serious ramifications to that concept, which if not overlooked, have been overly minimized. First, nobody really knows what this vast undermining might do to the water tables in those two beautiful states, along with other environmental considerations. Second, the almost inestimable amount of raw material needed for such a massive project will have to come "out of the hide" of our nation:

If nobody happens to know it yet, a shortage of plain, old, simple cement is going to be one of our nation's coming "crisis." And with the world's steel consumption rising at a rate that is 3 times higher than its additions to steelmaking capacity, we might also throw in that item. The point, of course, is that we should be devoting a great deal more effort toward getting-thru to the Russian people to halt this insanity. Particularly, since the completion of "MX," if it is undertaken, still lies several years in the offing. Unfortunately, neither can Americans fall back on Salt-II as a "security blanket." It is apparent from the overwhelming majority of **retired** high-ranking military officers (those who no longer have to be "team-players" with Mr. Carter) vehemently oppose the treaty as being disastrously imbalanced in the favor of Russia. But regardless of nuclear parity, it is still, and will always be, conventional military forces that take — hold — and defend ground, and therein lies our greatest weakness today.

It is imperative that the United States adopt whatever measures are necessary to rebuild America's conventional military services into a powerful and effective armed force — high in quality, discipline and training. There is only one possible hope that we will not need them in the near future, and that lies solely in the deterrent effect of overwhelming superiority. If we maintain a credible deterrent, we should avoid the aggressor's attack, even though much of the rest of the world may decimate itself in aggressive actions against easier opponents.

America's present concept of an "all volunteer" armed force has proved to be a disaster. Our military departments are not getting the quantity — much less the **quality** — of personnel upon whom the very life of our nation depend. As inducements to enlistment and retention of volunteers, the armed services have mistakenly lowered their standards of qualifications, conduct and discipline to the point where the morale factor has backfired. Too often, the category of person the services desperately need to retain, can hardly wait until the moment of his discharge, recognizing that to a large extent, our military forces have become little more than a "job corps" for the underprivileged.

Even the increased emphasis on the use of women to help compensate for this manpower shortage is but one more step in the wrong direction. Contrary to currently popular notions (TV programs included), women do not work out well in jobs involving physical prowess, danger, and violence. And this includes other positions, such as those in law enforcement and fire fighting, except in those capacities where they have always been utilized. This fact does not mean that women are substandard or "bad people." With only 60% of the physical strength of man, it simply means they are women. At the present time, women constitute approximately six percent of our armed forces, which is a higher percentage than is found in any other country in the world, including the Soviet Union.

But over the next couple of years the Pentagon expects this percentage will rise to somewhere between 10 and 15 percent, further aggravating what has already become a serious problem within the military services, and that is the **pregnancy** of its so-called "fighting force." This dilemma was dramatically illustrated during a major tactical operation by our European army units during the winter of 1978, when it was found that a great many women couldn't "move out" as soldiers because they were either pregnant or were caring for small children. And many officials within the services believe the pregnancy rate runs well above ten percent most of the time.

The chief question that logically arises is: "Whose responsibility should it be to bear arms for the United States? Those in the higher academic circles tell us it's not theirs, for they are too involved in the arts, the humanities, and abstract thinking, to concern themselves with such barbaric activities. The affluent will rightfully point out that a tour of military service might hamper the chances of their offspring becoming millionaires before the age of thirty. And so on down the line: Each will have a fairly plausible excuse. So let's put it another way: Those who do not benefit from the blessings of United States citizenship should not have to serve. (But they should also be invited to emigrate to a nation that is more compatible with them and their beliefs.)

U.M.T. (Universal Military Training) is the only answer to this dilemma, and it should be interpreted and implemented in the literal sense: "universal." There should be no deferments for college, occupation, wealth, or religion of those who are physically, mentally, and morally acceptable to the services. The only exceptions should be in proven cases of extreme dependency hardship.

A period of two years of active military service for every able-bodied male should begin within one year from high school graduation, or upon his reaching his 19th birthday. The idea that such service would represent "two wasted years out of my life" is a totally invalid premise. There is virtually no occupational field that does not have a compatible counterpart in one of the military branches. Nor is there any reason for such service to be spent digging post-holes and fillng them up again. In addition to direct military activities, civil defense and disaster training would be a logical part of the overall curriculum. It is an undeniable fact that at the present time the United States is totaly unprepared for any kind of truly major catastrophe. The recent accident at Three Mile Island nuclear power plant is both a warning and a typical example of the variety of peacetime "holocausts" that could result from our rapidly accelerating technological lifestyle.

If no other reason existed, a period of service at this point in an individual's life would be well spent in acquiring a knowledge of the realities of the world situation. It would help provide him an understanding of how such situations might logically progress to those more aggravated conditions requiring a strong and unified America, in which the responsibilities of citizenship are at least commensurate with the privileges and rights afforded by that citizenship.

Such military forces, including the Coast Guard, might even be used to a limited degree under the direct **supervision** and **control** of other government agencies. As an example: this would certainly be a practical and economic approach to meeting the incredible manpower shortage of the Border Patrol of the INS. That particular agency has been gravely short-changed by the Congress over the past two decades, with the result that America now has upwards of twenty million illegal aliens adding to our nation's woes, while another million or so invaders arrive annually.

We have already seen how the cost of government services, in many instances, has become almost prohibitive. Why not utilize the **training function** of our armed forces, whenever possible, in a dual capacity, so that their service also accomplishes meaningful and needed tasks?

Such a concept would almost certainly draw the ire of the labor unions, of businesses seeking fat contracts for such services, and of course would also bring cries of "police state" from those subversive elements whose primary mission is to raise such outcry about anything designed to strenghten our nation. But a **responsible government** — if we were ever again to have one — would tell such power blocs to "go to hell," and would get on with the business of shoring up America's defensive posture along with our economic stability.

If the military services could not effectively use the full manpower resources generated by the draft, then a "lottery" provision within the UMT act should be applied to deliver the exact proportion necessary. However, all **"first term"** recruits must come from the **draft,** and not **volunteers,** if we are to avoid the "quality crisis" which now plagues the forces. Surely, many will condemn this provision as absurd, saying: "Why not take those who want to serve in place of those who don't?" And on the surface this would appear to make sense. However, for the reasons already mentioned above — and particularly in the long run — it does not: America desperately needs a representative cross-section of its population, not only exposed, but also participating in our national defense effort. Only in such a manner can we even hope to rebuild a qualitative armed force on which the nation can feel secure — and one in which those who serve will feel proud and honored to do so.

Last, but not least, let those who would oppose compulsory military training on the grounds that it breeds a "war mentality" ponder the evidence: Switzerland can hardly be termed an aggressive "war-monger," yet that nation has had UMT longer than any other country on earth. As a result of their extremely strong defensive posture, the Swiss have not **had** to fight a war in **over 400 years.** It simply illustrates the fundamental truth of that cardinal rule which has shaped the course of history since mankind first appeared on this planet: Strength **deters** aggression; weakness provides an irresistible **invitation.**

CHAPTER 21
ITS TIME WE TOOK A "SECOND LOOK"

As we have endeavored to point out in this text, from its very beginning our nation has derived its strength and vitality from the liberty and freedom of its citizens. That liberty and freedom is exercised through what we commonly refer to as the free enterprise system; a political-belief that was once central to our concept of government. But as we have altered the concept, we have altered as well what the system is capable of doing.

For a mechanical analogy, we might consider the free enterprise system as the engine of our country which develops the **power,** and government, per se, as accessories on that engine which operate by draining away a portion of the engine's power. We all know what happens to the efficiency of an automobile engine as we add power brakes, power steering, automatic transmission, and air conditioning; the mileage plummets. And so it is with the power plant of our nation. We keep adding more and more accessories (many of them utterly ridiculous luxuries), until we have finally not only reached; but passed the point at which our engine is able to develop any net horsepower. How do we know this? Like the torque-meter on an aircraft engine, there are three guages in our economy that register the **actual** horsepower of our nation: (1) the size of our **national debt**; (2) the size of our **balance-of-payments deficit**; and (3) the rate of inflation.

All of which raises the question: "If the above is true, then how have we managed to keep our nation running?" The answer to that question isn't difficult, if we stop long enough to examine the evidence at hand. First, we know that we have been able to do so by mortgaging the future **productive output** of our citizens (national debt); second, we have recently done so by selling off America's gold reserves (and as we should all note, given the current price of gold, we did that at a handsome **loss** of billions of dollars; third, we are continuing to do so by selling off the **physical assets** of our country, which, exclusive of our people, **are** our nation. To understand this last point, we must realize that for the past several years America has managed to kite its high standard of living, to a large degree, upon an ever-increasing balance-of-payments **deficit** in international trading. This factor, coupled with the billions of dollars that our politicians have literally **given away** (and they continue to do so), has provided foreign nations (and individuals) with well over 600 billion American dollars that are currently being presented at our national cashier's cage for payment:

Yes, the day of reconciling irresponsible management with the facts of life is upon us. Foreigners with U.S. dollars are now buying up American homes and American apartment houses. Across the nation they are acquiring American businesses at an ever accelerating pace — and they are known to have purchased well over **10 million acres** of American farm land. (How many other purchases of land have been made through dummy corporations and third or fourth parties is not known, but are believed to be substantial.) And just how big is 10 million acres? It is approximately **twice** the combined land area of the states of Delaware, Rhode Island, and Connecticut.

But, lest it be concluded we are preaching an anti-foreigner rampage, let us review the facts: With the exception of the billions of dollars that our politicians have actually **given away,** those foreigners have earned their money the same way that Americans **used to** earn theirs — i.e., by the sweat of their brows. As a typical (but by no means the only) example: while America's automobile industry has declined to such a point that many workers (or potential workers) have had to resort to unemployment insurance or even welfare, we have been purchasing foreign-made vehicles at the rate of over 2½ million units per year, at costs ranging from four to 40 thousand dollars each. And how have we paid for them? With I.O.U.'s (U.S. dollars) which are redeemable (literally) in vast portions of our **nation.** And since it was foreigners who did the **work** that produced those vehicles, it is also foreigners who are legally and morally entitled to whatever those dollars will buy.

Now, in no way is the above to imply that our government should impose trade barriers to protect the auto industry, or any other industry. Such barriers are artificial remedies that often backfire, doing more harm than good to our overall economic posture. Even more important, such measures tend only to screen from view serious ailments and deficiences within the very industries they are designed to protect and preserve. The real point here is that across the board we must drastically reduce the overhead portion of every function and operation if our nation is to maintain a competitive stance in world trade, or even in our own domestic marketplace.

So, it is evident that the Pied Piper who gave us **so much** for **so little** (just our votes) has, in reality, betrayed the citizens of this nation at every turn. Even as this is being written, the cry is going up in Washington that if Congress fails to pass a 1.5 billion dollar subsidy for home heating oil, our nation's poor and elderly will freeze to death this winter; at the same time, subsidized housing units are increasing at the rate of 10 percent annually, and the President of the United States is creating another new bureaucracy under HEW, whose function will be to "study the problems facing the American family." What problems?

Is it a problem that millions of American citizens can no longer feed themselves without food stamps? Is it a problem that millions of Americans can't pay their rent without the assistance of HUD? Is it a problem that millions of our citizens aren't able to see a doctor or get into a hospital without a Medicare card? Or is it a problem that the average American can no longer afford to buy a home in his own country?

Succinctly stated, our nation's economic crisis can be traced to one simple fact: America is suffering from a "productivity crisis," and until we recognize that this is the **root** of our economic problems, all attempts to remedy the situation will merely aggravate the basic malady. First, however, we must understand what is meant by **productivity** and its relationship to **economic solvency.** Productivity is not "total output," nor is it to be confused with "technology." And economic **solvency** has nothing to do with size, but rather indicates the **health** of the economic body. To understand

211

this point, consider the following example: One hundred years ago, it can be said, the United States was a nation **high** in productivity but **low** in technology (by today's standards). There was virtually no "national debt." Percentagewise, corporate (business) and personal borrowings amounted to only a tiny fraction of our useful gross national product. Whatever we as Americans had, to a far greater degree than today, we owned outright — "lock, stock, and barrel." Now, to achieve this without the aid of modern technology required most of our citizens to work 10 to 14 hours a day, six — and often — seven days a week. In addition to the "breadwinner," everyone in the family, to the limit of his or her capability, contributed to doing the "chores," making life more fruitful for all concerned. Thus, in spite of a lack of technology, America was an **economically solvent nation** by virtue of its **high productivity factor.**

We shouldn't pass over the above too lightly. Think of it! At a time when roads were built with pick and shovel, when fields were ploughed with the aid of a mule, when clothes were made by a seamstress or tailor, and when huge buildings were erected with little more than bricks, mortar, and a hammer and saw, the American people were able not only to support themselves, but a reasonable and responsible government, too. Now, are we to believe that the advent of modern technology has lessened our ability to do so? No, such an answer couldn't make sense. Or could it be that more efficient ways and means have created a surplus of labor for which there are no jobs? Again, a closer examination of that question reveals that for every job eliminated in the past century through advances in technology, no less than a dozen new jobs have been created in the process. All of this has greatly raised our standard of living, while it has also substantially reduced the required number of hours in our work day. Since there is obviously no physical reason for our present financial plight, we must look elsewhere for answers. We must examine especially that element which has been most active in tampering with and altering the natural progression of economic matters, namely, government.

First, we know that the proper and legitimate role of government under a constitutional republic such as ours is that of a **public servant.** Like any servant, a government must never be imposing, obtrusive, or over-demanding, and above all, it must be affordable. We might also add to this list of desirable traits, a relative degree of honesty, along with — if not loyalty to its **employer** — at least loyalty to the **terms of its employment.** Needless to say, neither our federal government, nor more than a very few of our state and local establishments, meet **any** of those requirements today. It is certainly obvious that government as conducted by its current practitioners is no longer **affordable.** Our present course of fiscal irresponsibility is leading us to economic collapse, and **rising inflation** is the **infallible** harbinger of such a catastrophe.

If the American people wish to salvage not only our economy, but our form of government as well (because the immediate aftermath of economic collapse of the magnitude America faces today would be anarchy, most likely followed by totalitarianism), then we must make a drastic change in our "housekeepers." We must bear in mind two extremely important factors relating to our ability to recover from the Great Depression of the 30's so that we do not confuse that situation with the one facing us today: First, in spite of "tough times," America then was still "economically solvent" in terms of our own **natural resources.** And second, we were then totally **solvent** as a nation, **internationally.** Today, we are neither, and we must immediately plot a course leading to both.

The citizens of this nation must demand that candidates for public office stop "wallowing around in generalities" as they have been prone to do in the past. We must demand **specifics** of them, and we must demand **time tables** for their achievement. "What month, what year, how many, and how much?" **Specifics!** And any candidate who cannot supply those specifics is not qualified for the job. But extracting promises alone will not suffice. Too many of our politicians are congenital liars who will "promise the moon" for a vote. We must therefore develop a system of **recall** from office that works. Since one way or another most of the nation's serious problems are the result — direct or indirect — of fiscal irresponsibility, "Taxpayer Associations" would seem to be the most logical groups to monitor government performance. There are other types of organizations, too, that can be effective, but taxpayer associations generally are the ones most concerned with the overall best interests of all citizens and tend to weigh most fairly and objectively both sides of an issue. Those who do not have the time to participate actively in such groups should at least support them through membership dues, which normally are almost negligible in comparison with their benefits.

We must also demand of politicians a declaration that every action taken will be geared towards improving America's **productivity factor.** In no way does this statement imply that we must set about producing ever increasing amounts of "four-on-the-floor, high fidelity, remote controlled **eggbeaters**" (a simple table fork will often suffice). It does mean, however, that whatever we produce in the line of goods and services must be provided more efficiently. But unfortunately, whereas in earlier days of only minimal government red tape, restrictions, and unreasonable social demands, America could look to increased technology for increased efficiency, today we can no longer do so. Why? Because the **overhead factor** of our life style has greatly surpassed the **efficiency gains** made possible through better technology — to the point where it has not only eroded those achievements, but now accounts for not less than 90 percent of the **inflation** problem.

With the above in mind, if we find we can't get out of this mess through improved technology, then the **only alternative left** is to **reduce** the **overhead factor.** As we have continually stressed in this text, overhead is everything that costs money but does not return a usable product or service. Admittedly, a certain amount of overhead is normal in any enterprise; it is simply part of the cost of doing business. Therefore, we must concern ourselves with abnormal overhead.

The **size** of government must be dramatically reduced. This in turn will affect the **cost** of government, in two ways: First, through the savings in salaries, building space, supplies, travel expenses and so on, which are required in support of such personnel; and second, by the elimination of wasteful spending of public funds which so many "public servants" find necessary to justify their existence. Such a goal of government reduction could be achieved in the following manner without any immediate "lay-offs": (a) By **stopping** the **growth** of government agencies. (b) By normal attrition through retirements and voluntary terminations by those who leave government to enter private enterprise. And (c) by reassigning personnel from bloated, unnecessary and non-productive bureaucracies to critical functions that even today are dangerously understaffed.

Typical of useless government functions that have literally mushroomed under the current administration is that of the First Lady's **personal staff.** Beginning with Eleanor Roosevelt who had one government-paid personal secretary, this staff has grown to three under Truman, nine under Johnson, ten under Ford, and then ballooned to 18 women (including a $56,000 "chief of staff") and two men on Mrs. Carter's staff, which the White House admits costs the taxpayers annually over $600,000 to operate. And still, this is only the tip of the iceberg regarding the actual cost of this operation, since many of the tasks previously performed by the staffs of Pat Nixon and Betty Ford are now assigned to, and paid out of funds from, other government agencies, such as the Executive Office and the National Park Service.

It's bad enough that the American taxpayer has to support a president of questionable value, but we do. There is, however, nothing in our Constitution which says we must also support a "Mrs. President" whose primary occupation appears to be flying around the country in "Air Force One," campaigning for the reelection of her husband. While "Roz's Army" is only a matter of a "mil" or so a year, in the aggregate these little "pittances" do add up.

The obvious requirement at this point in our history is learning to distinguish between normal overhead, and that which has been forced upon us; usually in a quite insidious manner. We must also understand that while abnormal overhead is bad for the general public, it is invariably profitable for a select few. To see how this works let us consider the following (but typical) example:

As of February 21, 1980, there were 67,377 attorneys registered with the California State Bar Association. And in that same month — 5,000 more legal aspirants were about to sit for their bar exams. That's another 5,000 people, who (for all practical purposes), will not be entering the mainstream of productivity, but rather, will be added to the **overhead factor** of California's citizenry. In the main, the efforts of these new lawyers will produce nothing of **tangible** value that can be shared in by the general population. To put it quite bluntly; they will be "feeding" off those who bake our bread, build our houses, and heal our sick. The purpose of emphasizing the role of the legal profession within our society, is that it is extremely unique among all other professions; or occupations.

As example, if we get sick we go to the doctor. But if we are fortunate enough to avoid sickness or accidents, there just isn't much that the medics can do to generate their own business. In fact, it is often to the contrary: We know that much of the practice of dentistry, such as flouride treatments, are actually **designed** to **reduce the need** for dental services. But such is not the case in the legal profession and it is precisely that capability which concerns us: Whenever the "legal pasture" becomes endangered from "overgrazing" — the rejuvenation process is simple: Another law is passed making something illegal or unlawful — and presto — their pasture is back in "clover" again. And often it doesn't even take a **new** law: A judicial ruling upon a certain aspect of an existing statute in many instances serves the same purpose, and does so without benefit or **permission** of the legislative process.

Although the inflationary impact of "legal-mania" is evident in every facet of our living, it is particularly disastrous in its application to criminal law. We note, for instance, an October 1979 newspaper account regarding a group of Hell's Angels about to go on trial. In the account it is estimated that the trial will last from four to six months, and although no cost estimates are given, we know from past experience that such a lengthy trial will cost the taxpayers well over a million dollars. And that's just for the first go 'round, which will naturally be followed by an appeal should there be a guilty verdict. That is absurd! No nation on earth can remain solvent with that kind of overhead built into the functioning of its legal and judicial system. And it should be needless to point out that if the total process were to be reduced by 50 percent in both time and cost, the defense would suffer no more than the prosecution, and no **less** justice would be dispensed.

But again, it is not just our legal system that needs a pruning, it is everything that constitutes unwarranted overhead — some specific categories that have been mentioned in this text, and a great many that have not.

Think of it! If millions of native-born American citizens cannot feed themselves, pay rent, improve their education after graduating from high school, gain the approval of their neighbors, see a doctor, or even heat their homes without government assistance, then, indeed, our nation does have problems, and it is time we looked **at the roots** of those problems rather than at the **evidence.**

Consider the saga of the Patel family, as recounted by a recent artricle in the San Francisco **Examiner**: this lately-arrived clan of Hindu immigrants now own and operate one out of every six motels and hotels in the state of California. Yes, it is indeed a serious problem when our nation can no longer compete with the other nations of the world. But when our native-born citizens can no longer compete with recently-arrived immigrants for subsistence in the country that virtually invented the free enterprise system, that is not a problem — that's a crime, and those responsible for such a situation should be punished accordingly.

Devisive Government Policies

No government on earth has ever been created that is capable of successfully "playing God" — or "taking care of its people" — without literally consuming the souls of its citizens in the process. This is not idle philosophy; this is fact! Look around the world, anywhere, in any corner of the globe, and see what happens when governments assume that they can replace the qualitative instincts of survival and progress which are inherent in normal humankind. The phenomenal success of the United States as a nation was not due to government programs, but rather to a system of government which, not perfectly, **but more perfectly,** allowed the natural development of its citizens according to their own individual merits and abilities. While such merits are never identical in any two persons, they do include such traits as ambition, initiative, resourcefulness, pride, competitiveness, personal responsibility, fear of failue, jealousy, family obligations, earlier rejection, willingness to make sacrifices, and a host of others — a list almost as endless as the combinations, and the combinations of combinations, that can be found in varying degrees in each of us.

Even severe physical handicaps have at times provided motivation to excel in a given field. And when we see the case of quadriplegics who become incredibly talented artists, holding the paintbrush between their teeth, it becomes abundatly clear that governments can neither bestow nor replace the qualities and the drive for achievement that are inherent in the human being.

Born a Negro slave 100 years before the enactment of the Civil Rights Act of 1964, Dr. George Washington Carver became one of America's most brilliant and noted scientists. In 1882, at the age of two, a serious illness had left Helen Keller both deaf and blind. But in spite of being a **woman,** a **deaf mute,** and **totally blind,** Miss Keller not only graduated from college, but went on to a life of greatness and achievements equalled by very few men. And neither of those idividuals owed their success to Title IV "protected" status nor to "affirmative action" programs.

The point, of course, is that with millions of hours devoted to theoretical research on the subject, and then billions of dollars to back up their findings, the assets and the best brains of the United States government have been totally incapable of duplicating what these two simple human beings achieved by themselves. We also know that at one time or another in our nation's history, the Irish, Jews, Hungarians, Japanese, Catholics, Italians, Chinese, and yes, even Germans, were, as groups, discriminated against. And again, without government assistance and without the support of government decree, they all managed to surmount this obstacle. But how? Did they do it as **groups,** or did they do it as **individuals** who were determined that they had something to offer society in general, and did so in a **competitive manner?**

Our primary concern is not so much with what is being "given" by government, as it is with what is being "taken away" in the process, both from those who receive and from those who must provide. While many will cite certain specific areas of progress attributable to government civil rights and nondiscrimination policies (and they would be right), we must nevertheless ask at what price to the basic principles upon which this nation was founded? We might even ask how many of these gains might have been achieved through **evolution** during this period, which would have been permanent progress, since they would have been based on a solid foundation.

Of equal concern, is how all that government intrusion into the normal functioning of our societal structure has become an enormous "overhead" burden that has not been vindicated or justified by the degree of meaningful progress attained. Perhaps it is time that we tried a completely diffeent approach to this problem, as illustrated by the following:

First, consider that the new Department of Education with its 17,000 employees has many years worth of "studies" behind it, all designed "toward solving the educational problems that particularly affect disadvantaged groups." Now, suppose we were to put those 17,000 experts out in the field, "teaching" rather than "preaching"? Even if they conducted classes of no more than 20 students each, this would amount to an annual input of some 340,000 formerly educationally "disadvantaged" persons into the mainstream of our productive society. And if these educators do their jobs properly, teaching, along with the "three R's," some good basic economics, then based on **merit** many of those "disadvantaged" will become not only valuable and sought-after employees, but even **employers** in their own right. And **that** would be **progress**.

In the meantime, the removal of **millions** of illegal aliens from this nation should open up more than enough **real** and **genuine** job opportunities for our citizens that we could dispense with all "affirmative action" programs and still have employment "left over."

Such a move would also virtually solve the "energy shortage" problem while at the same time reducing our balance-of-payments deficit to zero, and perhaps even put it on the **plus** side of the ledger.

Now that would seem to be a practical approach toward solving a great number of the major problems facing this nation. But as we have noted from past experience, government does not like to **solve** problems, it would rather **create** them.

In considering the desirability of a gradual return to the basic and fundamental concepts which made our country something special in the first place, we might also ponder the ramifications of **not doing so.** While the initial thrust of the "special rights" programs was intended to upgrade the status of our black population, just look how the number of special categories singled out for "protected status" has been expanded to include Orientals, Hispanics, women, and in some instances even "gays." But still the list for **special legislative protection** hasn't even begun to approach its full, even awesome, potential. How about left-handed people, the tall, the fat, the short, the ugly, the bald? And of course, sooner or later we would have to consider religious sects, social clubs, political groups, and ideological cults as well. It is obvious that if we continue this march long enough (and that's not too far away now), we will eventually come "full circle" to the point where each **checkmates** the other, and there we'll be: right back where we started, with the "right to life, liberty, and the pursuit of happiness" applying to all equally, and with accomplishment realized primarily according to their individual merits. But in the meantime, what is the cost of administering these often unworkable programs? What are they doing to our national productivity factor in terms of unwarranted "overhead" for government, for industry, and even for every individual in the general population?

And ERA (the Equal Rights Amendment for women) is no exception to this folly. Admittedly, there are still some inequities for women in our society which need to be rectified. But those who cite them in support of ERA conveniently seem to ignore the fact that there are also **many advantages** for women in our traditional social structure. It is interesting to note that most organized opposition to ERA comes not from men, as might be assumed, but from women who recognize that ERA would signal the end of traditional family life in America.

The primary objection to ERA is that it is not at all what it appears to be. It is simply a noble-sounding phrase (permeated with fraud and deceit) that will deprive women of virtually every safeguard, or "right," which they now enjoy while providing absolutely no additional protection. As example:

1. It will not guarantee women "equal pay for equal work," this is already covered by the Equal Employment Opportunity Act of 1972.

2. It will not help women to establish credit in their own right. The Equal Credit Opportunity Act of 1974 took care of that matter. (It would, however, deprive wives of their present ability to obtain credit in their husband's name.)

3. It will not protect women against "sexual harrassment" at work, because, in essence, ERA says there is no difference between men and women — they are simply — one each "thing."

4. It will not improve the educational opportunities of women, this area is covered by the Education Amendments of 1972.

Those are just a few of the things that ERA will **not** do. Now let's look at some of the **actual** ramifications of the Eual Rights Amendment:

1. It will deprive women in industry of their **present legal protections** against being involuntarily assigned to heavy-lifting, strenuous, and dangerous men's jobs, and compulsory overtime.

2. It will invalidate all state laws which require a husband to support his wife.

3. It will impose on mothers the equal (50%) financial obligation for the support of their infant and minor children.

4. It will eliminate present **lower** automobile and life insurance rates for women.

5. *"Not only would women, including mothers, be subject to the draft, but the military would be compelled to place them in combat units alongside of men."* — U.S. House Judiciary Committee Report, No. 92-359 on the impact of ERA.

Senator Sam Ervin of Watergate fame described ERA thusly: "My view that the ERA is the most destructive piece of legislation to ever pass Congress still stands." (And considering its stiff competition in the field of destructive legislation — being the "most" is indeed an achievement.) The Equal Rights Amendment failed to achieve ratification by the required number of states in order to become law, and was slated for a "natural death" on March 22, 1979. In the preceding seven-year limitation period for ratification, several states that had initially ratified the Amendment, later withdrew their ratification. But Mr. Carter (that great "family" man), has pressured Congress into extending the ratification period for yet another 3 years, while at the same time trying to get the Supreme Court to rule as "illegal" the actions of those states that withdrew their ratification.

The pathetic part of the ERA farce is that its backers are primarily among the so-called "feminist" movements. Now let's run that one by again! What could possibly be "feminine" about the kind of "uni-sex" society that ERA would create? And for the few women who have been taken in by the feminists distorted propaganda — let them consider the real — and the awesome potential of this folly. With only 60% of the physical strength of the opposite sex, there is just no way that women could survive (with any degree of dignity whatsoever), in a society devoid of the traditional respect and preference that has always been accorded them.

We might also note that while there has been a general "exodus" of women over the past couple of decades — from family life to "career-mindedness" — there appears to be a reversal of that trend taking place: In 1979, there were over 90,000 American women who entered motherhood for the first time — that were **past the age of thirty.** And many of these women will never return to the business world.

As we continue piecing together isolated facts, one after another, a rather frightening picture of the "whole" begins to take form. We note for instance, that in 1979 and 1980 respectively, both the California Supreme Court and the U.S. Supreme Court established the right to absolute privacy of a minor child's belongings in the home of their parents. The case which brought on this landmark decision was that of a 17-year old drug-pusher. The boy's parents had been advised by neighbors that their son was selling drugs to other children. After finding a small quantity of what they suspected to be illegal drugs in the house, the parents decided that it was time to call in the police. With the permission of the father, and in the presence of the boy, officers opened the boy's toolbox and found a large cache of illegal drugs. But the court ruled the boy's right to privacy had been violated and the evidence was inadmissible.

So that we don't lose sight of the principles involved in this case, let us review them: We know that parents are responsible to feed, clothe, house, educate, and provide medical care to their minor children. We also know that they can be held accountable for their actions. But yet, according to this ruling — it is perfectly alright for children to set up a criminal activity within their parents domicile with complete immunity. So we see in this particular case, the courts not only encouraging criminal activities, but severely restricting parental authority in the process.

On January 14, 1980, a nation-wide study of drug use in America's high schools was made public by the University of Michigan. This survey which had been in progress since 1975 revealed the following statistics: Although the rate of increase in the use of marijuana seemed to be leveling-off, it showed that 60% of the seniors had tried the drug — 50% had done so in the last month — and 10% use it daily. Even more alarming, however, was the dramatic increase in the

223

use of hard drugs. While 6% of the students had used cocaine in 1975, this figure has risen to 12% in 1979.

The point, of course, is that something very "weird" is taking place in this country, and it's time we paused long enough to find out what is really behind it. We know for example, that government only "plays" at stopping the drug traffic. That is, they furnish a lot of money to the cops to catch drug pushers and smugglers, but then turn them loose again in the courts. And if the smuggler is unfortunate enough to get caught south of the border (where they take a dim view of such activities), then people like Congressman Pete Stark spend hundreds-of-thousands of taxpayer dollars getting them freed from those nasty jails. And then, too, we have people like Assemblyman Willie Brown who has spent a large part of his long career in the California legislature; introducing bill after bill that would legalize the home growing of marijuana. And of course, with the "weed" available and growing in backyards and from every balcony, we could fully expect that even 9 and 10-year olds would soon be rolling a "joint" or two each morning before heading off to grammar school. That is, if they decided to go at all.

To see how all of this is affecting our culture and our behavior, we might consult a couple of similar examples that were separated by a great many years: During the Klondike gold rush, tens-of-thousands of miners who were literally "burning-up" with "gold fever" descended upon Alaska. They were, however, prevented from tackling the snow-covered Chilkoot pass (which led into the Yukon) without first proving to U.S. Marshals that they had at least 60 pounds of provisions with them. There were no exceptions made, and no hassles either. And once in the Yukon Territory, all that it took was a couple of Canadian "Mounties" to keep the entire area virtually violence and crime-free.

In contrast to the above, in 1979 we find a group of people in Cincinnati — also with a "burning fever" — this time stomping to death 11 of their own trying to get into a rock-concert. And in spite of the fact that 11 people had just been stamped to death like bugs (and dozens more injured) the concert took place anyway with everyone having an absolute "ball."

The obvious concern here, is not so much the drug-problem, per se, but rather, how this growing phenomenon will affect our nation's survivability-factor: We know that in a world in which its population is mushrooming like a gigantic nuclear explosion, that America's right to survival as a nation is sure to be challenged within this very decade. And will we be able to respond to this challenge with any degree of clarity of mind and action?

CHAPTER 22
CONCLUSIONS AND RECOMMENDATIONS

It is later than we think! In an era of satellite communications, laser beams, computer technology, and ICBM's — the time honored fashion in which Congress and the administration have been able to cocoon themselves in laborious "studies" and "hearings" - will no longer suffice. Without exception, every candidate for public office virtually swore that they "knew exactly what to do" when they applied for their jobs.

Apparently they did not — and the evidence to support such a conclusion is overwhelming.

With the interest of our national debt consuming almost 10% on the 1981 federal budget ($67.2 billion), those **habitual** "big spenders" in Congress must be removed as quickly as possible if this nation is to stave off bankruptcy. (Regardless of who is president — it is still Congress that appropriates the money to be spent.) But as deadly serious as the inflation crisis and other fiscal matters, shoring-up our perilous immigration posture must become America's #1 -PRIORITY concern. If we don't resolve this crisis first — attempting to solve the others can be no more than an exercise in futility.

Many citizens are finding it difficult to reconcile America's past, as exemplified by the Statue of Liberty (1886), with the frightening realities of today's world. Remembering the past is a fine and noble way of enriching the present. But to blindly dwell on the past is the surest way to forfeit the future. We should pause for a moment to put these era's into perspective:

In 1880, the United States was a nation of approximately fifty million people. Land was often available for the asking. Smog and pollution were unknown. Life was uncomplicated, and the population was very self-sufficient. While 85 percent of our inhabitants lived in rural areas, the 15 percent classified as city dwellers were a far cry from those of today. The majority of those "city folks" maintained a vegetable garden, often chickens and rabbits, and occasionally even a milk cow or two.

Just as the family home of today usually has an extra room, designated as the "TV" or "leisure" room, the home of the 1880's also had an extra room: the pantry, or larder. It was customary to keep this room stocked with a supply of home-canned foods, dry stuffs, and other necessities of the day, enough to last for several months. Whatever the occasion, the population was well prepared to contend with the situation, for this was an era of unavoidable self-reliance and responsibility.

That was the America of the 1880's, a country with what appeared to be inexhaustible supplies of natural resources, and with a margin of error capability that seemed boundless.

Almost 100 years later we find ourselves no longer a nation of self-sufficient people. In fact, we are not even a self-sufficient nation. We live in a complicated technological society in which we are all interdependent upon one another for everything — including the ability to sustain life itself.

Our constantly increasing energy demands far exceed our domestic fuel supply — a single but vital factor which, of itself, proclaims that our once boundless margin of error capability is now but a memory.

A 330 percent increase in the last century has swelled our population to some 230,000,000 people, along with several hundred million automobiles, trucks, buses, airplanes, tractors, and factory smokestacks pumping pollutants into the atmosphere, endangering our ability to breathe, and in many ares blighting the vegetation of the surrounding countryside. In the words of the immortal Bard of Avon, we may "have lived well, but not too wisely."

In order to gain a better understanding of the amazing transformation taking place in our way of living, we must first understand the process. The improvements we naturally accept without question, but it is the serious deterioration of many other areas of our lifestyle that warrants concern. Deterioration that we often accept without challenge. The insidious part of this change for the worse is that it occurs on an almost daily basis, with no sudden shock or impact to sound an alarm.

In this process, our country is only a fraction less habitable each day than it was the previous day. Roads are a little more crowded, prices are slightly higher, and it is a little harder to find a suitable place to live. Taxes ease upward, the air becomes a bit dirtier, and one more item has been added to the growing list of shortages. Imperceptible changes, but changes indeed!

The effect of immigration upon our lifestyle is also easier to assess over an extended period. To those who ask, "What difference will a few hundred thousand more immigrants make?" this number may not seem enormous when viewed as a single figure (over 500,000 legal immigrants in fiscal 1979, for example). However, if we consider that, since 1960 alone, more than enough **legal** immigrants have entered this country to populate the entire cities of Boise, Pittsburgh (Pennsylvania), Tampa, Minneapolis, Albany (New York), Dayton, Hartford, Honolulu, Reno, Oklahoma City, Portland (Oregon), Omaha, San Francisco, New Orleans, Anchorage, and Fort Worth (cf. 1970 census; not including offspring born since 1960), we see the cumulative impact of this factor on our growth. But remember, we are speaking here only of **legal** immigration.

Population growth is extremely difficult to forecast and is particularly susceptible to under-estimation. As example, the 1938 "Year in Review" of the Encyclopedia Britannica in noting that America's population (1937) was 129 million, states the following: "... *according to recent forecasts, the population of the United States will grow more slowly in the future, until a probable maximum of about 153 million is reached around 1980."* Unfortunately, the impact of accelerating illegal immigration has played a major role in shattering that dream.

Mere numbers, alone, however, are not America's only concern regarding the illegal alien problem.

Professor Arthur Corwin, who has studied the illegal alien problem intensively for both the U.S. and Mexican governments during recent years, suggested the migratory wave may have grown uncontrollable. He postulated as geopolitical facts of life four political "models," and expressed deep concern at the degree to which newly-arrived Mexican immigrants were being absorbed into the militant new political activist groups emerging among Spanish-speaking elements in the U.S.

The four models he cites as:

★ the **Crystal City Model**, exemplified by Crystal City, Texas, where the **raza unida** movement has organized its own political party, seized complete control of the city and county government, and driven off a large part of the old **anglo** community;

★ the **Laredo Model**, in which the long-time, generally "Americanized" Spanish-speaking community has acted as a buffer and intermediary for the new arrivals and kept them in line through lukewarm advocacy of their interests;

★ the **Big City Model**, in which the immigrants have become ethnic political blocs embraced and exploited by big bosses (notably Mayor Daly of Chicago) who encourage their cultural distinctiveness as a means of controlling their votes; and finally,

★ the **Quebec Model**, which Corwin suggested is as yet hypothetical, but which he foresees as a possible powerful separatist movement along our Southwestern border.

If the population explosion continues in Mexico, and if the U.S. fails to effectively control massive illegal immigration, then in Corwin's view, the United States faces the alarming prospect of the "Latin Americanization" of its political system.

Citing illegal immigration as both a cause and an effect of our growing welfare state, Corwin noted that immigrants and their children were being indoctrinated in **raza** political ideologies, including the "Reconquest of a Southwestern Aztlan," and often this was being accomplished through our educational and antipoverty programs, funded by federal agencies. ("Whether we like it or not," he believes, "the Mexican War smolders on.")

Unless the federal government controls both the illegal immigration from underdeveloped countries, and its own massive social assistance spending programs, Corwin foresees a bleak future for American social institutions, with the American taxpayer breaking down under the growing load imposed by social costs and poverty migration.

As Corwin notes, most of the illegal immigrant families, and no few legal ones, who enter the United States today can be found immediately eligible for Great Society programs and assistance. They do not necessarily go through the same struggling stages of most past immigrant assimilation — peasant, bluecollar, middle class — but commonly, as in the border states, become proletarian wards of federal programs, political patronage bosses, and indoctrination groups. They are to vote in their own language, and be taught ethnic pride in their native tongue, as "subsidized pseudocultures."

It is obvious that something must be done immediately to rectify this insane situation: Illegal immigration was illegal when Congress began studying the matter over a decade ago, and we don't have to wait for the results of yet another study to tell us that it is illegal today.

In 1950 the Immigration and Naturalization Service was authorized a force of 6,717 personnel. Since then their normal workload from rising tourism (both American and foreign), the manifold duties associated with administering to dozens of new cultural exchange programs, an enormous increase in legal immigration, plus an assortment of refugee programs - ad infinitum - and all **legal**; has increased by several thousand percent. Yet, this organization today (including their Border Patrol units) is authorized (but not totally funded) for only some 10,000 employees. Indeed we see here, a classic example of a genuine need being bypassed by Congress — in favor of thousands of their utter frivolities. And we still haven't touched on the INS's increased workload from skyrocketing illegal immigration.

In terms of priorities, the federal government's "first order of the day" (which should begin tomorrow morning), must be to bring the INS's manpower and funding in line with its responsibilities. And "responsibilities" is indeed the key word here. It is obvious from world conditions that the Immigration Service will increasingly become a more vital service with each passing year. Even today, in terms of being

critical to our **national survival**, it is matched only by the Department of Defense. This fact becomes starkly evident when considering that the number of illegal aliens already within our borders — exceeds the standing armies of Russia and Cuba combined. Something to think about!

Perhaps the first step in recognizing the needs of the INS would be to remove this agency from control of the Justice Department, which itself, seems to suffer from a paucity of **quality** in its leadership. Without a doubt, this vital function deserves to be a full-fledged Department. And if our government happens to be short of "Department" spaces — we could certainly eliminate the "D" of Education which was never needed in the first place. With immigration under control we probably won't need the "D" of Energy half as much as we think we do; and HUD (Housing and Urban Development) would fit in quite nicely under the Department of the Interior, or Commerce.

Next, we had better start taking a "hard look" at politicians who invariably seem to favor "alien interests" ahead of those of our nation and our citizens. We note for example, that in December of 1979 Mario G. Obledo, California's Secretary of Health and Welfare, proposed that America open its border to all Mexicans in order to help alleviate that nation's population problem. Yes, Mr. Obledo is paid $66,000 per year by the citizens of California, many of whom are being driven from their homes by sky-rocketing rents, pollution, inflation and taxation; but it is obvious that his heart and allegiance lies elsewhere.

And such is the case with those who advocate amnesty for America's illegal alien population: They are playing "ethnic-politics" with the rightful inheritance of our children. The concept of amnesty is obviously wrong for the following reasons:

1. It legalizes **unlawful** entry at the expense of honest applicants for immigration, many who have been waiting patiently for years.

2. We have absolutely no idea of the numbers we would be talking about, nor of the future "domino effect" of such a program.

3. What criteria could we possibly use that would be fair, honest and accurate — and above all, practical to administer? A three-year — six-year — or ten-year period of residency in the U.S.? The ease with which false affidavits of residency could be obtained from within the alien communities, would render such criteria a farce. And the administrative workload of adjudicating such requests would surely be astronomical.

At some future date (after our immigration posture has regained its equilibrium), we might consider an amnesty program for exceptional cases, but indeed not at this time. However, **all costs** associated with the process (administrative, judicial and investigative) should be borne by the applicant.

Next in line of priority actions; it has been known for years that America needed legislation that would make it unlawful to **knowingly** hire an illegal alien. Almost every other nation on earth has some kind of a safeguard which accomplishes the same purpose — why not the U.S.? And since this concept has already been studied in both houses of Congress for at least a full **decade** — it shouldn't take more than a couple of weeks to accomplish this. Should it?

To complement the above, and for a number of other reasons, too, Americans definitely need a **non-forgible** Social Security card. We know, for example, that this card is the "pass-book" to virtually the only bank account that millions of Americans have. It seems kind of "nutty" then, to pass them around as though they were little more than cigar-coupons. And when we find illegal aliens with a pocketful of SS cards, we know they are not that difficult to come by.

An equally sound reason for such a valid document, is that it could serve as "proof of citizenship" when registering or voting. There have, however, been objections raised to this idea in the past, on the ground that it would constitute a "police state." Now that's an alarming phrase — but what does it mean? We know that millions of people have been slaughtered in "police states" throughout the world — but it is doubtful that any of them carried a Social Security card, forgible or not.

With counterfeiting of other types of documents so flagrant today, it is difficult to understand why any American citizen would oppose the idea of a tamper-proof Social Security card. Similar cards would be furnished to legally resident aliens, but such identification would clearly indicate that the holder was **not** a citizen and therefore **not entitled to vote.**

As mentioned earlier in this text, a very large percentage of America's foreign aid programs have ranged from a simple waste of money — to the aiding and abetting of inevitably greater future tragedies. It is time for our nation to pull in its global "glad hand" and start directing at least some of that aid to where it will do some good, not only for the recipient; but for ourselves as well. The United States should adopt and pursue a policy of exceptional aid and cooperation with Mexico, designed to create an economic environment that will keep our neighbor's children at home.

While at the moment this may sound like the classic story of the "blind leading the blind," it makes far more sense than continuing to pour billions of dollars into nations located half-way around the world, whose allegiance at best are questionable, and temporary. While many persons might argue that "charity begins at home" (and they would be right), we might also point out that by helping to create jobs in Mexico for Mexicans — we would also be opening-up job opportunities for Americans in the United States. And if we can substantially reduce the **abnormal** overhead-factor of our nation's "modus operandi" — we will soon find that any job and every job — will indeed pay a living wage. Our nation has the productive capability to provide an excellent standard of living to all of our citizens. We need only to apply that capability in the manner in which our system was designed to operate: That is, as free **as possible** from the extraneous handicaps imposed upon it by government.

The late Mike Todd (producer of the movie "Around the World in Eighty Days") was once quoted as saying: *"I've often been broke — but I have never been poor."* If we can rid this country of politicians who love "poor people" so much that they have **created** them by the millions — then such a philosophy might become a personal motto leading to the economic salvation of our nation.

In spite of the incredible number and variety of disastrous consequences looming on our nation's horizon (all brought on by mis-management of our political-house) - America **can** survive the challenge. But first, we must accept the fact that we have been "sold out" by those we entrusted with such awesome authority, and resolve that never again will we as citizens be so blindly trusting. With a national election at hand, there could be no finer opportunity for Americans to pierce the nebulous veil of campaign rhetoric, by demanding from candidates — specifics. Particularly, how they stand on the issue of American rights — American interests — and American needs — versus those of foreign demands.

"Have a nice day."

AUTHOR'S NOTE: No other problem or issue so lends itself to emotional distortion than the subject of immigration. Unfortunately, unlike most problems it cannot be accurately examined solely on the basis of its own merit, for the impact of immigration directly affects every part of our daily life, the future of our children and the American posterity. The purpose of this book therefore, is to find what immigration "does," rather than merely what it "is."

In April of 1980, while an armada of 25 American warships patrolled the **Arabian Sea**, small boat owners "thumbed their noses" at U.S. authorities as they brought hundreds of **boatloads** of Cubans illegally into Florida. These were not refugees from the Cuban revolution which occured **20-years ago**, but simply relatives, friends and acquaintances of hundreds-of-thousands of other Cubans who have fled that country in recent years. And they will later be joined by their friends and relatives still in Cuba, who will then be joined by theirs in a never ending migration.

These defiant smugglers who were picking up $1,000 a head for their passengers, were warned by U.S. authorities — "Golly, gee-wiz — don't you know we **could** prosecute you for violating U.S. immigration and smuggling laws" — and such was the sum and substance of our nation's defense. But the Cubans are only a small fraction of some 3 billion other inhabitants of this earth who are also not too happy with their present place of residence.

It should be obvious that a government that refuses to protect its own citizens and its own territory against invasion, has no business wondering why it has lost the respect of the world-at-large. And it is equally true that the citizens of a nation that refuses to protect itself while it still has the power to do so, will soon lose that ability.

ABOUT THE AUTHOR: James Farrell, 58, is a retired United States Air Force officer who is thoroughly dedicated to the beliefs expounded in this treatise. His intense interest in the subject of immigration was aroused quite incidentally by the November 8, 1973 issue of the San Francisco Chronicle. The front page of this issue was covered with frightening accounts of an impending "fuel crisis," while buried on the third page was a virtually unnoticeable one-inch item reporting that the administration had authorized the admission of 25,000 additional immigrants above our normal immigration quotas. In the conflicting elements of these news stories, the author perceived governmental management not in the best interests of the American people.

Researching the immigration question further, Farrell became convinced that the average American citizen had no idea of the magnitude or impact of our present rates of immigration, both legal and illegal, and that our politicians were not about to tackle seriously such a volatile issue. His first book *Give Us Your Poor (The Immigration Bomb)* published in 1975, accurately predicted the present inflation crisis. The fact that politicians still choose to ignore the obvious relationship inherent in massive immigration — shortages — and inflation, now causes him to examine the underlying motives behind this enigma.

A military man with 25 years of service (including nine years of foreign service duty), Farrell has better than average first-hand knowledge of world conditions and their relationship to the well-being of our own country. As a rated Command Pilot credited with 525 combat flying hours, he obviously believes the United States of America is a nation worth trying to save.

With the future of his children foremost in his concern, Farrell has now taken to the pen in defense of his country, attempting to place the various facets and ramifications of immigration within the realities of today's world.

As a youth during the Depression, he worked in the fields of mining, logging, and construction, helping to support his family. Perhaps it is his knowledge and appreciation of the clean air, fresh water, and serene beauty of America's open spaces which has led him on this crusade to help preserve as much as possible these qualities of this great nation, with all of its inherent opportunities, for his and the other children of this country to inherit.

THE INEVITABLE CHANGES IN OUR LIFESTYLE
IF OUR POPULATION CONTINUES TO GROW

Personal pets and pleasure animals; dogs, cats, birds and race horses, etc., will be illegal. Even though we have nowhere reached that point of necessity in the U.S.—their very substantial food requirements have already been challenged.

A permanent BUREAU of RATIONING as large as any of our other major government agencies will be established. Rationing will eventually encompass virtually everything.

"Medallions" or Permits of Residency will be issued every citizen designating a specific city, county or metropolitan area of authorized permanent residence. A request for a change in locations would be handled in much the same way as an inter-company transfer is today. Ample justification along with a need and certification of ability to accommodate at the other end would be required.

Golf courses because of their large and generally fertile acreage as well as huge water and fertilizer requirements would fade into oblivion. There would be no need to "outlaw" the game, the land area would simply be taxed out of business.

Milk, eggs, meat, poultry and dairy products will be a thing of the past. All nutrition will come directly from the feed source rather than from the lesser efficient by-products of the feed.

Visits to National Parks and recreation areas will be strictly by "reservation only." Waiting times will gradually increase to perhaps as much as 5 to 8 years in many instances.

All forms of personal freedom and choice will be greatly reduced. Of necessity—the "state" will make most decisions regarding our fields of employment as well as assignment to schools of higher education.

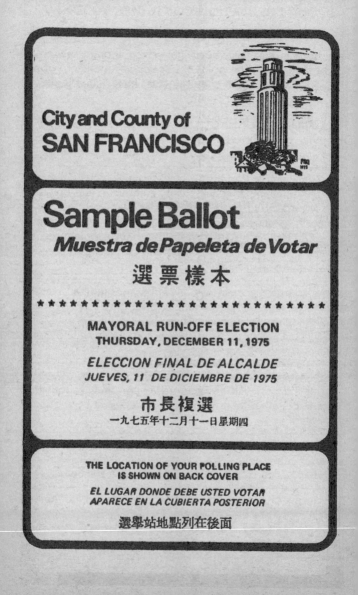

City and County of SAN FRANCISCO

Sample Ballot
Muestra de Papeleta de Votar
選票樣本

* *

MAYORAL RUN-OFF ELECTION
THURSDAY, DECEMBER 11, 1975

ELECCION FINAL DE ALCALDE
JUEVES, 11 DE DICIEMBRE DE 1975

市長複選
一九七五年十二月十一日星期四

**THE LOCATION OF YOUR POLLING PLACE
IS SHOWN ON BACK COVER**

*EL LUGAR DONDE DEBE USTED VOTAR
APARECE EN LA CUBIERTA POSTERIOR*

選舉站地點列在後面

EMERGENCIA
EMERGENCY

緊急事故

🔥	**FIRE** INCENDIO 消防局	
🛡	**POLICE** POLICIA 警察局	
✚	**AMBULANCE** AMBULANCIA 救急車	
	DOCTOR DOCTOR 醫生	
	HIGHWAY PATROL	TO REPORT EMERGENCY CALL OPERATOR: ASK FOR ZENITH 1-2000
	PATRULLA DE CARRETERAS	PARA DAR AVISO DE EMERGENCIA LLAME A LA OPERADORA Y PIDA ZENITH 1-2000
	公路巡警	報告救急請打電話接線生： 請求 Zenith 1-2000
		OR IN ANY EMERGENCY DIAL OPERATOR. O EN CUALQUIER EMERGENCIA LLAME A LA OPERADORA 或其他緊急事故打电話給接綫生。

🔔 **Pacific Telephone**

SAN FRANCISCO UNIFIED SCHOOL DISTRICT

DATE (Fecha)
日期

DEAR PARENT OR GUARDIAN:
Estimado Padre de Familia o Tutor:
貴家長或監護人：

THIS IS TO INFORM YOU THAT YOUR APPLICATION FOR FREE OR REDUCED-PRICE MEALS OR FREE MILK
Esta es para informarle que su aplicación para comidas gratis o a precio reducido o leche gratis
這是通知閣下關於貴子弟的免費或減費食物及牛奶申請表

FOR YOUR CHILD _____ HAS BEEN:
                              (NAME) 姓名
para su niño _____ Ha sido:
                              (Nombre)

_____ APPROVED FOR FREE MEALS AND FREE MILK
        Aprobada para comida y leche gratis
        批準免費食物及免費牛奶

_____ APPROVED FOR REDUCED-PRICE MEALS AT 5¢ FOR BREAKFAST AND 10¢ FOR LUNCH
        Aprobada para comida a precio reducido (5¢ por desayuno y 10¢ por almuerzo)
        批準減費食物，早餐每份五仙，午餐每份一角。

_____ DENIED FOR THE FOLLOWING REASON:
        Rechazada por las siguientes razones:
        為以下原因被拒絕

        _____ OVER INCOME
                Familia con suficientes entradas monetarias
                過多入息

        _____ INCOMPLETE INFORMATION
                Información incompleta
                資料不足夠

        _____ APPLICATION NOT SIGNED
                Aplicación no firmada
                申請表沒有簽名

YOU MAY APPEAL THIS DECISION BY CALLING OR WRITING THE OFFICE OF COMMUNITY RELATIONS
Si deseas, esta petición puede ser reconsiderada. Llame o escriba a la Oficina de Relaciones con la Comunidad
如果閣下對於此決定有異議或請求，請打電話或寫信到三藩市洞衙
AT 135 VAN NESS AVENUE, SAN FRANCISCO, CA 94102. TELEPHONE: 863-4680, EXTENSION 208.
Situada en 135 Van Ness Avenue, San Francisco, Ca. 94102. Teléfono 863-4680, Ext. 208.
一百三十五号,公共閣係部聯絡。電話號碼是八六三四六八〇,分綫二〇八号。

SINCERELY,
Sinceramente,

Richard H. Farrar

RICHARD H. FARRAR
DIRECTOR OF FOOD SERVICES
主持人

IN ORDER TO BE SURE THAT YOU HAVE RECEIVED THIS INFORMATION, MAY WE REQUEST THAT YOU
Para estar seguros de que usted recibió esta información por favor firme esta carta
為請確知道閣下曾收到此通告，請在此通知書上簽名及交回　貴子弟
SIGN THIS LETTER AND RETURN IT TO YOUR CHILD'S SCHOOL.
y devuélvala a la escuela con su hijo(a).
就讀的學校

_____   _____
DATE   PARENT OR GUARDIAN'S SIGNATURE
Fecha   Firma del Padre de Familia o Tutor
日期   家長或監護人簽名